FEMINIST ACCOUNTABILITY

Feminist Accountability

Disrupting Violence and Transforming Power

Ann Russo

NEW YORK UNIVERSITY PRESS

New York

NEW YORK UNIVERSITY PRESS
New York
www.nyupress.org

References to Internet websites (URLs) were accurate at the time of writing. Neither the author nor New York University Press is responsible for URLs that may have expired or changed since the manuscript was prepared.

Library of Congress Cataloging-in-Publication Data
Names: Russo, Ann, 1957–   author.
Title: Feminist accountability : disrupting violence and transforming power / Ann Russo.
Description: New York : New York University Press, [2019] | Includes bibliographical references and index.
Identifiers: LCCN 2018020948| ISBN 9780814777169 (cl : alk. paper) | ISBN 9780814777152 (pb : alk. paper)
Subjects: LCSH: Feminism. | Responsibility. | Feminist theory. | Women—Violence against. | Sex discrimination against women.
Classification: LCC HQ1155 .R87 2019 | DDC 305.42—dc23
LC record available at https://lccn.loc.gov/2018020948

New York University Press books are printed on acid-free paper, and their binding materials are chosen for strength and durability. We strive to use environmentally responsible suppliers and materials to the greatest extent possible in publishing our books.

Manufactured in the United States of America

10 9 8 7 6 5 4 3 2 1

Also available as an ebook

For Frannie and Cece

CONTENTS

Introduction

Cultivating Feminist Accountability

> If we ask ourselves the most simple questions, such as where do we get our food from, we can see that we are tied up in networks of relationships with millions of other people. Our actions are constantly creating, recreating, challenging and transforming the networks of relationships that make up the fabric of our shared world. We influence the fabric of society by the choices we make, about whose actions we choose to acknowledge and whose we choose to ignore; by where we take a stand and where we choose not to; by how we treat others and how we expect to be treated.
> —C. Kaufman, *A User's Guide to White Privilege*

What does it take to build communities to struggle against the multitude of injustices we face and to create the social change we envision necessary for the world in which we want to live—a world with love, liberation, and justice at its center? How do we work together to transform the deep historical, structural, and interlocking systems of oppression and violence that shape our relationships with one another without reproducing these same systems and the violence they produce?[1]

In thirty-plus years of participation in antiracist, feminist, and queer antiviolence critical-consciousness community building, organizing, and activism, the most important lesson I have learned is that our praxis often reproduces the very power dynamics that we are seeking to transform. So often the hierarchical and inequitable divides produced by global capitalism, imperialism, white supremacy, patriarchy, and heteronormativity get played out in our relationships and communities as well as in our organizations, activism, and advocacy. In teaching, writing, and organizing around the everyday oppression and violence that saturate our communities locally and globally, I am often haunted by the questions Aimee Carillo Rowe poses in her book *Power Lines*; she asks, "Whose well-being is essential to our own? And whose survival must we overlook in order to connect to power in the ways that we do?"[2] I would suggest that these questions are integral to building theory, research, and action against the entrenched violence that shapes the conditions of our lives. They reveal how much our choices—as individuals, organizations, and communities—are often embedded within these systems, rather than resistant to them. They are questions thus that compel us to become more critically aware of and to take accountability for the impact of the ways we imagine, embody, and live the world that we envision for a future not yet here.

They are also questions I ask myself daily as I make my own choices in the midst of pervasive interpersonal, community, and state violence produced by the interlocking systems of oppression and in the context of my lived experience as a white, professional-class, queer, cis-gendered, monolingual, English-speaking woman with US citizenship, with deep love, belonging, and commitments within my multiracial and transnational families, communities, and movements for change. Because of how embedded I am, and we are, in these systems, our emotional, intellectual, and political responses to oppression and violence as well as our strategies and visions for change may reproduce the very violence that we are striving to transform. This is the case not because we are individual failures but rather because of how enmeshed we are in the very systems we are organizing to change. As Morgan Bassichis, a former collective member of the Oakland-based Communities United Against Violence, so aptly notes, "the very systems we are working to dismantle live inside of us."[3] And yet we often act as if these structures, ideologies, and power lines are outside of ourselves, our groups, and our efforts, and so we do not consistently question how they are shaping our identities, our relationships, and our organizations, as well as our ideas, strategies, and visions.

These inequitable divides and the culture that supports them are the fault lines that undermine, fracture, and disable feminist antiviolence efforts. For instance, despite the critical efforts of many, the most prominent and funded feminist and LGBT antiviolence organizations have become mainstreamed into social service, advocacy, and policy reform projects. These projects tend to replicate, rather than undermine or disrupt, the institutional, structural, and community-based power lines built through historical and interlocking systems of oppression. They tend to resist naming the multiple power lines that differentially shape the lives of the different communities they serve, that structure the relational hierarchies within the organizations, and that shape their agendas and practices. Their work is often embedded in the dominant ideologies, norms, and perspectives of neoliberal capitalism. This means they often approach violence through a social service and criminal legal lens that understands violence as an individual and interpersonal issue, rather than a social and political one. This means they often ally with, rather than significantly challenge, the state institutions, policies, and systems that underlie and contribute to the endemic violence we are facing.

The results of these dominant approaches are that under the broad rubric of feminism and LGBT activism, we witness uncritical commitment to entrenched carceral frameworks that rely on the police and the criminal legal systems for protection, incarceration, and punishment despite their brutal impact on poor, immigrant, queer, and trans communities of color. We witness support for US militarism and war grounded in Islamophobia and anti-Arab racism as a way of securing women's and LGBT rights. We witness silence in the face of police brutality and murder of people of color in the United States and of US militarist violence and occupation through the war on terrorism, including violence against women and queer, gender-nonbinary, and transgender people. We witness the white middle-class heteronormative ideology and practice of antiviolence social services and legal advocacy turn away from women, queer and trans people, and/or immigrants who are impacted by the sex trade, who are non-English-speaking, who live in the United States without legal documentation, who live with disabilities, who are formerly incarcerated, and/or who are struggling with drug or alcohol addictions, and more. We witness rape crisis agencies that do not speak out or offer support and advocacy for women, queer, and trans folks raped and assaulted by the police, immigration officials, and prison guards across the world. We witness resistance to creating the necessary space for front-line workers, often working-class women of color, to process the trauma, grief, and exhaustion connected to the work and to the daily impact of oppression and violence because our accountability is to the funders and their expectations, rather than to those most impacted by violence. And we witness resistance to the voices and perspectives of feminists of color, queer and trans feminists, and transnational feminists who seek to address internal power lines within the movement that contribute to the pervasive violence facing those most marginalized in the service of preserving the framework that serves the organizational funders, including the state.

At the same time, many activists, writers, healers, artists, and scholars are organizing projects and movements of Black, Latinx, Asian, Indigenous, and Arab feminists, including queer, transgender, and disabled feminists of color as well as antiracist and transnational feminists (e.g., #BlackLivesMatter, Assata's Daughters, Incite! Women of Color Against Violence, Transnational Feminists against the War) that offer significantly different analyses, organizing frameworks, strategies, and actions in response to interpersonal, community, and state violence. These projects are based in the interconnected historical legacies of women of color feminisms, third world feminisms, and antiracist/anti-imperialist feminisms responsible for the theoretical lenses of intersectionality, community accountability, transformative justice, and transnational feminisms. They challenge the carceral and imperial feminist frameworks that have become so dominant in the US mainstream, and they offer ways of building community to transform violence that do not rely on policing, surveillance, punishment, or state and military violence. Rather than building feminist antiviolence projects around singular issues or unidimensional homogeneous identities, these projects seek to build relational accountability for the power lines and structures that create the endemic and ongoing oppression and violence that differentially impact our multiple, heterogeneous, and interconnected identities and communities.

Intersectionality as a Bridge to Accountability

Over the past thirty-plus years, many feminist, queer, and transgender scholars, writers, and activists of color have developed the theoretical and analytic lenses of interlocking systems of oppression and privilege, antiracism, and postcolonial and transnational feminisms.[4] These lenses foreground the way the historical structural systems of patriarchy, white supremacy, capitalism, compulsory heteronormativity, ableism, colonialism, and imperialism are integrally related to one another, albeit differently depending on the historical and social context. They shed light on how these systems simultaneously shape people's lives, ideas, relations, and politics. Most importantly, they underscore the significance of taking accountability for our differential relationships within these systems as a praxis of critical analysis and action as well as alliance, coalition, and solidarity.

A feminist accountability approach, according to Fellows and Razack, makes visible how interlocking "systems of oppression (capitalism, imperialism, patriarchy) rely on one another in complex ways." They draw critical scrutiny to the ways that these systems "came into existence in and through one another so that class exploitation could not be accomplished without gender and racial hierarchies, imperialism could not function without class exploitation, sexism, heterosexism, and so on."[5] Viewing the matter through this lens enables the recognition that each of us is shaped by and implicated in these systems—our identities, our experiences, our ideas, our actions—and that our relational ties are guided by the power lines that link us together.[6] As Mary Elizabeth Hobgood also suggests, "[P]rivilege and oppression do not simply coexist side by side. Rather the suffering and unearned disadvantages of subordinate groups are the foundation for the privileges of dominant groups."[7]

This approach draws our attention to how, for instance, in a white supremacist, capitalist, heteronormative patriarchy, white women and women of color are situated in hierarchical relationship with one another, and so our lives and relationships are interconnected through these hierarchies. This is evident, for instance, in the differential interpretation and response to sexual violence against women. Within the US system, social institutions idealize white, middle-class femininity by associating it with purity, virginity, and passivity, an image that is set up against social constructions of Black and Brown femininities as associated with criminality, sexual promiscuity, and aggression. This socially constructed idealization/criminalization binary produces the differential institutional responses to sexual violence, such that the criminal legal system, the media, and educational as well as gender-based social service and advocacy institutions are more likely to criminalize men's violence against white, middle-class, heterosexual, able-bodied women when it is perpetrated by men of color, whereas they respond with si-lence, social apathy, and/or victim blaming when men commit violence against women of color, including queer and trans women, trans and gender-nonconforming people, poor women, and women in the sex trade, particularly when perpetrated by white men.[8] White, middle-class, heterosexual men's violence against white women is mostly de-nied, minimized, ignored, and/or treated as an individual anomaly.

Feminist theories, analyses, and strategies that do not approach these issues through an intersectional lens often contribute to systemic in-terpersonal, community, and state violence and the social and struc-tural power systems that fuel it. Beth Richie's book, *Arrested Justice: Black Women, Violence, and America's Prison Nation*, offers a power-ful analysis of the brutal and painful consequences of an institutional-ized feminist antiviolence movement in which poor Black women and gender-nonconforming people's genders and sexualities are devalued and stigmatized. She shows how institutionalized antiviolence efforts contribute to the pervasive interpersonal, community, and state violence that Black women experience, both by reifying white, middle-class femi-nine innocence *and* by remaining largely silent about and unrespon-sive to pervasive intimate, community, and state violence against Black women. By not critically struggling against the racism, classism, and heteronormativity of the criminal legal system, she argues, the service and advocacy organizations have bolstered the development of a prison nation, including the buildup of the prison industrial complex, the "war on crime" and racist criminalization of Black people and people of color more broadly, policies of gentrification, and more.

Relatedly, while the so-called protection of the fragility and inno-cence of white women is held up as a justification for the buildup of a prison nation through incarceration, as well as through imperialist war and occupation, white, middle- and upper-middle-class, heteronorma-tive women are simultaneously positioned as heroic and superior in re-lation to women of the global south. As a result, US neoliberal feminist projects often feed into the US imperial project of "saving" poor women of the global south that actually reproduces and expands the systems of oppression and the violence that they experience. Organizations like the Feminist Majority Foundation or CARE, for instance, approach women's rights– and gender-equity-development projects through gender-myopic lenses that are oriented to changing "other cultures" to become more like "us," but do not account for the ways US militarism and global capitalism have contributed to pervasive conditions of poverty, ill health, illiteracy, and violence. The so-called superiority of white western women and men that shapes these "civilizing projects" mostly feed, rather than challenge, US foreign policy and development projects that work to control the future of these communities and countries to serve US interests. In each of these contexts, neoliberal feminist projects thus contribute to the structural inequities and subsequent injustices and violence experienced by women most marginalized by these interlocking systems.

Intersectional approaches to violence make visible how our responses to some forms of violence contribute to other forms of violence and to the systems that underlie them. In this way, a praxis of intersectionality builds a path toward accountability in that it requires that we name and take responsibility for the power lines that connect us to one another through hierarchical structures and the logics, discourses, and actions that maintain them. It makes more visible how our feminist theories, research, and activist work maintain, reproduce, and/or challenge and transform these systems of oppression. According to Razack, accountability is a "process that begins with a recognition that we are each implicated in systems of oppression that profoundly structure our understanding of one another."[9] By centering structural relationships between ourselves and others, as well as by focusing on how our praxes maintain these systemic hierarchies, Razack suggests that feminists move from a politics of *inclusion* (come join us on our terms) or *saving* (we'll come save you so that you can become more like us) to a politics of *accountability* (we work in solidarity, recognizing that our lives are interconnected and that we are responsible for the shape of that interconnection). As she writes, if we recognize how we are implicated in the "subordination of other women," then our "strategies for change" will "have less to do with being inclusive than they have to do with being accountable."[10]

The significance of this framework was made apparent to me ten years ago when I heard about the struggle of a group of immigrant domestic laborers in Chicago to find an organizational home for their work to address low wages, lack of health benefits, sexual and racial harassment, and violence, among other issues. A wide array of organizations they approached did not see the immigrant women's identities, lived experiences, or issues as significant to their agendas. Women's employment organizations would say that they do not deal with immigration issues, immigration organizations would say that these were women's issues, and labor organizations would say that these were women's and immigrant issues, not labor issues. In other words, each organization suggested that this group of women and its particular set of issues belonged to some "other" organization.

Their struggle was not an unusual one, and underlined for me the ongoing necessity of shifting from the compartmentalized, identity-based approach of inclusion to an approach grounded in intersectionality and accountability. When feminists who are US citizens and white, middle-class, monolingual speakers of English understand the realities of immigrant domestic laborers as simply different and separate from ours, we may simply ignore their struggles or offer to "help" them. In the latter case, we might plunge into a hierarchy by seeing their issues as located in their identities and cultures, unrelated to our own locations of structural privilege and entitlement. On the other hand, if we start from the premise that we ourselves *are implicated* in the dynamics and structures that shape the experiences of immigrant domestic laborers, then we might stand a better chance of recognizing our direct relationship and accountability to their plight.

In other words, if feminist scholars and/or projects took account of how we are implicated in the structures supporting low wages for domestic labor with no healthcare or Social Security benefits, and/or in the global capitalist system that creates the conditions for migration and flight, our responses would be quite different. Rather than locating the problem in the immigrant identities, our work of accountability would focus on the places of feminist complicity with the systems of oppression that are shaping their lives. This would require reexamining organizational assumptions of "women's labor issues," "immigrant issues," or "violence against women." It would mean making it a priority to challenge the devaluation of paid housework and childrearing that leads to very low wages and lack of benefits. It would mean working to address the transnational conditions that underlie sexual and racial abuse and mistreatment of immigrant women, including social isolation, the hostile racist and xenophobic climate against immigrants from the global south, and/or the marginalization of immigrant domestic workers in liberal feminism.

Another powerful example of the difference between a politics of "inclusion" and one of "accountability" is given by Simona Sharoni in her book *Gender and the Israeli-Palestinian Conflict*. She offers an analysis of alliance efforts between Palestinian and Israeli feminist groups during the first Intifadah.[11] She found that the alliances were quite fragile, particularly when Israeli Jewish women came to alliance building under a rubric of shared identities, experiences, and oppression *as women*, and did not want to discuss the Israeli occupation and its impact on Palestinians. This approach rubbed up against Palestinian women who came seeking allies in their struggle for justice. For them, the differences between them were political, structural, and economic, not cultural. As Sharoni writes, "Because their long-term goal was to bring about the end of the occupation, they saw their encounters with Israeli women as an important vehicle for influencing public opinion in Israel in that direction. For them, dialogue was not perceived as a means for overcoming differences and establishing personal relationships with Israeli-Jewish women, but rather a tool of social transformation and political change."[12] They were looking for a solidarity based in accountability, not simple inclusion based in shared experiences as women with an assumption of political neutrality. The alliance efforts that most succeeded were those grounded in collaboration and solidarity, where "the differences, injustices, and inequalities separating Palestinian and Israeli-Jewish women" were recognized from the outset.[13]

A praxis of accountability draws our attention to the ways in which identities, cultures, and communities are produced through historical, structural, and systemic inequities.[14] It draws our attention and action to the ways in which historically based power systems produce identities and differences, structure our relationships to one another, and become internalized into our individual and collective identities and consciousness as well as our political analysis and strategy. Rather than evading how these systems shape our collective work within communities, organizations, and movements, and rather than locating the causes of oppressive behaviors and actions in individual "bad apple" behavior, a praxis of accountability makes the inequities and divides open to ongoing collective scrutiny, intervention, and transformation. This process of scrutiny is not about calling out individual or organizational failures as anomalies, but rather about making visible the fault lines of structural inequities that distort and undercut the relational possibilities for individual and social action and transformation. If we cultivate critical and compassionate consciousness and skills to address these structural inequities as they manifest in our identities and relationships as well as in our theorizing, research, organizations, political visions, and strategies, we build more collective accountability within our antiviolence work to transform rather than to deepen these systems of oppression and violence, and to create the spaces where we can practice creating the world we envision.

Cultivating Accountability

The feminist intersectional and transnational theories and praxes that have gained visibility across the United States over the past forty-plus years are the ones at the heart of *Feminist Accountability.* In the book I bring together three areas of work around the concept of accountability—antiracist feminisms, community accountability and transformative justice efforts to end intimate and interpersonal violence, and transnational feminisms. I explore some of the emerging praxes of accountability, transformative justice, and transnational feminisms that have arisen in response to institutionalized carceral and imperial feminisms that reproduce rather than undermine the interlocking systems of oppression and privilege that produce pervasive violence. Each chapter draws from these emerging practices and tells stories about living, theorizing, analyzing, strategizing, building, and organizing that seek to build feminist individual and collective accountability for the ways in which we may participate in and contribute to these systems while we are also seeking to dismantle them. The chapters overlap in ideas, themes, and arguments, although they are purposefully given different emphases so that they can stand alone outside of the other chapters. Throughout the book, I share stories from my own experiences of teaching and organizing as well as from the many community organizers and scholar-activists, mostly women and queer, trans, and gender-nonconforming people of color, who have been developing these intersectional and accountability-based approaches to endemic interpersonal, community, state, and imperialist violence. These stories build upon and expand the possibilities for critically engaging and developing an ethics, politics, and practice of accountability across inequitable divides as a way of strengthening communities and movements for change.

In the book I emphasize the term "cultivating" as a reminder that accountability is a practice, not an end, and it is a continuous process, rather than a single act. As I try to remind myself and the reader throughout the book, this process of taking individual and collective accountability is an ongoing one, and it requires a willingness not only to name oppression but to understand our relationship to its perpetuation. In other words, rather than a practice of locating the problem outside of ourselves and the movements with which we affiliate, it is a practice of awareness about how our ideas, organizations, policies, and activism are often embedded in the logics and structures of power. This awareness creates the potential for taking active accountability in ways that lead to change and transformation.

This book is grounded in my experiences of learning about and practicing different methods of accountability—personal, interpersonal, communal, and collective—through my living, writing, teaching, strategizing, and organizing with others against oppression and violence. Most of this experience has been in the context of my involvement with feminist-of-color-led, queer, antiracist antiviolence efforts in Chicago. It is also informed by my participation in efforts to challenge US feminist contributions to US wars and occupations connected to global capitalism, white supremacy, and imperialism and to engage in transnational feminist efforts toward accountability for our contributions to and complicity within global divides. I am indebted to the amazing knowledge, wisdom, practical strategizing, community-building approaches, and vision of so many feminists of color within Chicago and across the United States whom I've had the opportunity to know, learn from, and collaborate with, as well as the many white feminist co-strugglers who are stepping up into the work of building solidarity, accountability, and new ways of living. The book would not be what it is outside of all those with whom I have been living in community and struggle. I am immensely grateful for the community, inspiration, ideas, and challenges from the following people, whom I am naming alphabetically by first name: Adaku Utah, Aimee Carillo Rowe, Alexis Pauline Gumbs, Alice Kim, Ana Romero, Andrea Ritchie, Barbara Ransby, Beth Catlett, Beth Richie, Brian Ragsdale, Cheryl West, Chez Rumpf, Choua Vue, Claudia Garcia-Rojas, Cricket Keating, Daisy Zamora, Deana Lewis, Erica Meiners, Erin Tinnon, Francesca T. Royster, Harvette Grey, Hiranmayi Bhatt, Iliana Figueroa, Jen Curley, Joey Mogul, John Zeigler, Laila Farah, Lara Brooks, Laurie Fuller, Lourdes Sullivan, Lourdes Torres, Manju Majendran, Mariame Kaba, Mark Hoffman, Mayadet Cruz, Michelle VanNatta, Mimi Kim, Misty DeBerry, Namita Goswami, Natalie Bennett, Penny Rosenwasser, Rachel Caidor, Rachel Herzing, Sandra Jackson, Sanjukta Mukherjee, Shakti Butler, Sharmili Majmudar, Sheena Malhotra, Shira Hassan, Sumi Cho, Tanuja Jagernauth, and Tony Alvarado-Rivera. I would also like to recognize my dear friend and collaborator Aparna Sharma (who passed away in 2013), who was a continuous support for this work. I also have deep gratitude for my community in women's and gender studies and the Women's Center at DePaul, particularly with the Building Communities, Ending Violence Project, a project that creates space for building knowledge and skills for community accountability and transformative justice. This is a project I co-initiated, -created, and -envisioned in 2010 with Michele Emery, an MA student in women's and gender studies at the time. Since then, I've had the great opportunity to work with many students and staff at DePaul who have contributed to creating this space for learning and practicing community accountability and transformative justice practices, including Anna Kochakian, Asher Diaz, Buki Ogundipe, Caitlyn Lomonte, Clare Stuber, Erin Tinnon, Hannah Arwe, Jill Kuanfung, Joy Ellison, Katie Heinekamp, Katrina Caldwell, Mary Hazboun, Michael Riley, N. A. Clark, Nihan Can, Olivia LaFlamme, Satya Chima, Shana Bahemat, Stefani Mikos, and Sydney Halliburton. I have deep gratitude for Laurie Fuller and Misty DeBerry, as well, who have been co-collaborators on the project at DePaul and beyond. I'm also grateful for the DePaul groups that have shaped my perspectives over the years, including Difficult Dialogues Committee, Feminist Front, SURVIVE, GRRRL House, and Dykes Against Oppression. Chicago-based organizations that I have learned and drawn inspiration from include Chicago Freedom School, Community Justice for Youth Institute, Dyke March Collective, Just Practice, Love and Protect, Project Nia, Queer to the Left, Queer White Allies Against Racism,

Survived and Punished, Women and Girls Collective Action Network, Young Women's Action Team, and Young Women's Empowerment Project, among many others. I am also deeply greatly for the learning I have gained through my engagement with groups outside of Chicago, including Communities United Against Violence, Creative Interventions, Critical Resistance, Generation Five, Incite! Women of Color Against Violence, Philly Stand Up and Philly's Pissed, Stop It Now, the Storytelling and Organizing Project, and Ubuntu, among others. And, as will be clear from reading the book, I am always learning from and being inspired by an amazing array of theorists, writers, artists, community organizers and educators, activists, healers, and more.

Organization of the Book

Feminist Accountability is a collection of chapters that reflect on what it means to engage in a praxis of accountability. The book is divided into three major parts: The first part, "Accountability as Intersectional Practice," consists of three chapters that explore accountability as a praxis of community and movement building that embraces critical engagement with the power lines of racism and white supremacy that shape our identities and politics. In this introduction, "Cultivating Feminist Accountability," I introduce the concept of cultivating accountability as a praxis that brings conscious awareness to how much our work as antiviolence scholars and activists is impacted by and implicated within hierarchical and intersectional relations of power. Chapter 1, "Building Communities," explores what it might look like to address everyday oppression and violence in communities by practicing, rather than avoiding, taking accountability for the impact of our words and actions. Chapter 2, "Navigating Speech and Silence," reflects on how the feminist call to speech as *the* method for personal and social transformation often reproduces rather than challenges inequitable power lines. It examines the compulsion both to speak and to be silent in feminist spaces, and offers strategies to resist structural and relational inequities in our efforts to build connections and solidarity across these formidable power lines. In the last chapter in this section, "Disrupting Whiteness," I reflect on my experiences teaching and my efforts to disrupt and resist the gravitational pulls of white-supremacist, patriarchal, imperialist capitalism that compel us toward the callous disregard of the pain and suffering of others in order to accept and assimilate into the hegemonic normative systems of power.

The second part, "Community Accountability and Transformative Justice," includes four chapters that explore the concept and practice of community accountability and transformative justice within the context of US-based feminist antiviolence movements. It begins with chapter 4, "Shifting Paradigms to End Violence." This chapter explores the 1970s shift in the feminist antiviolence movement from radical social change to institutionalized social services and exclusive reliance on the criminal legal system as a method of accountability for the perpetuation of violence, and the more recent shift in the 2000s toward (re)politicizing the movement with innovative approaches based in community accountability and transformative justice. These approaches have emerged from grassroots radical women and queer people of color antiviolence efforts. Chapter 5, "Collective and Communal Support," explores communal and collective methods of support and healing. Rather than seeing support as something offered to an individual as they cope with the experiences of interpersonal or state violence, a community-based approach to support recognizes the power of healing in community, and that when violence occurs within or against a community, all suffer, and thus all can benefit from participating in collective healing and justice. Chapter 6, "Everyday Responses to Everyday Violence," opens up the possibilities for collectively responding to everyday harassment, abuse, and violence. Rather than perceiving that the only option is calling the authorities (e.g., police), this chapter explores the possibilities of building knowledge and skills for everyday individual and collective interventions that do not rely on the police or other external authorities. Chapter 7, "From Punishment to Accountability," explores alternative methods of creating individual accountability for the harm of violence that do not rely on punishment, shaming, and oppressive systems of violence such as the criminal legal system. Recognizing not only the failures of the criminal legal system in fully supporting and affirming survivors of interpersonal and intimate violence but also the ways in which the system itself only perpetuates oppression and violence through its implementation, this chapter asks, what are the alternatives?

The third part, "(Re)Imagining Feminist Solidarity," includes two chapters that explore how a framework of accountability can help to disrupt and disentangle US-based feminist storytelling about the issues facing women of the global south that are embedded in US imperial discourses, logics, and social policies. Such a shift is essential for making visible the deep and historic relationship between and across these global divides and for creating possibilities for a solidarity based in mutuality, reciprocity, and respect. In chapter 8, "Disentangling US Feminism from US Imperialism," I explore how enmeshed mainstream feminist discourses are in US empire building, and offer ways of disentangling US ideas about solidarity from efforts of imperial conquest. The chapter takes as a case in point the "war on terrorism" as it has played out in the US occupation and war in Afghanistan since 9/11. Then, in chapter 9, "Resisting the 'Savior' Complex," I offer critical reflections on the book by Nicholas Kristof and Sheryl WuDunn, *Half the Sky: Turning Oppression into Opportunity for Women Worldwide.* In the chapter, I critically interrogate the underlying white-supremacist, capitalist, patriarchal, imperialist discourses in the book. Drawing upon transnational feminist theories, the chapter offers an oppositional rereading of the stories through a lens of accountability. Putting the book in the context of an increasing focus on the "empowerment" of women and girls in western development projects and in US militarism and foreign policy, this chapter deconstructs the myths of western superiority embedded in these discourses and builds toward a critical lens of accountability, rather than pity and altruism.

PART I

Accountability as Intersectional Praxis

1

Building Communities

What would it look like to cultivate accountability as an everyday practice of addressing harm to strengthen our communities? Rather than inflicting shame and punishment, accountability calls us to take responsibility for our contribution to and/or complicity in the harms of systemic oppression. Connie Burk of the Northwest Network in Seattle, Washington, frames accountability as "an internal resource for recognizing and redressing the harms we have caused to ourselves and others" rather than as "something that happens to bad people."[1] Similarly, Carolyn Boyes-Watson, in her book *Peacemaking Circles and Urban Youth*, suggests we understand accountability as "an active experience, not a passive one" in that "[i]t is something we do, not something done to us."[2] This approach to accountability disrupts the dominant carceral logic that reserves punitive and shaming responses for groups of people designated as the "bad people" while offering everyone else immunity from any responsibility for wrongdoing. Instead it calls for the recognition that all of us are capable of harm and complicity in systemic oppression, and so we all could practice taking accountability for our involvement in the perpetuation of oppression and violence.

This praxis of accountability is a decisive shift away from a "zero tolerance" approach to the harms of everyday oppression that offers no room for recovering from mistakes and that "relies on fear to motivate good behavior."[3] A zero tolerance approach assumes that people's racist, sexist, homophobic, and/or xenophobic words and actions are individual aberrations in an otherwise equitable and just community, and that oppression can be easily prevented and stopped by punishing, shaming, and/or ostracizing individuals who are oppressive. By contrast, through a lens of accountability, we recognize that the roots of oppression and violence operate on intimate, interpersonal, institutional, and systemic levels, rather than beginning and ending with the individual. These systems impact our lived realities and are always at work on our psyches, identities, relationships, and communities. From this perspective, racist behavior is an outcome of ongoing racial inequities, injustices, and abuses of power that are always/already operating in our lives, including in feminist, queer, antiracist, and social justice communities. When one of us perpetuates the harm of racism, then, we approach it not as an individual and unchangeable moral flaw from which we cannot recover but as an action for which we can take responsibility and make amends, and that we can commit to change. If we cultivate an ongoing praxis of accountability within our relationships and communities, we are much more likely to take responsibility for our actions, to learn from our mistakes, to make changes to prevent future harm, and to build deeper relationships in the process.

From this approach, taking accountability can become something we yearn to do rather than something we run away from. In other words, instead of causing us to try to pretend we are above perpetuating harm, a praxis of accountability directs us to recognize how our words, actions, and decisions are always embedded in relations of power and to act from that recognition. We can then approach the manifestation of oppressive systems in our lives as an opportunity to strengthen our skills of accountability and to practice disrupting systemic power and building toward change. As bell hooks in *Teaching Community* writes, "To build community requires vigilant awareness of the work we must continually do to undermine all the socialization that leads us to behave in ways that perpetuate domination."[4]

By making it a daily practice to name the ways white, male, heteronormative, able-bodied, and/or class privilege and supremacy inform our actions and manifest in our lives, we are better able to undermine their work in producing divisions, inequities, and violence. This requires that we become less afraid of recognizing how we are implicated in the everyday injustices and more eager to shift and transform power lines and the structural oppressions that maintain them. In our relationships, then, instead of responding to oppression through a framework of innocence and guilt to be met with approval or punishment, we encourage one another to take accountability for the systemic impacts and pulls of oppressive systems so that we can disrupt and transform them. When taking accountability becomes an active practice, it becomes less of a painful process that we mostly try to avoid.

The ways these systems manifest in our everyday words and actions, even when we are struggling against them, is indicative of the strength of the systems. Our mistakes, blunders, and complicity shed light on the gravitational pulls of systemic oppressions and illuminate the need for more work, struggle, and change. I am adopting this notion of "gravitational pull" from Chris Crass, a white antiracist activist and author of *Collective Liberation*.[5] He uses this term as a reminder that these forces are always at work pulling us into logics that normalize systemic oppression. Part of the necessary social change work is to lessen the power of systemic oppression over our identities and choices, and for this we need each other.

A *communal* approach to accountability means that we build relationships and communities that can hold the inevitable conflict, oppression, and difficulty that we will inevitably experience given the ongoing work of interlocking systemic oppression. This puts us in a better position to work collectively to engage, understand, process, and transform these systems and their impact. Such an approach, Sharon Welch suggests, offers a more modest "hope for resilience in the face of ongoing and new challenges." Within such a space, Welch envisions, "Rather than denouncing or bemoaning the partiality and weakness of others' responses, let us see them as something to be responded to, played with, and worked with."[6]

In this chapter, I draw on a praxis of accountability for building accountable communities of struggle that is fundamentally different from the current carceral logic that is often embedded in feminist and queer antiracist and antiviolence organizing. In it, I explore practices that help cultivate our willingness to take accountability for the ways we participate in and/or are implicated within systems of oppression and privilege. They call us to recognize, challenge, and transform the impact of systemic racism and white supremacy on our identities and relationships as well as our ideas and visions for social change. A praxis of accountability can build a community's capacity to address the harms of interpersonal and intimate violence, which are explored in the second section of this book.

Refusing Innocence, Embracing Accountability

One of the formidable barriers to owning up to how we are implicated in systems of oppression is the binary framework of guilt/innocence that pervades the dominant culture in the United States. The queer, antiracist feminist projects that I have been involved in over the last forty years have often mimicked carceral and punitive responses to the manifestation of endemic racism, white supremacy, heteropatriarchy, ableism, and other systems of oppression within and outside of our communities. We tend to divide people into two distinct and rigidly defined subject positions—victim or perpetrator. This binary framework leads feminist, queer, and antiracist scholars, educators, and activists to want to present ourselves as "innocent" in relation to structures of oppression and domination in order to evade the determination that we are guilty. And thus, as Ellen Kaye Scott suggests, we "tend to vie for membership in the victim category and attach a great deal of shame to belonging to the perpetrator category."[7] This response among white folks doing antiracist work, Tema Okun argues, is the "logical consequence of a cultural binary where we are taught we can only be one of two discrete choices rather than a muddy and chaotic mixture of both."[8] As a result, when people tell us that our words and actions are racist, sexist, homophobic, xenophobic, transphobic, or when they point out our complicity, we defend ourselves as a victim of some other oppression and/or we defend our individual intentions as innocent. We often present ourselves as one of the "good" ones located on the side of those marginalized, oppressed, and silenced, and we do this, in part, by primarily focusing on how we experience oppression.[9] Relatedly, even though queer and antiracist feminists recognize that oppression is systemic and structural, we often respond to oppression as if it is rooted in our individual attitudes and behaviors.[10] We tend to defend our individual intentions, rather than address the impact of our behavior and its relationship to broader systemic oppression. In order to dis-identify ourselves from systems of oppression from which we benefit, we resist examining how deeply entrenched these systems are in our identities, relationships, and interactions. These defensive and evasive responses block our ability to address the harms within and between us.[11]

A practice of accountability, on the other hand, encourages us to shed critical light on how these systems are manifesting in our lives and in our communities, rather than silence conversations that might reveal their impact. This makes it more likely that we are able to collectively build critical consciousness *and* action that would work to undermine and disrupt these systems. In other words, a practice of taking accountability for our acts and/or complicity can free us up to act, to change, and to transform ourselves. I have deeply appreciated the story that Aurora Levins Morales shares in her book *Medicine Stories* in the context of her family's complex, contradictory, and painful history of oppression, privilege, and resistance. In her essay, "Raicism," she shares how after growing up with her mother's struggles around poverty and racism in the Bronx, New York, she traveled to Puerto Rico and learned that she came from "five generations of slave-holding ancestors among the petty landed gentry of northeast Puerto Rico."[12] While this initially led her to feel shame, upset, and discomfort, she realized the deadendedness of this response. She decided to shift out of guilt and denial and move toward accountability.[13] For her, this translated into a commitment to break the family silences around slavery: "to acknowledge publicly and repeatedly my family debt to their coerced labor, to expose and reject family mythology about our 'kind' treatment of slaves . . . [and to make] African people visible in every discussion of Puerto Rican history in which I participate." Taking accountability, she suggests, frees us to act, and "leads to greater integrity and less shame, less self-righteousness and more righteousness, humility and compassion and a sense of proportion."[14]

This practice of tracing our locations and actions within structures of oppression and privilege was brought home to me in an antiracism training in 2000 for an LGBT group in Chicago called Queer White Allies Against Racism.[15] The trainers had us watch a short film, *Space Traders*, based on a short story by Derrick Bell (1993) from his book *Faces at the Bottom of the Well*.[16] Briefly, the story is as follows: an alien group lands in the United States and offers the following: "Give up all African-Americans and in return they will leave for America the contents of their ships—enough gold to retire the national debt, a magic chemical that will cleanse America's polluted skies and waters, and a limitless source of safe energy to replace our dwindling reserves. Following roughly two weeks to consider the offer, heated public debate leads to a referendum that when approved, consigns all blacks to the traders."[17] As the story develops, almost all of the white leadership and the majority of white people (70 percent) vote for the tradeoff on the basis of its benefits for whites; some even frame it as patriotic for Black people to do this service for the nation because it would restore all natural resources to the United States. While the film also shows people of color and liberal whites resisting the resolution, ultimately their efforts are ineffective.

After showing the film, the antiracist trainers asked our group of queer, white antiracist activists, with whom did you identify? Most of us expressed identification with the African Americans in the film—with their struggles, the dilemmas they faced, the pain of being betrayed by friends, the experience of being singled out and/or targeted. None of us spoke about our relationship with the white people in the film; instead, we distanced ourselves from them and their actions, particularly given the outcome of the film. The trainers challenged our dis-identification and asked us to explore more specifically how the white people in the film upheld or resisted white supremacy. They encouraged us to compare the white people's choices and actions in the film to our own decisions, relationships, actions, and allegiances we make in our lives, in our workplaces, political organizations, and educational institutions. Rather than placing ourselves outside of the system, or solely identifying with the experience of being oppressed, we were directed by the trainers to critically understand how embedded we are in the engines of white supremacy, and how our lives and decisions are impacted by as well as aligned with and/or resistant to that system. And it is within such a context of naming that we can best see where we are able to contribute to change and act in solidarity against racism and white supremacy.

Similarly, Leslie Roman, in her essay "White Is a Color! White Defensiveness, Postmodernism, and Anti-racist Pedagogy," argues that white people need to locate ourselves "*in* the stories of structural racism" rather than outside of them. We need to create narratives where we "fully account for the daily ways we (whites) benefit from *conferred* racial privilege as well as from our complicity in the often invisible institutional and structural workings of racism."[18] Such a process opens up paths for action in relation to these systems of power that we might

otherwise see ourselves as outside of. By recognizing rather than denying the places where we may be complicit in these systems, we can make
conscious choices about taking actions that would disrupt and shift
power lines. In so doing, we can act more decisively in solidarity with
people of color to resist, challenge, and transform these systems and the
devastating harms they create in people's lives, and to build a world, as
Shakti Butler from World Trust suggests, that would work for all of us.
Within this context, everyday accountability is an important reminder
of our interconnectedness in these systems, and of how our liberation is
bound up with one another, rather than isolated and distinct.[19]

From Identifying Privilege to Co-struggling

In the 1980s, in response to feminists of color calling for white feminists
to address racism, I joined other white feminists as we began to name
and make visible our relationship to racism and white supremacy. We
began to critically examine our unearned privileges, our consequent
sense of entitlement, and our active and passive complicity in interpersonal and institutional racism in order to critically understand how
these systems had shaped our feminist communities, organizations, and
political work. This practice of naming systemic privileges eventually
expanded to include class, ability, citizenship, gender, and other areas of
privilege.[20] Naming our privilege, dominance, and entitlement in systemic inequities and injustices, and their impact on people of color and
people of the global south, is important as these are underscrutinized
in dominant US and western culture. And yet, as the practice has been
assimilated into normative logics, it often translates into a static listing
of identities associated with privileged structural location, rather than
critical active engagement in response to our complicity and involvement in these historical systems of racism, white supremacy, capitalism,
patriarchy, and imperialism. Naming privilege became a process of
ascribing a passive identity attribute or status, rather than as something
we understand as systematically propped up, produced, reproduced, or
alternatively disrupted, challenged, and transformed through our daily
choices, actions, ideas, and/or our knowledge production. The listing
does not prompt people to reckon with the impact of white supremacy on our own identities and lives, nor the substantial and devastating

impacts our dominance and entitlement have on those oppressed, marginalized, and excluded through this privileging. Nor does it direct us to act or to resist.

In relation to action, many white antiracist educators and activists, like myself, also began to take up the term "ally" to signal our commitment to taking responsibility for our privileged locations and the associated harms. And while this too moved us out of evading our role in systemic oppressions, over time the term began to be used as an identity label and a role, rather than a praxis of action. Mia McKenzie, Black feminist blogger, aptly suggests in "No More 'Allies'" that we must approach allyship as a practice, "as an active thing that must be done over and over again, in the largest and smallest ways, every day."[21]

The word "ally" also locates those made dominant by systemic oppression as outside of their impact. In practice, it does not necessarily direct us to take accountability for how we are actively participating in the system, for the ways in which we are both implicated and impacted—physically, emotionally, intellectually, economically, socially, legally—by systemic oppression and violence; instead, it directs us to "help" less privileged "others." The result is that being an "ally" often reproduces the normativity of white supremacist patriarchy, rather than challenging it. For instance, when "allies" uncritically assume that we are in the best position to "do good" and "to help" those harmed, the concept reproduces the myth of superiority and does not challenge the inequity that structures our relationships. Within this framework, struggling against racism becomes something that we do for "others" and around issues that are separate and disconnected from "ourselves."

The conceptual frameworks of "privilege" and "ally" have not necessarily compelled us to recognize the distortions and devastation that result from our complicity with the systemic machinations of these systems. They do not illuminate the significant impact of active participation and complicity in racism and white supremacy on our identities, relationships, and communities. As Mab Segrest offers,

> What we miss when we only calculate our privilege is insight into the profound damage racism has done to us, as if we as a people could participate in such an inhuman set of practices and beliefs over five centuries of European hegemony and not be, in our own ways, devastated emotion-

ally and spiritually. The indigenous Hawaiian term for white person is *haole*—which means "without breath, or spirit, or soul."[22]

Instead of seeing white privilege as something *everyone* should have, Segrest reminds me that it is more important to see it as a systemic location and experience that creates callous disregard and ignorance for others as well as for ourselves. She challenges me—and other white people—to recognize the impact of our active and passive complicity in endemic racism and white supremacy on our humanity. When we only name a set of privileges, we act as if racism and white supremacy are positive for white people, rather than understanding how our passive and active complicity in them contributes to systemic oppression. She gets us to consider the impact of our investment in denying, minimizing, and turning away from the pain and suffering caused by institutional and structural violence and the impact of actively participating in harming, marginalizing, and ignoring those targeted by racism and white supremacy. Segrest suggests that white supremacy disciplines and controls our hearts, our capacity for empathy and connection, our ability to connect across power lines by producing a callous disregard for the well-being of people of color, poor people, and anyone defined as "different" and "other." A praxis of accountability, on the other hand, encourages us to recognize the stakes of those of us privileged by race or class or citizenship or gender in disrupting, challenging, resisting, dismantling, and transforming oppression and the violence it produces.

As the concept of "ally" has come into sharper focus for its limits, activists and writers offer up new terms that cultivate the taking of accountability through active engagement. Black feminist educator, writer, visionary, and scholar Mariame Kaba calls for "co-strugglers" who are actively engaged in collective action for structural change.[23] Co-struggling, as I understand it, implies that the root of solidarity is in people's active participation in collective efforts and struggles to transform these systems, working side by side with those most impacted, not as privileged outsiders. Co-strugglers are compelled to action not because of a privileged identity as ally but because we have vested interests in challenging and transforming these systemic injustices because of their profound impact on people's identities, relationships, and communities, including our own. Other community organizers and activists also use the terms "accomplices," "collaborators," and "co-conspirators" to call folks into action and solidarity. Each of these terms conjures relationships of mutuality and responsibility, rather than "helping," and most significantly, they imply active engagement in solidarity across the power lines of structural and interlocking systems of oppression.

Instead of seeing ourselves outside of the impact of systemic oppressions, co-struggling centers a recognition that we each have a stake in working together to intervene, disrupt, challenge, and transform these conditions of endemic violence, and that we must do so with a recognition of our differential relationships within these systems. It is placing ourselves in the struggle for freedom with others across inequitable divides that offers us opportunity for transforming the structural roots of the problem, including transforming who we think we are in relation to these identifications. Within the context of co-struggling, we must be mindful so as not to perpetuate the power dynamics that we are simultaneously seeking to dismantle, and to take accountability when we do.

Mistakes Are Integral to the Process

Given that we are living, breathing, and relating with one another within multiple and interlocking systems of oppression, we need a praxis of accountability to address their impact. Power lines cannot simply be willed away, and they are manifest in everything we think and do. The result is that it is inevitable that we will disappoint and hurt one another either through our oppressive words or actions, through our silence and complicity, or through our responses of punishment and shame. This has been the place of heartbreak and disappointment in so many of the feminist, queer, and antiracist programs, organizations, and classrooms that I have participated in over the years. We are so often hurt, angry, frustrated, and sad when everyday racism, homophobia, xenophobia, ableism, or another system of oppression manifests in a women's and gender studies class, and/or in a feminist and/or queer organizing meeting. We can feel the tensions in the room rise, the pain and anger flare, and the defenses set in. Sometimes people are called out, at other times they are ignored, avoided, and/or sidelined, and at still other times they are defended and protected from critique. Sometimes only a few notice and retreat from the conversation, sometimes those responsible become defensive and shut down, sometimes the group splits up without ever creating the space to address the conflicts. These responses are indicative of how difficult it can be to address these power lines and the harm they produce when we are in community with one another.

These default responses are linked to a carceral logic of establishing innocence and guilt. This is a logic that roots oppression in individuals and tries to control spaces to exclude or control such individuals. An accountability approach opens up processes of engagement and change. Rather than trying to control whether oppression will manifest, the focus is more on how we will respond *when* it manifests. Drawing on the recognition that we live within these social and systemic structures of oppression, we must recognize the manifestation of oppression in ourselves or others as inevitable, rather than surprising, and to understand that our work is in the everydayness of addressing and transforming these systemic manifestations of oppression, dominance, and power. As bell hooks writes, "[White people's] commitment to anti-racism does not mean they never make mistakes, that they never buy into race privilege, or that they never enact in daily life racial domination. . . . What it does mean is that when they make a mistake they are able to face it and make needed repair."[24]

In 2011, a multiracial group of students, staff, and faculty attended the twelfth annual White Privilege Conference, "This Land Is Whose Land? Defining Citizenship, Understanding Access, Taking Action," in Minneapolis, Minnesota. We were looking forward to gathering with thousands of others to learn about racism, white privilege, and white supremacy and to build skills to help us engage and expand social change and justice.[25] This conference creates space to share, imagine, and practice strategies with which to critically examine, disrupt, shift, and dismantle systemic racism and white supremacy, to heal from their impact, as well as to recognize how much our identities, relationships, and actions continue to be embedded in these systems. As the conference proceeded, our group met and began to share our upset with how facilitators or participants in workshops were perpetuating racism, white supremacy, patriarchy, and heteronormativity. Anger, disappointment, frustration, and defeat settled into our conversation. As a group, we began to build a narrative about the failure of the conference and its participants. We caught ourselves midnarrative and challenged one another to shift our conversation. We reminded each other that we were part of the picture we were painting of the conference, and that there were more than likely ways that our own complicity in "isms" was also manifesting, including in our desire to distance ourselves from others.

Rather than staying in our self-righteous critique, we began to grapple with how our distancing was also contributing to the perpetuation of the racism and white supremacy manifesting at the conference. We reminded ourselves that no space is free of these systems and none of us is completely outside of them. Moreover, we reminded ourselves that the conference does not promise a space free of all oppressive systems, and that the goal is not to be "perfect" or to create a "perfect" gathering. The desire for purity and for perfection, as Sharon Welch so aptly suggests, "is itself part of the logic of domination, the illusion that imperfection and error are solely negative and not part of the ingredients of creativity. We do not reach 'truth' by transcending error, by defeating enemies, by containing chaos; we do not reach 'truth' in spite of our particularity, our frailty, our finitude. We reach 'truth' through error, through chaos, through responding to cruelty and exploitation."[26] And so we began to reconceive of the conference as an opportunity for us to engage in the messiness of this work to disrupt and transform these systems and their perpetual impact on our identities, relationships, and communities. In this, we are bound to make mistakes, to be complicit with systemic privilege and/or oppression, and to use our words or to act in ways that are flawed and contradictory in relation to our vision. The recognition that "this is the work" and it is all of our work offered us a way out of either abandoning the project or ignoring the problems.

Our group then shifted from complaining about and distancing ourselves from other conference participants to exchanging strategies for how we could engage ourselves and others on what we were seeing and observing. A few of us decided to find the people with whom we were upset to engage in a conversation about our concerns. Some of the people of color (POC) in our group decided to use the POC-identity-caucus space to process their experiences, and some of us who are white decided to use the white-identity-based caucus space created by the conference to process and strategize around our concerns.[27] I appreciated going to the white identity caucus at the time. Instead of helping white participants sharpen our critiques of other white participants, the caucus space cultivated critical and compassionate reflection on how whiteness and white supremacy were manifesting in our own responses, including in our response to other white people's racism. This redirection of white people's energy contributed to our understanding that we ourselves are in a change-making process. Engaging one another from a space of collective movement building, rather than individually distancing ourselves from manifestations of racism and white supremacy, strengthened our ability to see how we could contribute to shifting the dynamics. We could then think about how our responses, actions, and inactions contribute to or diminish the ways in which whiteness and white supremacy were manifesting in the conference.

As a result of participating in these conferences and other antiracist events, I have become much more humble in my approach to cultivating accountability for the racism and white privilege of white people, including myself. Sharon Welch, in *Sweet Dreams*, writes,

> To move out of our identities as the dominant race, we must learn to fail—because we will, often and embarrassingly and repeatedly. It is not easy to dismantle centuries-long structures of racial oppression, a self-definition predicated on racial divisions. And yet, as Myles Horton knew, and celebrates in his work *The Long Haul*, it is often in our failures that we learn the most, often in our failures that we discover deep ties with people, in our failures that we plant the seeds of later victories.[28]

Embracing and learning from mistakes—my own and others—have strengthened my understanding that if we collectively support and practice accountability, we can much more effectively contribute to disrupting and dismantling systemic impacts of oppression. In other words, if we collectively engage conflicts, divisions, and the systems that fuel them, instead of avoid and deny them, we can create the change we envision as part of our community and movement building.

Deepening Relationships as a Praxis of Accountability

Given the default carceral punitive and individualistic approach to everyday harm, we tend to disinvest, shame, and punish those who act in oppressive ways, or we defend them by ignoring and/or denying the impact of their actions. A praxis of accountability, on the other hand, supports people to take accountability for everyday harm. This includes inviting and encouraging people to take responsibility for the harm and its impact, to make efforts to repair the harm, and to commit to transforming ourselves and the situation to prevent future harm. It encourages us to lean in to our relationships with one another to address oppression and its harmful consequences.

Ngọc Loan Trần, writing in the context of queer antiracist movement building, suggests that we learn to lean in to those we love and care about when they have caused harm through oppressive words and actions. Trần argues that the practice of "calling out" people is embedded in the logics of hegemonic power. Trần asks, "[W]hat does it mean for our work to rely on how we have been programmed to punish people for their mistakes?"[29] As with the current criminal legal system, Trần suggests, our resort to punishment and prescriptively rigid lines makes little room for the many times we mess up in our lives and hurt one another. And it does not encourage us to step up to accountability for harm. Rather than offering a place for change, it tends to contribute to lasting divides within our communities. As Trần notes, "[W]hen we shut each other out we make clubs of people who are right and clubs of people who are wrong as if we are not more complex than that, as if we are all-knowing, as if we are perfect. . . . [W]e resort to pushing people out to distract ourselves from the inevitability that we will cause someone hurt." Instead of offering a path for change, these default responses make it difficult for people to step up into accountability.

A praxis of accountability calls for engagement when we or others have caused harm, rather than defaulting to shame, blame, and rejection. This is particularly important when harm occurs within our close friend, familial, and community relationships. When people we care about cause harm, we want them to take responsibility, to understand the impact of their actions, to make it right, and to commit to change. In this context, Trần writes, "I am willing to offer compassion and patience as a way to build the road we are taking but have never seen before."[30] In such relationships, Trần approaches conversations grounded in shared values and experiences. This provides a context where we can encourage one another to recognize how our words or actions are not in line with our shared values and expectations, and offer support for realignment.

The goal is to deepen our understanding of each other and our shared values, rather than to shame and/or push out someone from our circle of caring.

Part of the work is to understand that we are living within systems that reinforce and reproduce oppression every day. Rather than viewing "mistakes" (that is, passive or active complicity within oppressive systems) as aberrations, then, we must see these mistakes as default normative behaviors. Given that we are living and breathing these systems of power and oppression every day, while simultaneously internalizing a carceral logic that blames racist and other oppressive behavior on individuals, we need to shift away from the idea that the oppressive words or actions are located within the individual. As a community building practice, Trần suggests "[c]alling in as a practice of loving each other enough to allow each other to make mistakes; a practice of loving ourselves enough to know that what we're trying to do here is a radical unlearning of everything we have been configured to believe is normal."[31] In a transformative justice class I teach at DePaul, we practice "calling in." Drawing on our own stories of everyday oppressive actions or words enacted by people we care about—our family members, our peers, our coworkers, our activist friends—we practice alternative responses to either ignoring the behavior or calling it out. I encourage us to practice using examples from our own lives. We engage in a process where we first reflect on why we care about the person we are upset with, we think about what we appreciate about them and our relationship with them, what common values we share, and why we are committed to engaging with them on what they have done or said. From this space of reflection, we practice calling them in to a conversation. Overwhelmingly, this shift in approach feels transformative as we are able to practice approaching people more holistically, and we can then imagine deepening our relationship with them rather than maintaining or deepening our upset with them.

This approach to harmful behavior creates the potential for deepening the work of social transformation. When there are paths that enable us to make things right and when we frame accountability in the context of a broader shared set of values and practices toward a more just community, we are more likely to take steps toward accountability. When I first started teaching women's studies in the 1980s, many feminist and social justice teachers, like myself, distributed no-tolerance anti-oppression guidelines to the students. Similar to the "zero tolerance" school policies developed at the time, the guidelines posited that oppressive words and actions would not be tolerated. The guidelines made it seem like "we" all understood and agreed on what was oppressive and what was not. They did not account for different perspectives linked to differential and intersectional relationships to power. The guidelines thus made it difficult for groups to grapple together with how systemic oppression is entrenched in our psyches and in our relationships. Instead, the guidelines made it seem that if I or someone else did not "get it" immediately, then I or the other person was "bad" and needed to be reprimanded and/or excluded from our community of belonging. While this approach sometimes silenced people, it did not create space for someone to take accountability, to make amends, to commit to change, nor did it produce a learning environment where we could explore the complexities of ideologies and their relationship to structural inequities and injustices.

Instead of setting up no-tolerance guidelines, I now follow a practice I have learned from community organizers in Chicago, including Mariame Kaba of Project Nia and Shira Hassan of Just Practice. It is a collective practice in which class members or workshop participants work together to build agreements that provide guidance on how to address the everyday oppression, privilege, entitlement, and power systems that will inevitably manifest in our work together. Participants share what they individually and collectively need in the space to allow us to engage in difficult conversations where we name oppressive behavior, where we take accountability for complicity in oppression, and where we can work through conflicts rather than avoiding them or letting them eternally divide the group. Rather than assuming that community is a given and that everyone is on the same page, I remind myself and the participants that *we are not the same*, that *we do not have the same experiences or interpretations of inequities*, and that *the differences in our experiences of interlocking power lines will rub up against one another*. From this space of difference, then, we look for values and practices that can hold our differences and the power lines that create them. The work this entails in both establishing guidelines and then practicing them in the face of conflict and/or oppression is often difficult, messy, and complicated.

While the list varies from group to group, the shared values and agreements we generate often include a commitment to engaging before immediately opposing one another, to responding to differences with curiosity and questions, rather than immediate judgment and dismissal, and to taking accountability for the impact of our words and actions, rather than defending them with the idea of our innocent intentions. We also often talk about being attentive to how responses to one form of oppression might in turn end up perpetuating another form of oppression. The hope is that we can create a context where challenging one another builds understanding as well as accountability, rather than proclamations about each other's "guilt" or "innocence." Ultimately, in classes and workshops, I encourage us to recognize that we are all shaped by the world we live in, that these systems are entrenched in our identities and ways of being in the world, and that it takes work to make it different.

It is important to recognize that such lists are not necessarily preventative, nor do they provide immediate resolution. And yet they are significantly important. What creating shared values does is to encourage participants to be mindful of how we engage with one another and to be more open to taking accountability for the impact of our words and actions. The process of creating these shared values early on in a class or workshop also allows people to return to the values when tensions or conflicts or systemic oppression manifests. In my classroom teaching, this has been the most valuable.

From Individual Critique to Collective Practice

Given the ongoing impact of systemic oppression on our psyches, ideas, actions, and relationships, our struggle to lessen this impact and shift the power lines that produce it requires more than individual engagement. Quite to the contrary, our struggle must be as much collective and communal as it is individual. It is this broader context of collective struggle that can sustain our resistance to these structures and that allows us to forge new ways of being in the world. In order to build this collective, we must shift out of the individualistic logic of blame and shame that so permeates the dominant culture. As Tema Okun suggests, we must view our self-awareness as a "collaborative, collective endeavor" rather than an individual one, where we could "help one another notice when we fall back into old behaviors until we gradually learn how to behave in accordance with our expressed desires."[32] By working collaboratively and collectively to support, build, and reinforce a communal critical consciousness as well as a vision of change and transformation, we are in a better position "to create a just world."[33]

In a keynote address at the White Privilege Conference in 2014, in Madison, Wisconsin, Chris Crass, a white antiracist activist, shared a story of how friends in his antiracist community work to support one another in living up to their expressed values. A friend of his had been doing research on anti-immigrant movements to develop strategies to counteract them, and in the process he began to feel the pull of some of their logics. He reached out to Crass to help him talk it through, to disrupt the force of the rhetoric, and to recenter his values and the social realities of those most harmed. He was able to do this because they had committed to helping each other stay accountable to their values and vision. Crass's story reminded me of how important it is to be intentional about building relationships in which we actively talk with one another about the impact of these systems on our psyches, ideas, and actions, rather than pretending we are above them. This would make it possible for us to more clearly address, disrupt, and dismantle their impact on ourselves and others. Community accountability, at its best, then, becomes a collective process and way of life, rather than an individual response to individual acts. Supportive relationships that center a praxis of accountability contribute to building and expanding a broader movement toward change.

Storytelling and Community

Storytelling in community can be a powerful method for cultivating critical consciousness and accountability. Through sharing stories we can recognize the social inequities among community members, rather than assuming a unity based in sameness. It allows us to see how we are integrally related to the abuse that others in our community are bearing, rather than seeing ourselves as separate and distinct. Richa Nagar and the Sangtin Writers document such a process in their book *Playing with Fire*. The Sangtins are a group of low-level workers in a women's empowerment NGO in the Uttar Pradesh district of northern India. The book tells the story of this group of women, who collaborated with Dr. Richa Nagar, a professor of women's studies currently residing in the United

States who was born and raised in northern India, in a storytelling and organizing project.[34] The project engaged the women in a process of sharing and documenting their stories, which in turn deepened their understanding of the interlocking systemic roots of oppression and violence within their communities, and it clarified what might best serve their organizing efforts for real change and transformation.

By attending to their individual stories, they made visible the intersecting power lines of caste, class, and religion in their lives—in their families and communities. This enabled them to collectively recognize how the power lines shaped the dynamics in their group, the NGO, and their broader interconnected communities. What emerged was a more nuanced framework that complicated the "women's empowerment" model of the NGO, which presumed that women share common experiences and common roots of oppression. This new framework made visible the complex power structures that shaped their relationship with one another, as well as with their communities and with the organization. Because they told their stories in relationship to one another, rather than as isolated and individual stories, they came to see how they were also implicated in the systems that were producing the oppression and violence others faced. For instance, some named how their family's mistreatment of them was connected with their family's low status and consequent mistreatment within their communities, a status shaped by their caste, class, and/or religion. This naming in turn revealed how other members of the group were also implicated in the mistreatment because of their higher status within the community. Their collective storytelling and analysis demonstrated that it is impossible to separate out the caste, class, and religious dimensions of their lives. This process enabled them to name the tensions and divides within their own relationships in and outside of the organization.

In other words, they came to realize that these divides were in fact integral to the structure and practice of the NGO. While the NGO is a "women's empowerment" organization, it, like many other NGOs, uncritically operates along the hierarchical lines of caste, class, and religion. These hierarchies are rarely challenged. As a result, the women of higher class or caste, for instance, automatically gained more structural and social power within the organization and within the broader community, while the contributions of women designated as of a lower class, caste, or religious status were structurally confined with no path to significant social mobility. Thus the organization reinforced the marginalization and low status of those women most marginalized in their communities.

By creating a space in which to talk about the differential impacts of these multiple structures, inevitably the women began to come to terms with how they were also implicated. This enabled them to make new commitments to trying to shift and transform these structures. The storytelling method cultivated accountability for how they viewed and treated one another and other women in the community. And it became a lens within which they began to respond to incidents of violence within their shared communities. Recognizing these differences and how they operated in the NGO, at the same time, caused tension and defensiveness on the part of the NGO, which then took action to shut down the critiques, relying on these same systems of power.[35]

Belonging, Community, and Accountability

In developing a shift in the way we approach harm, hierarchy, and oppressive systems, it has also been important to recognize that our identifications, relationships, communities, and loyalties are not necessarily bound by these prescribed hierarchical categories of identity. A key refrain within transformative justice work is that categorical identities do not determine whether one experiences or does harm; instead, people have the capacity to enact harm as well as to experience harm. This is not an erasure of our identities nor of our positionality within hierarchies and interlocking systems of oppression, but a recognition that our lived realities are complex and interconnected. These categories that we have inherited are not the end of our stories, and the way we live them in and through our relationships with others can shift what they mean.

While our identities inform our critical consciousness and politics, they are not fully determinant. Our life choices, relationships, communities of belonging, and actions can disrupt, shift, complicate, and even transform our consciousness and our politics. In *Power Lines*, Aimee Carillo Rowe suggests that the possibilities for alliances and solidarity across power lines is linked to a communal accountability that emerges from the knowledge grounded in relationships and communities as much as from individual identity and social location. She argues for a politics of relation because it undermines the individual and isolated nature of most feminist understandings of how we come to know and understand the world and one another. She writes,

> A politics of relation seeks to . . . provide a point of entry to theorize experience and agency as collective processes. . . . The broader cultural forces in which we are situated provide a vital layer of meaning through which we come to know experience. But as we make sense of our experiences, we turn to those we love and trust for guidance, and we provide this for others.

She calls us to recognize, then, "that how we insert ourselves in community produces a range of options not only for what kinds of experience become possible (experience), but also for how we come to understand those experiences (consciousness), and how we seek to transform, challenge, and resist the conditions which produce it (agency). A politics of relation, then, entails understanding agency, experience, and consciousness as collective and interrelated moments within a circuit."[36]

This reminds me of my ongoing shifts in critical consciousness and action that continue to evolve and expand. If I lived the life envisioned and initially built by my conservative, Roman Catholic, upwardly mobile, middle-class, white family in the late 1950s and 1960s, I would not have lifelong commitments to social justice, embedded in relationships and communities that I have chosen, with others, to build across inequitable divides produced by the interconnected systems of patriarchy, racism, capitalism, heteronormativity, ableism, and imperialism, among others. And similarly, if I had simply fallen in line with the liberal feminism and/or lesbian and gay politics associated with my particular identity and location—white, middle-class, lesbian, professor, able-bodied, US citizen—I would not be living the life I am living within chosen families, communities, and movements that cross multiple identities, spectrums, and communities and that are integral to my everyday life and commitments to broad-based social and political change.

The path I have come to forge is not one of individual consciousness and action, but rather a deeply collective process—embedded in the relationships, community, and alliances I continue to build with others within and across power lines, in the service of social justice and transformation. These continue to transform who I am, how I think, what I do, and what kind of world I seek to build with others. The social and political life I continue to forge with others is always in struggle with and against a backdrop of how I grew up. Even as a young child, I felt, and often fought against, the injustices around me—I knew there was something deeply wrong with oppression and violence, even as I also felt so entrenched in its dynamics given my white, middle-/upper-middle-class, heteronormative family and community. It is finding and building community with others that have fed my deep yearning for connection and community in a "remade world."[37] And, of course, the choices I make have been and continue to be interconnected with my sources of pain and anger, oppression and privilege, both—not one or the other, but both. And none of it is neat or clear or easy; instead, it is complex, messy, and always a process of making mistakes and trying again. This leads me to Sharon Welch's question and reflection:

> Where does this leave us in our work for justice, in our attempts to build and sustain community?
>
> We are not ushering in a new age.
>
> We are not part of a grand cultural revolution.
>
> We are not fighting the war to end all wars.
>
> We are, quite simply, like all the generations before us, and all the generations that will come after, learning to walk.[38]

2

Navigating Speech and Silence

In the 1970s, when I first got involved in feminist movement, I felt compelled to speak to everything and everybody. Speaking was my resistance. I had started speaking out as a kid in my white, middle-to-upper-middle-class Catholic family in Central Illinois. I was mad at the injustices I experienced and observed as they were perpetrated by my father, by the Catholic Church, by the schools, and by people within my communities. I was one of those white, middle-class girls who sometimes talked back and often got punished for it. But that did not stop me from speaking. I was ecstatic to discover feminism when I was a college student. The white, middle-class, liberal, socialist, radical, and lesbian feminisms I found on campus validated my anger at the everyday patriarchy, homophobia, racism, and classism I experienced and/or observed in my family and in my community. Feminist organizing provided me with access to the social theories and critical analyses that helped me to name and understand the systems and practices that I found oppressive and unjust, and with the relationships and activist communities where I found support and courage to develop ideas, strategies, and visions for change. In many ways, these feminist, socialist, and lesbian communities provided me with spaces from which to collectively organize and talk back to unjust power.

As I came into feminist speech, I equated silence with oppression and speech with liberation. I came to assume that my socialist, radical, and lesbian feminist politics, in combination with my experiences with oppression and violence, gave me the authority to speak out in whatever contexts I chose. It did not occur to me at the time that my taking up space, my sense of "authority," and my comfort with speaking in generalities could be connected with my race, class, able-bodied, and citizenship privileges, located in the predominantly white, middle-class university setting, or that my speech and action could serve to marginalize the voices and perspectives of women of color; working-class, poor, and/or immigrant women; and queer, transgender, and gender-nonconforming people of color, including those living with disabilities. Nor did I realize how the unspoken *privileges* of my identity and location were implicated in and could serve to reproduce the very systems and relationships of power that I thought I was combating.

It has been through my experiences of intentionally building relationships and community across "power lines"[1] that I have come to understand how the praxes of speech and silence are intricately connected with the power systems we are working to dismantle and transform. Through my living and working in multiracial and transnational feminist communities, I have come to rethink the call to speech as *the primary method for transformative change*. I no longer assume that my speaking up is *the path* to liberation and freedom. Instead, I remind myself to critically interrogate both my compulsion to speak and my compulsion to be silent, particularly in terms of how my choices are situated within inequitable power relations. In addition, I am more critically reflective of my presumption of feminist "authority." I recognize how the sense of entitlement to speech is intricately connected with my simultaneously privileged location as a white, middle-class, lesbian, and queer feminist scholar in the university. As importantly, I recognize how my "inhabited silences" may reinscribe, rather than disrupt, the power lines that inform and shape alliances and coalitions. In this chapter, I reflect on the practices of speech and silence as they relate to cultivating accountability across the power lines embedded in feminist movement building.

Disrupting Speech as Entitlement: The Practice of Listening and Embodied Silence

Talking, speaking out, demonstrating your knowledge, and making yourself known are often taken as the signs of "real" engagement, leadership, and contribution in many middle-class, feminist, queer, and/or social justice organizations. The cultures of these groups often privilege those quick to demonstrate their powers of knowledge and expertise, and those who presume to command authority in any given situation. The power lines produced within these organizations often follow along the preexisting lines formed by structural and systemic oppression and privilege in terms of race, class, education, and language, even when the stated goal is to dismantle and transform these structures of oppression.

In speaking to what is needed to shift these power dynamics, María Lugones and Elizabeth Spelman offer suggestions for white feminists seeking to build theories and consciousness with women of color in ways that do not reinscribe asymmetrical power relations; they write,

> So you need to learn to become unintrusive, unimportant, patient to the point of tears, while at the same time open to learning any possible lessons. You will also have to come to terms with the sense of alienation, of not belonging, of having your world thoroughly disrupted, having it criticized and scrutinized from the point of view of those who have been harmed by it, having important concepts central to it dismissed, being viewed with mistrust, being seen as of no consequence except as an object of mistrust.[2]

The experience of being decentered within multiracial feminist spaces, for instance, can cultivate critical consciousness building centered in the lived experiences of women of color. And this practice is one of many that contribute to a feminist organizing that does not reproduce the inequitable power divides created by racism and other interlocking systems of oppression. It disrupts the hegemony of white privileged power and the relational dynamics it produces within feminist, queer, and social justice movements.

One of the simplest, most profound, and yet consistently difficult practices that disrupts the automatic entitlement to hegemonic speech is active listening. Stepping back from speaking, and stepping up to active listening is one method of undermining the presumed entitlement to be at the center of the conversation, to speak in universals, and to determine the direction of the agenda. Active listening creates potential for an equitable collective process, one in which those most privileged are not at the center, and one in which our ideas and our selves are open to modification, change, and transformation. This is not simply about the physical act of hearing without speaking, or making space for "others" without real engagement. As Lynet Uttal laments about her experience as a woman of color speaking in white-dominant feminist spaces, "I am tired of feeling that my words were given space, but they might as well have not been said because they didn't get built upon or incorporated into the conversation."[3] Active listening implies a willingness for our identities, ideas, theories, and actions to be transformed in the process of dialogue. Megan Boler offers a useful distinction between "passive empathy" and "testimonial reading." She writes, "The primary difference between passive empathy and testimonial reading [listening] is the responsibility borne by the reader [listener]. Instead of a consumptive focus on the other, the reader [listener] accepts a commitment to re-think her own assumptions, and to confront the internal obstacles encountered as one's views are challenged."[4] For Boler, this includes the willingness to "recognize oneself as implicated in the social forces that create the climate of obstacles the other must confront."[5]

Engaging in active listening, however, does not necessarily mean power dynamics will shift. Audrey Thompson, in reflecting on the asymmetries of listening, writes, "[W]e [white people] have a hard time finding ways to listen that do not simply reinscribe our sense of entitlement."[6] One of the manifestations of such entitlement is the conditions placed on our willingness to listen, for instance, saying that we will listen as long as we do not feel bad, or excluded, or blamed. Thompson suggests that this form of listening is based on the idea of "formal reciprocity" where "everyone is to be treated identically."[7] It does not consider the differential stakes in conversations, particularly those regarding racism, classism, and public policy. By way of example, Thompson offers the story of a white student who "once protested that her concerns were not being given the same validation as black people's" in the class. This student struggled with Black students who argued that, for them, it was a priority to increase the number of Black teachers in schools with predominantly Black populations; the white student felt that her desire for racial integration through the experience of having white teachers was necessary *for her* to unlearn racism, and so it was *as important* as the desire of the Black students for Black teachers. She resisted the idea that there were different stakes involved for her as a white woman than for the Black students who were also her peers. It was through a subsequent commitment to deep active listening that "she came to appreciate the differences in power and privilege at stake." Through the process, she came to understand that accountability to the African American students and to their goal of creating the best environment for the education of Black children was more important than her own needs and desires.[8] In reflecting on her process, she shared with Thompson, "'All I could see at first . . . was what *I* needed and wanted.'"[9]

These practices of listening, decentering, minimizing intrusiveness, and stepping back often create discomfort, particularly for those with internalized entitlement to structural advantage. In my own efforts to decenter myself in multiracial feminist spaces, I often feel "less important" as a participant as defined by the standards of normative power relations, and yet simultaneously I feel it is another opportunity for living in ways that disrupt, rather than contribute to, white supremacy. For instance, in 2002 and again in 2015, Incite! Women of Color Against Violence organized national conferences in Chicago. Their goal for each conference was to create a woman-of-color-centered space for the event. This decision, while controversial to some, has been an important intervention given the history of white, middle-class dominance in feminist antiviolence work, including the marginalization of the identities, experiences, perspectives, and approaches of women of color, lesbian, queer, gender queer, and trans people of color, poor people, and women from the global south, among many other groups. In order to interrupt these power relations, Incite!, organizers decided in 2002 that white women and male-identified allies would contribute to some aspects of planning (e.g., fundraising and logistical support) and deliberately withhold from participating in others (e.g., planning the program, attending workshops). Some white women and men of color, like myself, who were working in solidarity with Incite! stepped up to talk with white women and men of all colors who were uncomfortable with or opposed to the centering of women of color. In 2015, white women and queer, trans, and gender-nonconforming people also contributed by creating guidelines for white participation, and we helped to implement them during the conference. The experience of participating in this way was a very good one. I respected the space being created, I understood its significance within the broader movement, and I felt honored to contribute in the ways mentioned. It also was uncomfortable at times, in part because I wanted to be in sessions to listen, to learn, and to participate. Through the practice of stepping back, I came to appreciate that decentering does not necessarily mean nonparticipation. Instead, it means another kind of belonging, a belonging not conditioned on my centrality, and yet nonetheless a deeply connected belonging contingent on a practice of accountability to the work of transforming, rather than reproducing, deeply entrenched power relations.

These transformational moments in my life have mostly occurred when I am intentional about how much space I take up speaking and how much space I give to listening—when I stop myself from thinking only about what I have to say, or assuming that what is most important in this moment is for me to reveal myself as knowledgeable. It happens when I listen with curiosity rather than simply for confirmation of what I think I already know. Cynthia Enloe talks about this disposition in terms of "being open to surprise," which she says "may be among the most useful attitudes to adopt to prepare one's feminist self for what lies ahead."[10]

Through active listening and striving to refuse the know-it-all feminist persona, I am reminded of how much I do not know or understand. This is a most humbling experience. It consistently deepens my awareness of how much a privileged location in the university has propped me up to be "all-knowing." It also provides me with opportunities to consider how distorted my race, class, able-bodied, nation-bound consciousness can be when left on its own, isolated from multiracial and transnational social justice and feminist relationships and communities.

This shifting of locations of "authority" and "knowledges" (my own included), in many ways is just as central to the process of transformation as is speaking to power. As M. Jacqui Alexander writes,

> There is something quite profound about not knowing, claiming not to know, or not gaining access to knowledge that enables us to know that we are not the sole (re)producers of our lives. But we would have to apprehend the loss that comes from not knowing and feel its absence in an immediate and palpable way in order to remake ourselves enough, so that our analyses might change. We have to learn how to intuit the consequences of not knowing, to experience their effects in order to reverse some of the deeply embedded deposits on which an imperial psyche rests—a psyche that still holds on to the idea of manifest destiny and the fiction of protection and safety from an enemy, who is either calculating on the borders outside or hovering on the margins within. We would have to visit the devastation of living segregated lives.[11]

The practices of accepting our not knowing, of stepping back, of committing to being "in conversation, not domination, with a range of relational knowledges,"[12] create new possibilities for transforming feminist movement building so that we undermine rather than entrench existing power lines within our relationships and organizations.

Interrupting the "Inhabited Silences" of Whiteness

Reflecting on the spaces between speech and silence and their relationship to power, I have also come to be more attentive to the spaces of "inhabited silences" that are implicated in my complicity with whiteness.[13] Here I am thinking about how keeping whiteness an invisible and unscrutinized presence reproduces inequitable power lines rather than disrupts them. White, middle- and upper-middle-class feminists, like myself, have often premised building solidarity on shared experiences of oppression and/or resistance, with less attention to the inequitable power lines that separate and divide people. There seems to be an active investment in sameness, as is evident in the "me too" that we may insert into this or that conversation as a way of commiserating, creating common cause, and building an alliance. While on the one hand the "me too" can be a way of creating connection, it also may serve to obscure the ways our experiences, perspectives, and actions are differentiated and fractured because of our differential locations within these hierarchical structures of oppression and privilege. In addition, the "me too" often deflects attention from our complicity with the systems that shape our different experiences, and therefore from becoming accountable to one another for the ongoing impact of these inequitable divides.[14]

By way of example, I remember being in a discussion focused on the dearth of leadership of faculty of color at the university, when a white woman faculty member, with significant institutional power relative to most faculty of color in the room, commiserated with the people of color in the room. She asserted a "me too" in response to the issue of institutional racism, by identifying herself as one of the "outsiders" in the academy (i.e., shared positionality of oppression). She then went on to narrate a story about how *despite* her "outsider" identity, she had ascended through the ranks of power through her own individual persistence and with good mentoring. This was her argument that the solution to the problem was better mentoring. And yet what was missing from her narrative was how her growing status as an insider had been, in part, contingent on the structural privileges she gained through relations of white heterosocial belonging.[15] These privileges are related to the networks of power she had been able to access through personal and then institutional relationships with white men in leadership positions in the university, relationships in part made possible because of whiteness and heterosociality.

This experience led me to deeper reflection on the politics of claiming for oneself an "outsider" (i.e., oppressed) identity when doing so serves to evade and/or resist oppressive power dynamics and our complicity with them. The claim to be an outsider does not necessarily lead to collective solidarity, nor to a commitment to dismantle the structures of institutionalized inequities that shape our differentiated experiences. Instead, it may function to evade taking accountability for our complicity in these structures. Ultimately, a discourse of shared oppression, and shared "outsider" identity maintains the "inhabited silences," in the case above, around the specificities of white, middle-class, and heterosexual privilege, and the power lines that are integral to the differentiated experiences of faculty within the academy.

Alternatively, breaking the "inhabited silences" by explicitly naming whiteness and white supremacy as a systemic hierarchy in which we are located might create possibilities for strategic alliance building for change. Such naming would shift the dynamics of what is being said and not said, examined and not examined. In the context of faculty of color and leadership at the university, it would shift the focus of scrutiny from faculty of color who are told that they just "need mentorship" to become an "insider" to a critical examination of the policies and practices by which white faculty so often ascend into leadership through their mostly white heterosocial networks and by which faculty of color are often marginalized.

And yet, as Ellen Kaye Scott found in her analysis of antiracism efforts within two feminist antiviolence organizations in California, naming does not necessarily break the silence with regard to the everyday racism within an organizational context. In her work, she found that while many of the white women were able to become race cognizant of their identity, it did not mean that they were able to articulate the everyday racism in their midst. As Scott writes, "[W]hile white women could problematize their white racial identity, they had a great deal of difficulty identifying manifestations of racism and the ways in which they perpetuated racism."[16] She attributes this difficulty to the entrenchment of a binaristic framework to address racism in the United States that focuses on determining whether someone is a victim or a perpetrator of racism. She suggests that even with the best of intentions, given this framework, many of the white women did not feel comfortable naming racism, were fearful of being wrong, and lacked the tools to articulate their own relationship to structural racism and its impact on the culture, dynamics, and relationships within the organization.[17] In *Teaching Community*, bell hooks argues that this binary approach makes it difficult to build antiracist community; she writes, "Either/or thinking is crucial to the maintenance of racism and others forms of group oppression. Whenever we think in terms of both/and we are better situated to do the work of community building."[18] hooks emphasizes an alternative approach to what it means to make a commitment to antiracism; as quoted in the preceding chapter, she writes, "[White people's] commitment to anti-racism does not mean they never make mistakes, that they never buy into race privilege, or that they never participate in racial domination. . . . What it does mean is that when they make a mistake they are able to face it and make needed repair."[19]

"Outsiders" and Relations of Belonging

Returning to the question of identification as "outsiders," I am interested in shifting what it means to be an "outsider" from an identity of shared oppression to a political praxis grounded in differential belonging with a commitment to coalition building. If we connect outsiderhood to a commitment to resistance and solidarity as well as accountability, then the possibilities expand to build alliances for collective liberation. In other words, we might intentionally coalesce around an "outsiderhood" grounded in accountability across differential and inequitable power lines. Within a frame of multiracial alliances, an "outsider" identification becomes less about shared identity or oppression, and more about a shared commitment to refusing a politics of exclusion grounded in respectability and hetero/homonormativity and their roots in interlocking systems of oppression. Such a shift might be in tandem with Cathy Cohen's intersectional and transformative approach to *queer* politics; in her essay "Punks, Bulldaggers, and Welfare Queens," she calls for a radical and imaginative politics in which queer is a signifier of nonconformity, resilience, and resistance to white, middle-class, heteronormative hegemony, rather than a static, unidimensional sexual-orientation identity that is always already implicated in existing power hierarchies.[20] Within this context, creating "outsider" communities might be accomplished through processes suggested by Cricket Keating for "coalitional consciousness building" that recognizes the differential relations of power operating in the world as well as the ways in which we are differentially implicated in them. Coalitional consciousness would require that we break "inhabited silences" and make these relations to power explicit, rather than invisible, used rather than evaded, and yet still from within a place of collective movement building. As Cohen's title suggests, what might it look like for "punks, bulldaggers, and welfare queens" to gather together to challenge structures of heteronormativity, classism, and racism, among other forms of oppression, from each of their unique vantage points?

Breaking Ranks with the Whiteness of Feminist Belonging

When whiteness becomes subject to scrutiny in the analysis of the interlocking systems of oppression, including white supremacy, the myths of meritocracy and individualism are diminished.[21] In her essay "Silence Speaks," Lisa Mazzei, drawing on the work of Elizabeth Ellsworth, suggests that silence about whiteness as a system of power becomes "a means of 'fitting in,' remaining invisible, protecting the vulnerability to emotional/intellectual exposure, or simply avoiding calling attention to oneself" and is linked to a broader cultural system of whiteness.[22] On the basis of her work with white students in the field of teacher education, she argues that they resist the naming of whiteness because it "means they risk a loss of privilege, identity, and comfort . . . A loss of identity when an undoing of white privilege means that their unspoken, unacknowledged, unnoticed position of whiteness is suddenly called into question and redefined, reinscribed, or refuted."[23] By naming and owning white people's everyday implication in a broader

system of racism and white supremacy, we lose our claims to innocence, ignorance, and distance from the problem. Such naming, then,
is uncomfortable, causes distress, and yet may be what will cultivate
more accountability.

Thandeka, in *Learning to Be White*, argues that the investment white
people have in deflecting conversations about race onto people of color
and in evading explicit discussions of whiteness is connected to the conditions of belonging mandated by most white families and communities.[24] She came to this conclusion through her experience of talking
with white people about their white racial identities. Her investigation
began in response to a query from a white colleague who asked her to
talk about "what it felt like to be black" but who was then flustered when
Thandeka responded to her colleague by asking her "what it felt like to
be white." From this exchange, Thandeka invented what she came to
call the "Race Game," in which she asked her white colleague to use the
word "white" whenever referencing white people in her daily conversations.[25] The colleague never met up with her to discuss the results. When
Thandeka asked other whites to engage in the "Race Game," most could
not or would not do it, and were equally unwilling to talk with her about
why it was so difficult. She wrote the book *Learning to Be White* in an
effort to explore the "feelings [that] lay behind the word *white* that were
too potent to be faced."[26]

Thandeka argues that it is shame that underlies white people's discomfort with examining our white identities, a shame that does not
preclude feeling comfortable talking about race in relation to people of
color. From her conversations with white people she found that many
had experienced rejection, discipline, and punishment from their white
families when they failed to follow the rules of whiteness. These rules
include uncritically going along with the racist mistreatment of people
of color as well as maintaining race-segregated relationships and communities. In order to avoid punishment and exile, white children and
adults comply with these rules. To be accepted, many white people will
resist naming whiteness and will avoid critical discussions of white entitlement, racism, and white supremacy with other whites. Adherence to
these rules becomes the condition of belonging in many white families
and communities. Thandeka suggests that the cost of *becoming white* for
white folks is to live with the shame of this complicity.

Thandeka's analysis prompts the question, are there conditions of be-longing to white dominant feminism? And I would say, "Yes!" I would suggest, in fact, that *silence* with regard to the practices and structures of racism is often a condition of membership in predominantly white femi-nist communities that are not explicitly antiracist. If you want to be part of the group, you must not speak up about racism within feminism, you must not explicitly name whiteness or white supremacy in relation to fem-inism, you must not align with women of color in critically engaging other white feminist women or organizations. I have certainly experienced such conditions when I have spoken up about racism within organizational contexts; for instance, when I have challenged feminist racism, I often have been accused of divisiveness and told that I am not a real feminist, that I do not care about women's issues, and/or that I am a race traitor.

These conditions of belonging to whiteness become evident when an-tiracist critique and/or women of color are centered within a feminist context and white feminists complain that we feel "silenced" or "vic-timized," or that the event or activity is no longer feminist. I have been in situations where white women say that "they" (that is—we) feel si-lenced, no longer feel "welcome," no longer "belong," or no longer have a place in feminism. Sometimes, such statements are made in response to programming and/or politics that highlight racism or multiple and interlocking systems of oppression, or that privilege particular groups of women of color, poor women, queer women, and transgender women, among others. I feel that such statements reveal an anxiety as well as an anger at having whiteness made visible, open to scrutiny, no longer a stand-in for individualized universality. I think these claims around these feelings of being "silenced" must be interrogated in the context of white entitlement and dominance, particularly since silence is so often equated with oppression.

A very good friend of mine shared this story about an experience in a women's studies program in which the faculty members were pre-dominantly white and there had been little to no direct conversations about race or racism. At a meeting of the broad interdisciplinary com-mittee, a relatively new woman of color faculty member made the ob-servation that there were very few faculty women of color involved in women's studies. She suggested that the group reflect on the situation and strategize ways to involve more women faculty of color. In response, a white woman faculty member began to cry and offered to drop out of the committee to make room for women of color. In response, all of the white faculty members' attention refocused on the white woman. They reassured her that her membership was very important and that they would never ask her to step down. It should be noted that the woman faculty member of color never asked any white faculty member to step off the committee. The concerns that she, the faculty member of color, brought to the table were immediately dropped, and of course, there was no similar outpouring of concern about her sense of community within the program, nor those of other women of color. The white woman's emotional outburst served to deflect attention away from the problem of exclusion and to shift it to the identity, experience, and feelings of the white woman, and by extension all the other white women in the program. Rather than address why so few faculty of color were involved in women's studies, the focus became making sure that white women feel validated. Rather than consider the harm caused by institutional marginalization, it became more important to protect the speaker and her membership in the community from scrutiny, to retain her "innocence."

Sarita Srivastava, in her essay "Tears, Fears, and Careers: Anti-racism and Emotion in Social Movement Organizations," explores similar situations in a variety of feminist organizations that she sees as governed by "therapeutic conventions" that uncritically privilege emotional expression over critical analysis.[27] She suggests that there is a pattern of white feminists responding to antiracist critiques with hurt feelings and claims that such critiques make the space less "safe." In these instances, Srivastava argues, the white women in leadership label the women of color as "angry" while they perceive themselves and other white women as innocent victims of antiracist critique, represented by the image of a "tearful white woman."[28] In these contexts, white women's expression of vulnerability shifts the locus of concern from the vulnerability and feelings of marginalization expressed by women of color to recentering white women's sense of vulnerability and simultaneous entitlement. Gail Griffin suggests that such dynamics simply perpetuate the "long, tiresome history of white middle-class women espousing 'weakness' as a buffer from consciousness, responsibility and struggle."[29] What is left unsaid in such instances is how these emotional disclosures themselves are "shaped by the inequitable relations of race" and serve to maintain the status quo.[30] They serve to deflect attention from white accountability for institutional racism. The uncritical, unreflective acceptance of white women's emotional outbursts in response to antiracist critique undermines efforts to engender structural shifts and changes in organizations.

What would it take to challenge and transform such dynamics? What would it look like to name the dynamics created by the "tearful white woman," as described by Srivastava, and to interrogate the systems such tears serve in the face of antiracist critique? Srivastava argues that feminists must rethink the role of emotion in organizations and address "the historical relations of power that prompt emotional resistance to discussions of race, and that allow white participants to openly express their tears, anger, and despair in the face of anti-racism."[31] This might include explicitly naming the segregated and white hegemonic histories that are called up in the defenses of women's studies and/or feminist communities.

I have certainly experienced these conditions. In the early 1980s, I remember my shock at how quickly my white, middle-class, liberal and radical feminist peers in a graduate feminist theories class turned against a few of us for simply naming feminist racism, following the lead of the radical women of color feminisms offered by Cherríe Moraga and Gloria Anzaldúa, bell hooks, and Angela Davis, among others. They accused us of being antifeminist and homophobic for simply raising the questions. More recently, during the Democratic primaries in 2008, I was surprised at how quickly white feminist leaders like Gloria Steinem and Robin Morgan, among others, questioned the feminism of so many of us for daring to support Obama rather than Clinton for president. Again, a litmus test for feminism—if you do not prioritize gender over race, then you are not a "real" feminist, and your status of belonging to feminism is made suspect. And yet this prompted many of us women of color and white allies to recommit ourselves to a multiracial feminism that refuses such false oppositions. For instance, Melissa Spatz, director of the Women and Girls Collective Action Network, and I issued a petition—"Stop the False Gender/Race Divide: A Call to Action"—that asked white allies to step up to refuse this divide and actively cultivate a broader intersectional and social justice politics.[32]

It seems that the rules of whiteness that Thandeka outlines apply within white feminist circles as much as they apply in other areas of

life, and if not challenged, they will continue to divide and immobilize
coalition and alliance building across inequitable divides. One question,
then, is what would it take to expand a politics of disloyalty to whiteness
with a simultaneous commitment to multiracial justice and community
within and outside of feminism?

What might be the risks involved, given contexts of power and privilege, with calls for white feminists, for instance, to name whiteness? One
of the risks might be that we recenter whiteness and reappropriate the
stage of authority and the space of all-knowing speaking-subject. Another risk might be that such naming is done in isolation from the perspectives and leadership of women of color. Our attentiveness to such
risks must be at the center of our practice; we must recognize that the
balance between speech and silence is always contextual, rather than
presupposed. In "White Identities and the Search for Racial Justice,"
Eichstedt explores the dilemma of "white antiracist activists" who "must
undermine white identity and white supremacy while they simultaneously must embrace their identification of themselves as white and un-
duly privileged."[33] As we work to "deconstruct whiteness as a system
of meanings and power distributions," we are also working against the
tendencies toward denial and silence with regard to our implications in
racism. She suggests that white antiracist activists "hold onto whiteness,
not as a place from which to act, but as a location of responsibility."[34]

In her essay "beloved community," bell hooks talks about the importance of making visible multiracial communities who share a commitment with one another to address everyday white supremacy within and
outside of their own community.[35] Building such communities offers
opportunities to practice the negotiations of silence and speech in relation to dynamics of power and privilege. What I have come to realize is
that it is not speech or silence that is liberatory on its own, but an awareness of how both can undermine or reproduce the unequal divides that
we are working to dismantle.

Conclusion

The question for me is how to critically interrogate the tensions between
speech and silence without making myself into the righteous one, the
all-knowing one, and the morally superior one. I believe strongly that

white people need to step up to the plate and speak out in the face of injustices, and yet do so without making ourselves the center of power and knowledge, and with a goal of deepening and expanding movement communities, not simply distinguishing ourselves as the "good white folks" (as distinct from all the rest who are racist). This is the challenge. I continue to explore ways to speak out about racism in a way that recognizes that I am implicated in the very system that I am trying to dismantle. In other words, I am learning to speak not as an "authority" but as a learner, to speak with humility as someone also implicated in the dynamics that I am simultaneously trying to undermine, and to engage people as a way to build relationships, not to shame them. All of this is dependent on and must be embedded within a commitment to compassionate witnessing and active listening as practices necessary to changing these deeply entrenched power relations and to transforming relationships and alliances across power lines. This path of negotiating both silence and speech must be one that undermines and resists rather than reproduces dynamics and structures of inequality. What I have learned is that I must accept that there are no easy answers and that, in any case, I alone will not be *the* one with the necessary "authority" or knowledge to offer them. And most importantly I have learned that it is through building relationships and communities across unequal divides that we are able to create the knowledge, strategies, and visions necessary for deep and expansive social transformation.

3

Disrupting Whiteness

> It is part of our task as revolutionary people, people who
> want deeprooted, radical change, to be as whole as it is pos-
> sible for us to be. This can only be done if we face the reality
> of what oppression really means in our lives, not as abstract
> systems subject to analysis, but as an avalanche of traumas
> leaving a wake of devastation in the lives of real people who
> nevertheless remain human, unquenchable, complex and
> full of possibility.
> —Aurora Levins Morales, *Medicine Stories*

I find Aurora Levins Morales's call for naming and facing the realities
of oppression, rather than obscuring their impact through abstract and
distanced language, to be a guiding principle in my teaching, maybe
now more than ever. With the recent election of Donald Trump, and the
simultaneous escalation of hatred and violence fueled by interlocking
systems of oppression, it feels as though everything has changed and
yet nothing has changed. We have been living with pervasive intimate,
interpersonal, community, state, and military violence for centuries.
This is not new, and yet that reality does not diminish the significance
of this historical moment.

When I think about my role as a teacher in this particular context, I
feel compelled to create classroom spaces for community building that
can cultivate collective critical and compassionate analysis about oppression and violence that emphasizes class members' interconnectedness
through and across power lines. I want to nourish students' commitments toward collective resistance and resilience as well as accountability for contributing to broad-based social change and transformation.
This seems imperative—for those of us most targeted, harmed, and marginalized who feel the impact of oppression every day, for those of us
who are impacted as witnesses to the harm to our loved ones, our com-

munities, all those we know and do not know, and for those of us who are situated within the interstices of race- and class-privileged power who may feel less impacted and less connected to the harms. It is often those most privileged within the interlocking structures of power who make choices to turn away from and distance ourselves from the everyday oppressions that do not target us directly, and it is this distance that I seek to disrupt.

As a white, middle-professional-class, queer woman who teaches women's and gender studies in a historically white-middle-class-dominant and private Catholic university in Chicago, I feel that the stakes are high. My classes tend to be peopled primarily by white, middle- and upper-middle-class students, who sit in community with students who identify as Black, Latinx, Asian, Indigenous, and mixed-race, students who are immigrants, and students who are working-class and poor. In any given class, there are students who identify across the gender and sexuality spectrum, and beyond. There are students who are living with disabilities and who struggle with various physical and mental health issues. This means that the students in my classes have differential relationships to the multiple and intersecting power systems impacting our lives, as do I, and so we have different experiences of and responses to intimate, interpersonal, community, institutional, and state violence. We also have differential relationships of belonging that contribute to the way we understand and engage the impacts of these systems on ourselves, those in our classrooms, and beyond. And so the classroom itself is also experienced differently, depending on who we are, what our experiences have been, and who we love and with whom we are in community.[1]

Part of my work as an educator is to create a space that cultivates a critical and self-reflexive awareness of these different identities, social locations, experiences, and communities of belonging, along with an awareness that we are also interconnected through these complex webs of oppression and violence. None of us exists outside of them, and they structure our relationships with one another, including in the classroom. In the context of any issue that we discuss, some of us in the class are more impacted, some are more complicit, some are more entangled in the webs of power that produce pervasive oppression and violence. With such recognitions, students are called upon to take accountability for the impact of our words, habits, practices, and actions in the class and beyond, as well as to resist and push against interpersonal, institutional, and systemic inequities and harms.

I believe that our willingness to take accountability hinges on our ability to recognize and account for how we are differentially impacted as well as implicated within these structures of power and to act from that place of recognition. Institutionalized systems of power work to diminish this awareness through what Mab Segrest calls the "anesthetic aesthetic" of whiteness and white supremacy. This aesthetic is a deeply engrained emotional stance that compels people, particularly white, middle-class and upper-middle-class, heteronormative people, to distance ourselves from the pain and suffering of people of color, poor people, immigrants from the global south, and trans, queer, and gender-nonconforming people, as well as from our own pain, in order to assimilate into the hegemonic normative systems of power and to resist any sense of responsibility or accountability.

In this chapter, I begin with a reflection on this "anaesthetic aesthetic" and its connection to training in whiteness and the ways it creates blockages to collective and relational accountability. I share some of my experiences in and outside of the classroom with seeking to disrupt and undermine the distanced and disembodied approach to racism, white supremacy, and other forms of oppression. I offer some of the methods and strategies I am learning, and try to practice, that encourage myself and others to name, understand, explore, and begin to heal from trauma and violence caused by historically based interlocking systems of oppression.

The thread that holds these ideas and practices together is that they each seek to cultivate an awareness that everyday structural, institutional, and interpersonal harms and violence impact all of us, though differentially, and that we all are implicated in the systems that produce these harms. In other words, these structures of power are deeply entrenched within our identities, experiences, and everyday actions. If we do not hold this awareness, then those of us who are white or otherwise privileged, who may see ourselves and are seen by others as not impacted by racism and white supremacy, often respond to learning about harm from a numbed-out distance or a defensive resistance, as if the racism and white supremacy that impact "others" is not directly interconnected with "us." This means that people of color who are more directly and negatively impacted by racism and white supremacy carry the burden of these harms, with no accountability from those of us implicated within them, and with no space to address the impact. When this happens, the injustices and harms become political or intellectual issues up for debate, a matter of information and objective truth, rather than a matter of life and death, of trauma and violence, of grief and mourning, of responsibility and accountability.

Recognizing and seeking to understand systems of oppression and their impact on people, including on ourselves, on the other hand, opens up space for relational belonging and accountability in a struggle against the devastation of endemic violence in our interconnected communities. It provides us with an opportunity to break out of the numbness that often accompanies our witnessing, experiencing, and being complicit in systemic trauma and violence. When we are able to do this in the context of a classroom or a relationship or within a community, when we hearten our responses to one another, I believe we are more able to recognize and take accountability for our relationship to these systems and to the harms they produce, rather than distancing ourselves from them, and to join in solidarity in the work to dismantle them.

Distancing and Disavowal: Rules of Whiteness

Mab Segrest, in her essay "Of Souls and White Folks," argues that the system of white supremacy disciplines white people's psyches away from recognizing and feeling the pain and suffering born of systemic oppression and violence. She says that the system compels white people to become numb to the pain and suffering of others, and to locate ourselves as distinctively separate from the historical legacies of ongoing violence and injustice and their devastating impacts on people of color. White supremacist culture discourages people from feeling, grieving, and mourning the everyday violence and oppression we witness and experience, and in fact trivializes such endeavors. Indeed, our social institutions—education, media, criminal, legal—socialize us to reign in, control, and ultimately squelch empathic, compassionate, as well as rightfully upset and angry responses when we witness and experience trauma, violation, violence, oppression. These institutions offer disciplinary logics along with social and economic benefits for diminishing our sense of responsibility for the harms of systemic oppression, particularly when we are not the ones directly targeted.

Distance and disconnection become conditions of assimilationist belonging that come with so-called protection and privileged status. Segrest reflects on her experience of the "massive denial" of racism in the white community she grew up in, where most "refused to acknowledge the reality, much less the moral significance, of the violent white resistance to black freedom movements."[2] This is the same denial so pervasive today that cultivates a callous disregard for the violence of white supremacy and capitalism on the many people targeted for mass incarceration, criminalization, and law enforcement brutality and killing. I appreciate her conceptualization of this as a "metaphysic of genocide" where "people don't need to respond to what they can pretend they do not know, and they don't know what they can't feel."[3] Creating collective spaces, including in the classroom, for embodied knowing and feeling, then, I have found to be one way of breaking up the system of callous disregard.

In order for people, particularly white, middle-class and upper-middle-class people, to accept and collude with the pervasive injustices, these systems work hard to dishearten us. As Mary Elizabeth Hobgood argues in her book *Dismantling Whiteness*, white supremacy compels white people—and all those aspiring to be white—to affirm, go along with, or refuse to recognize what María Lugones refers to as "'the mechanisms of a white racial state.'"[4] It requires "emotional reserve and constraint"[5] in the face of violence and so produces systemic numbing of emotional pain, willful ignorance of others' pain, and a refusal to know and to take accountability for our own participation in the dailiness of violence and oppression. Within these systems, Audre Lorde so aptly writes, "[O]ur feelings were not meant to survive."[6]

The training in white supremacist, capitalist, imperialist patriarchy that requires distancing, numbing, and disconnection from those defined as "other," particularly in the context of oppression and violence, begins in early childhood in this society. Thandeka, in her book *Learning to Be White*, through her interviews with white people, finds that white children *learn* to be *white* through the white adults in their lives who disciplined and punished them whenever they expressed anger at injustice, or compassion for people of color in the face of injustice, or when they dared form relationships with people of color outside of hierarchical structures of power. A prerequisite for belonging within their white families and communities was to distance themselves from those defined as "different" and "other" and to be indifferent to or complicit with the harm, oppression, and violence they witnessed.[7]

I remember these childhood lessons well. In the white, middle-to-upper-middle-class, Catholic, conservative, and right-wing family and community where I was raised, my parents, teachers, and peers shamed and punished those of us who challenged the gender, racial, and class injustices we witnessed and/or who formed relationships outside of the very narrow power lines within which we were being raised. To diminish any spirit of solidarity with those marked as "different," they disciplined us away from cross-race and cross-class relationships. They trained us to ignore and to be ignorant of the systemic and daily harms we witnessed or participated in (consciously or unconsciously) and to evade responsibility for our own complicity in these harms. They also trained us to minimize and/or deny the patriarchal and heteronormative violence within our own families and communities, accusing us of making a big deal out of nothing and urging us to just "get over it" while they simultaneously projected violence and criminality onto people of color, poor people, and LGBTQ people, among others. This despite the fact that, in families like my own, it was white, middle-class and upper-middle-class family members, neighbors, teachers, nuns, priests, and others who were most responsible for the physical, sexual, verbal, and emotional abuse that we experienced, and whose social and political power protected them from any scrutiny, much less accountability, for their behavior and actions.

Tellingly, as we grew older, one of the epithets used to pathologize our care for others was to call us "bleeding-heart liberals" whenever we brought attention to these injustices—a term that marked us as "overly sensitive," "thin skinned," and "too soft" on people suffering from discrimination or violence. It became a label that those of us who broke ranks would jokingly use in reference to ourselves. Looking back, I can see how we ourselves began to reproduce the disavowal, even though we yearned to resist the mandate. Similar to "political correctness," the phrase "bleeding-heart liberal" comes from the racist, homophobic, and xenophobic right wing to diminish solidarity and connection across power lines, and to shut down any critique of the multitude of injustices we are witnessing. James Westbrook Pegler, a well-known journalist in the 1930s and 1940s, adamantly opposed to the New Deal and labor unions, popularized the term in his diatribes against Eleanor Roosevelt. The online *Free Dictionary* perpetuates this legacy by defining such a person as one "who is considered *excessively* sympathetic toward those who *claim* to be underprivileged or exploited" (emphasis mine).[8] Inherent in the definition is the impulse to mark connection as "excessive" and to deny oppression by referencing it as a "claim" rather than a reality.

This training in looking away from and denying the brutality of white supremacist, capitalist, heteronormative patriarchy, maintained through structural racial and class segregation, contributes to the dominant gravitational pull to ignore, deny, overlook, justify, and/or rationalize domination of people in our communities, including sometimes ourselves.[9] And this process is integral to the maintenance of oppressive systems—otherwise we would not, could not, tolerate its systemic injustices. As Aurora Levins Morales writes,

> In order for the thing [oppression] to work, the humanity of almost everyone must somehow be made invisible. Who could bear to hold privilege that meant the suffering and death of others if they had not been trained from early childhood to see these others as not real? Who would tolerate, for even an hour, the inhuman conditions imposed by the privileged, if they had not been trained from early childhood to feel themselves not fully entitled to life?[10]

The system is set up socially and structurally to undermine the possibility for relational accountability and responsibility in relation to endemic pain and suffering in US society. Mistreatment, abuse, and violence that reinforce social hierarchies are understood through the logics and discourses that rationalize them as normative, seemingly inevitable, and therefore acceptable. The pedagogical effort to undo this training is what marks women's and gender studies as suspect as detractors derisively dismiss our circles, our use of creative arts, our focus on feelings as well as thoughts, and our investment in care and support for one another.[11]

In my life and in my classes, I witness the impacts of this training—the ways it shapes our responses to the oppression and violence we are working to understand and disrupt. I witness white students in particular, though not exclusively, who struggle to resist their training to turn away from and to distance themselves from care for others, and yet also feel troubled by seeing themselves, and their communities, as directly implicated in the oppression and violence we discuss. I also witness them struggle with how their education rubs up against the familial and social relationships with their white friends and family members who resist and fight against their growing critical consciousness. This can be a painful pedagogical process for everyone—for those most targeted who can feel the distance and disavowal in some students, particularly those most trained in whiteness as a condition of belonging, and for those who have been trained and are not sure of a way forward. And of course it is even more difficult to witness for those most impacted by racism, transphobia, xenophobia, and ableism, among other systems, who become witnesses to a struggle that is over their right to exist, to be considered fully human, to be considered a valuable member of the community worth care and consideration.

This awareness hits home as I listen to students of color describe what it is like to live and learn in white-dominant university settings, including those focused on addressing racism. In a workshop on the ways that the public safety department at the university participates in the racial profiling and criminalization of students of color, a multiracial group of students and faculty are thinking through responses for witnesses and co-strugglers to support the persons targeted as well as to address the situation as a whole. As the discussion moves to talking about the problem with the public safety department, an African American student shares that what hurts him most is not the constant police surveillance he experiences at DePaul, but the white faculty, staff, and students who are witnesses to it and who simply turn the other way, who disassociate themselves from him so as to not have to address the mistreatment they are observing. His statement shifts the energy in the room. Rather than solely focusing on the racist practices of the public safety workers who are not present in the room, he is asking those of us who are white to turn the spotlight on ourselves and other white witnesses, to challenge our compulsion to turn away from the behavior of the officers as well as the person being harmed. He wants us to understand that the distancing from the situation—even in the context of our workshop—is noticed, is felt, and impacts everyone involved. The issue, for him, was not abstract, nor should it be for those of us who are witnesses. Instead it is deeply concrete and personal—not in an individualistic way, but in the sense that it has an impact on real people, and that we are all involved, whether we want to admit it or not, and so any action that we take—including being silent, turning away, disengaging, or responding, intervening, documenting, supporting—has an impact.

This leads me to reflect on a common refrain in my classes from African American, Latinx, Asian American, and other students of color who share their confusion and upset in response to white students who do not seem to understand the painfulness of the issues that we are discussing. They are responding to the ways in which white students often approach and treat the issues as abstract, separate, and outside of the classroom, the way this contributes to the hurt and sadness of those most impacted who are also in the room struggling to learn and understand. This recognition pushes me to hold space within classes for recognizing how we are feeling in relation to what we are learning, at times to create space for grief and mourning about everyday oppression and violence and its impact on our everyday lives. This is hard in this society that is so quick to want to make everything light and easy and objectively the same.

The social logics in this society train us against feeling, against experiencing compassion around each other's vulnerabilities even when given the opportunity. One aspect of this dynamic occurs when students are not mindful of their own differential relationships to the issues, their impact, and what it means to have them under discussion in a classroom community. This was brought home to me in a very painful way in a spontaneous and impromptu discussion of Halloween and racism on the Internet in a class on antiracist feminisms. It started when one white student shared a few examples of racism on the Internet, including images of racist costumes and caricatures that were being circulated. Once this white student started sharing, more and more white students jumped in with additional examples. The level of animation among the white students increased, and it almost felt like gallows humor. Their conversation felt completely disconnected from any embodied awareness of the pain and hurt that these images and language cause. The white students sharing the stories distanced themselves from the examples by pointing the finger at and laughing at "the racists." The storytellers, then, set themselves outside of the scenario—not the one being racist, and not the one who is the target of racism. This distancing inhibited any reflective awareness about the impact of the discussion and the stories on people of color, including those present in the room. The practice of poking fun at "the racists" kept the acts themselves and the actors at a distance, rather than close to mind and heart.

As my own discomfort increased, I asked the white students telling the stories to step back, and to think more reflectively and mindfully about not only what they were talking about but how they were talking about it. A number of students of color in the class then expressed upset, hurt, and anger at the flippant and mocking responses that they felt did not account for the harm being perpetrated, both in the scenarios and in the telling. The white student storytellers were at first confused because they felt that they were on the "right side." They had not thought about the impact and harm of the stories themselves on their peers of color in the room. Making fun of people who are racist does not challenge the insipid and deeply entrenched nature of racism, and does not help to shift the power structures and the culture that maintains it. In a way, it does not take the harm seriously. And most importantly, it does not account for the impact on those most targeted.

What does it feel like to face the oppression and violence that surround us, not as an intellectual exercise, but as an exercise in bearing witness to the impact of harm and the ways we are implicated in it? What might it look like to engage each other with a recognition that each of us has something big at stake in changing it—not for our own self-gratification, but because what is going on is so hurtful, harming, hostile, violent, and abusive to people that we know and do not know, and because we want to create a loving and just community. I have become convinced that facing the pain and suffering that surround me, rather than trying to will it away, or covering it up with explanations, or distancing myself, is integral to my ability to respond. And so when I find myself distancing, I make an effort to sit with what I have witnessed or heard or read, to recognize the people most impacted and the pain and suffering caused. Why is this important? When I sit with it—then my relationships with all those involved changes. I become less distant, less outside of the situation, and more within it. The ways in which I engage it also change. The stakes are higher when I understand my relationship to the oppression and violence fully and deeply. I then have space to think about what might be needed to cultivate support and caring for those immediately harmed and all those impacted, and also to try to think about the people doing the harm, what led them to it, what forces or structures or power lines produced it, and how my lived realities may be related to these forces and structures.

Sometimes people will say that they do not feel they have any right to speak to an issue because they are not a member of the group being oppressed, and instead they are part of the group that is privileged and/or that is involved in the dominance and entitlement being enacted. Some say that because of this, we can never know what it is like to experience racism. And this may be true, and yet this does not mean that we are not impacted or implicated. Alternatively, when we recognize our integral relationship to the harm and to the people being harmed—we can more readily access how we might contribute to addressing the harm through support, intervention, accountability, and activism for social change. This may take many forms, including being present, showing up, speaking not as an expert but as someone who is invested in addressing the situation or as someone who feels the pain and is also grieving, finding ways to join with others struggling to change the systems and structures that produce the violence.

I can share in the anger and rage—the upset—even as I recognize that I have a different relationship to it, and my relationship to these systems has also changed over the years because of my own changing relationships and communities of belonging. And it is important to engage not from a space where it is *about* me individually, but from a recognition that it is about a communal, collective us, an us that is also complex, heterogeneous, and yet interconnected. As Chris Crass, a white antiracist activist, suggests to white people wanting to be in solidarity with Black communities against police violence and murder,

Take a moment to appreciate the fact that you are devastated by brutal racist injustice and that while your heart is broken, another alternative is that your heart has been hardened by the scarring of internalized white supremacy that has divested you from loving your own full humanity and the humanity of others.

Your devastation is the result of your heart being alive and refusing the socialized indifference, amnesia, and straightjacketing of your consciousness that post–Civil Rights movement white racialization aims for. Your internal capacity to be devastated by this murderous racist system is a source of power that serves you well and is what can help you be part of bringing this system down.[12]

Our ability to be in touch with the devastation of the harms of these systems and the people who benefit from them is essential, and it is what the system consistently works against.

Embodied Pedagogy: Brokenheartedness and Accountability

Creating learning spaces that allow for an emotional, heartfelt recognition of the interconnectedness of our lives in terms of the devastating realities of oppression and violence has the potential to deepen and solidify accountability for the pain and suffering of others as well as ourselves.[13] It is within such contexts that we have the opportunity to remap our identities and affinities and, in turn, to expand the possibilities for building mutuality, for living within an ethic of interconnectedness, and, most significantly, for taking accountability for our own role in maintaining and reproducing the power lines that create such harm and violence. It is within such spaces that we can be in community with others as we grieve and mourn the impact of devastating oppression and violence in our families, in our neighborhoods, in our university, in the many institutions across the broader city, country, and world. And this grief derives, in part, from the deep recognition of how much I am implicated in the oppression and violence of these systems, structures, institutions, and everyday realities, not only how I am targeted by them. I believe this leads to a deeper sense of responsibility to intervene, disrupt, and transform the systemic injustices that cause this endemic pain and suffering. Cultivating empathy and accountability in classrooms around the devastating impact of oppression and violence, rather than running away from it, disrupts the numbness, disassociation, and abstraction that mute and silence the way I, and I suspect many others, respond to this violence. It lays bare the cognitive dissonance between what we are told is the world we live in and the actual world that we live in.

This is what I have come to call a practice of brokenheartedness—a practice that cultivates our ability to face what the dominant culture and structural logics encourage us to evade, ignore, and distance. It opens opportunities for empathy across our differential relationships to power and violence, and it cultivates an ethic of accountability in the way we grapple with how we are implicated within these systems of violence. In my own experience of such spaces, I find myself heartbroken in response to the harms of violence—the impact on those harmed, those who witness the harm, and those of us who are complicit and accountable, either directly or indirectly, in the systems that produced them. Our political and social analyses are essential, and yet not enough in terms of compelling people toward action; along with many others, I believe that embodied engagement—emotional, spiritual, felt through and in the body—is what motivates action and change.

My yearning for such learning and activist spaces led me to the frameworks of transformative and healing justice practices created by women, queer, gender-nonconforming, and trans people of color activists, healers, and artists who are developing more holistic approaches to movement building. In the guide *Healing Justice Practice Spaces: A How to Guide*, Autumn Brown and Maryse Mitchell-Brody define healing justice as "an evolving political framework shaped by economic, racial, and disability justice that re-centers the role of healing inside of liberation; that seeks to transform, intervene and respond to generational trauma and violence in our movements, communities and lives; and to regenerate our traditions of liberatory and resiliency practices that have been lost or stolen."[14] Healing justice practitioners seek to create spaces for grief and mourning in response to the violence of racism, white supremacy, patriarchy, and capitalism as well as for critical analysis and action. They seek to build internal accountability practices for people to be able to process and address the harms that we create and reproduce within social and political movements and organizations and communities. Locating the roots of oppression within historical structures of power, rather than in individuals, they embrace the compassionate witnessing of violence with a recognition of its cumulative and collective harm and its roots in these larger systems.

Healing justice centers the experience and knowledge of those most impacted in order to shift our knowledge base and to deeply undermine the frame that has led us to disassociation, distance, objectivity, dominance, and superiority. Again, I find Aurora Levins Morales's framing of healing processes so valuable; she writes, "The only way to bear the overwhelming pain of oppression is by telling, in all its detail, in the presence of witnesses and in the context of resistance, how unbearable it is. If we attempt to craft resistance without undertaking this task, we are collectively vulnerable to all the errors of judgment that unresolved trauma generates in individuals."[15] She argues that if we want to transform the traumatic, we must be able

> to mourn, fully and deeply, all that has been taken from us. . . . [O]nly through mourning everything we have lost can we discover that we have in fact survived; that our spirits are indestructible. Only through mourning can we reach a place of clean anger in which we stand with all the abused and hold the abusers accountable. Only through mourning can we reconnect to the love in our lives and lose our fascination with the ones who harmed us. And only if we fully acknowledge and grieve the hurts can we possibly find genuine compassion for the perpetrators.[16]

In my work as a teacher, I seek to create learning spaces where participants—teachers and students alike—can see ourselves individually and collectively as deeply embedded in the systems that we also have a stake in changing. And our stakes in changing the world are not about gaining the so-called privileges of dominance and entitlement; rather, our stakes in change are that we cannot tolerate the injustices that we experience and witness, that create such pain, sadness, and brokenheartedness, and that are caused by these systems of domination. This is the work of embodied pedagogy—a pedagogy that creates space for participants to share, to witness, to cultivate empathy and accountability in response to systemic pain and suffering.

Storytelling Circles and Community Building across Power Lines

I often hold my classes in the structure of peace circles, as I believe they cultivate our collective ability to face and hold onto the embodied and layered emotional realities of violence that we are seeking to understand. Circles can disrupt the gravitational pulls of white supremacy, capitalism, and imperialism as they go against the compulsion to evade, minimize, and ignore these realities. In 2009, I took my first restorative justice circle training with Project Nia, a Chicago-based organization founded by Mariame Kaba. The training was led by Cheryl Graves and Ora Schub of the Chicago-based Community Justice for Youth Institute. I was deeply moved by the sense of community and belonging we created given that we had very different identities, experiences, and perspectives. Since then, I have taken more trainings, and I have participated in and kept many circles, including in many of my classes. The power of circles is rooted in the shared values developed by participants, in the emphasis on storytelling as a way to build understanding and community, and in the opportunity for each person in the space to speak their truth and to deeply listen to each other. These components create a space for people to share their unique experiences and perspectives on the world rather than to assume that participants share the same experiences, ideas, or perspectives. The circle allows for differences to arise in a context of shared values, such as respect, active listening, and meeting people where they are.

With an emphasis on community building and storytelling, in circle, participants begin to see each other's ideas as rooted in our experiences and in our social locations, rather than as abstract, disembodied ideas, and we begin to build an understanding of the differences between and among us, including the power lines, as well as the ways our identities and lives are interconnected. Additionally, because we have created a space of curiosity and active listening to each other's truths, when disagreements arise there is the potential for understanding, openness, and willingness to listen and change. The disagreements become part of the process of the circle, rather than only related to those in immediate disagreement.

Circles create a context for a more embodied experience of learning and communication. Through the sharing of stories, class members come to recognize and understand their differential relationships to systems of power and to each other. Deeply listening to one another's stories can cultivate what I would call a brokenheartedness that has the potential to break up the gravitational pulls of white supremacist, capitalist, heteronormative patriarchy. Across different issues, class members can come to see how they are both impacted and implicated in the harm that others are experiencing quite directly; and they can come to see that others have the potential to listen, care, and take accountability for their ignorance, complicity, or participation in these systems of oppression. The circle has the potential to provide a ground for students to begin to take steps toward accountability, to be more present and engaged with one another, and to understand the importance of acting in solidarity with others against these interlocking systems of oppression. I have often witnessed the transformative potential of circles, and I have also experienced circles where it feels impossible to move forward or where conflicts remain.

In the spring of 2015, I was teaching a class in Transformative Justice and Prison Abolition. The class was made up of over twenty students with varying degrees of knowledge, interest, and agreement regarding oppression, violence, and the prison industrial complex. Students in the class identified in many ways, including African American, Nigerian, Palestinian, Mexican, Chicana, Puerto Rican, Bulgarian, Indian, Italian American, white, Muslim, Catholic, queer, gender queer, and bisexual, among others. Each week we met in circle—sharing our stories of experiencing and/or witnessing injustices, supporting each other, reflecting on the inadequacies of how we and others have responded to injustice, and practicing responses that would not rely on police and other external authorities and would not avoid or escalate the violence. My goal was, as always, to deepen the class's understanding of how we each are differentially impacted and implicated within everyday oppression and violence, to create a space for grief and mourning as well as accountability, and to expand our skills to promote collective healing and transformation. While most students actively participated in and embraced the circle process, a few remained disconnected and distanced.

Toward the end of the class, we attended a performance of "It Gets Bitter" with Dark Matter, a South Asian transgender art duo. The performance was deeply moving; the stories and poetry they shared addressing white supremacy, white people, everyday transphobic, racist, sexist, xenophobic oppression and violence, and familial sexism and misogyny evoked many complex feelings—sadness, anger, shame, hurt, guilt, accountability, and more. After the event, we returned to the classroom to reflect. Not interested in a debate about the "facts" of the political analysis offered by Dark Matter, I asked the class to draw and/or write out their feelings and responses to the performance. We then sat in circle and shared our responses.

What happened in that next hour was powerful. As each person shared their reflection on the event, we witnessed each other express many different feelings and responses. Our social locations and experiences informed our particular relationship to the stories they were telling and to the structural systems of oppression being illuminated. Each reflection was important to hear both on its own and also in relation to one another. One of the more skeptical students in the class, who identified as white, middle-class, and heterosexual, presented his drawing of a big question mark. He began by saying something along the lines of, "Wow, I have no idea what to say." For the first time in the class, he invited us into his internal struggle over the event and the class. He wanted us to know that he never would have taken this class or gone to this performance if it had not been fulfilling a requirement. He said he needed to do "a lot of thinking and self-reflection." He said that as he walked back to the classroom after the performance, he found himself asking "who am I?" and "what am I doing in this world?" It felt like, for the first time in this class, he allowed himself to be vulnerable in the circle with his classmates and to share his feelings and responses. From what he said, I also gathered that he recognized himself in the stories of harms perpetrated. As he spoke, I could feel that the other students in the class witnessed his breakthrough with surprise as well as with compassion and care. Our sense of community both expanded and deepened.

Following him was another student—an African American woman who had also held back in the class. She shared that she had never felt so affirmed in her life as by the performance of Dark Matter. She said the artists said things that she had felt so many times, but was afraid to say. For her, the event confirmed her anger, grief, and upset in response to living in this world. She felt supported and affirmed by the performance, and in turn, the circle's responses prompted her to want to share her truths with the class. She too seemed to feel freer to share this in the class, as she listened to others share their own truths. A South Asian student shared that she deeply resonated with the storytellers and their experiences, more than she had originally thought. She reflected that since she identified as heterosexual, she was not sure if she would connect. Several white women and gender queer students talked about feeling guilt and shame at their own relationship with the white supremacist, capitalist patriarchy that was responsible for the harms produced in the storytellers' lives. They expressed a desire and commitment to take more steps toward actively disrupting and shifting the contexts that produce the racist, xenophobic, and transphobic words and actions described by "It Gets Bitter." They saw themselves implicated in the stories about white LGBTQ and feminist activists and about white people riding the trains who remain silent in the face of harassment.

By going around the circle, we each sat with our differential responses shaped by our own lived realities, pain, and relationships of belonging. The circle created space for those targeted by such violence as well as for those who have witnessed and/or been complicit in such violence. That evening something shifted in our relationships to one another in the present as well as in our futures. What I experienced—at least in the moment—was the potential for building a learning community that creates space for us to understand and feel and/or empathize with the harm of the devastating realities of violence, to witness our role and relationship to each other's experiences, and to cultivate a sense of individual and collective accountability for our future together.

Circles do not always lead to transformation, and they are almost never comfortable spaces. The differences within any given class can feel quite painful, frustrating, and unnerving. And yet these are also the spaces that reveal what is hard about this work, what needs to change, and what might be possible. In another transformative justice class, in the aftermath of a campus visit on May 24, 2016, by an avowed white supremacist misogynistic white man who identifies as gay—Milo Yiannopoulos—we created space in the class to process the event.[17] As a result of his visit to DePaul, which was shut down by student protesters, he and his followers engaged in verbal and physical attacks against protesters and all those who supported them, with subsequent harassment and threats, including death threats, through the Internet, phone lines, and the white supremacist press. After this event, the campus environment felt different to many of us, or, for some, the difference was that the racism, xenophobia, and sexism were more visible and audible. There was an increase in up-front white racist hostilities and violence that ensued. When I opened up space in my class in the context of a circle a few days after the event, students of color in my class—African American, African immigrant, Palestinian, South Asian, Latinx—expressed their upset, fear, and anger about the event, about the university's criminalization of the protesters of the event, rather than the racist and misogynistic speaker and his supporters, and about the broader university community that had once again let them down. Some white students who participated in the protests and were in community with students of color expressed deep upset and anger, with some shock. The remaining white students had a variety of responses—some expressed shock, many expressed confusion and upset about the speaker and the violence, and some did not have much to say at all.

As we went around the circle, and the different responses were spoken, I could feel the tensions rise. It felt disheartening and uncomfortable when some white students seemed distant and uninterested in what had happened, even though students of color and queer and trans students were talking about being targeted and attacked. The circle held us as these responses then became the subject of discussion. Some students of color openly expressed their hurt as well as frustration with this distanced and apathetic response. Some said it deepened their sense of fear and alienation that they were already experiencing. A South Asian student said that white students' surprise or shock was indicative of their privilege; she noted that she was not only not surprised but had never felt safe at the university, including in our classroom. For her, white supremacist and misogynistic behavior was not at all out of the ordinary. An African American student said she was sick of being both the person targeted and the person asked to educate and transform the situation. I could feel that many of the white students struggled with what was being said about their response. Some seemed to wake up to how their reticence and discomfort with the situation only confirmed to the students of color that the white students were not invested in their well-being. Others seemed paralyzed and unable to open up. The circle held these conflicting relationships to the situation and each student had to wrestle with what this meant for them and for the class.

While these tensions were not resolved in the circle that evening, the circle gave voice to and held these tensions. Some students of color expressed that they appreciated the space to be able to articulate their anger and upset, including in relation to the community of the class. Some white students reflected that they began to shift their response. Some began to say that they did have a role in and a relationship to the impact of the situation on the students of color in our class and beyond, and that they had a role in the broader issues of institutional racism at the university. Some responded more openly with compassion, care, and support, and others offered, albeit awkwardly, to be more present and alert around what was going on. Again, the circle did not resolve everything, and yet it created a space for these tensions and difficulties to be spoken and addressed. For some, it created some bridges and deepened some relationships within the classroom community, and it set the tone for the rest of the quarter.

For those of us who are white and otherwise privileged, these systems train us to see ourselves as outside of the situation and so distant and separate from the people harmed and from these structural power lines, inequities, and injustices, and yet that is the gravitational pull of white supremacy. This is what must be disrupted. It has become one of my pedagogical goals in every class to encourage students (and myself) to be persistent and consistent in asking ourselves always, how am I feeling about what has happened? How am I impacted by this situation? How am I implicated within the specific situation and in the broader one? How can I act from that location and with the knowledge and perspective of those most impacted?

What We Can Learn from Our Differential Relationships to Harm

One obstacle to recognizing our role and responsibility in these systems of oppression is the rigid fixity and polarized understanding of the positions of oppressed/oppressor, victim/perpetrator, innocent/guilty, and our desire to never be perceived as someone who is an oppressor or perpetrator, or who is responsible for oppression or violence. These binaries do not encourage people to take accountability. They provide little to no incentive to engage in a process of transforming conflicts and oppressive behaviors. In a class I teach on transformative justice, I often use an activity I learned through the Chicago-based Community

Justice for Youth Institute. In the exercise, I ask class members to meet in pairs and share one story of a time when they were hurt and another story of when they hurt someone else. After sharing stories in pairs, the group gathers back to generate four lists on post-it paper—one is a list of the feelings experienced when they were hurt, one with the feelings experienced when they hurt someone else, followed by a list of what they needed when they were hurt and a list of what they needed when they hurt someone else. We put the lists side by side up on the wall, and what we find is that often there are shared feelings and needs for when we have harmed and when we have done harm—including the feelings of fear, of being out of control, of feeling alone, isolated, and powerless, and needing understanding, support, space for reflection.

In this process, class members inevitably recognize that all of us have been in both positions—harmer and harmed. Through reflection, we come to recognize the humanity—the feelings and needs—of the people on multiple sides of any given conflict or incident of violence. The purpose is not to dismiss or excuse the harm caused, nor to say that the impact, meaning, and consequences of the mistreatment, abuse, and/or violence are the same; instead, the exercise provides us with an opportunity to recognize the humanity of one another in the room and beyond. And it provides a space to realize that there may be ways to meet the needs of people who have been harmed as well as those who have harmed, and to find ways toward healing and justice.

It matters that we begin the exercise by sharing our own stories of harm—when we harmed and when we were harmed. In one workshop I co-led with a colleague and friend, Laurie Fuller, we made the mistake of skipping the storytelling. When listing out the feelings and needs of an abstract person who did the harm—not those of us in the room—the group responded much more harshly. They expressed little tolerance for the feelings and needs of anyone who caused harm. They completely distanced themselves from this abstract group of people—they derided them, dismissed them, and made fun of them. The takeaway was that it matters that we begin this work by recognizing that we ourselves have caused harm, that we are capable of causing harm, and that we may cause harm in the future; none of us is immune. By sharing our own stories of doing harm, we may be more apt to come to the work of community and justice with humility, honesty, and love, and we may learn that the practice of taking accountability for the harms we perpetrate and/ or are complicit in is one that we all must learn to build and embrace.

When we draw rigid lines between oppressor and oppressed, those of us drawing the lines tend to locate ourselves solely on the side of the oppressed. There is a reluctance to own up to how we are implicated within systems of oppression as well as privilege, and yet this is an important space to self-reflect about complicity and to engage in resistance. The reality is that we are all located in the interstitial structures of oppression and privilege, and each of us is related in one way or another to the many forms of violence within and across contexts. For me, this means that each of us must consider our complicity in and accountability for our own role and relationship to the perpetuation of oppression and violence.

In order to build these personal-political recognitions within my classrooms, I often engage students in an activity I learned about from the curriculum *Something Is Wrong: Exploring the Roots of Youth Violence*, edited by Mariame Kaba, J. Cyriac Mathew, and Nathan Haines, and a collaborative project among Project Nia, the Chicago Freedom School, and Teachers for Social Justice in Chicago.[18] It is a popular education activity—"Oppression/Privilege Workshop"—adapted by Mariame Kaba from an activity of Anne Bishop. In my classes, it has become a powerful way to create a shared understanding and recognition of how we—as members of the class—are impacted as well as implicated within these systems. It lets us know that these systems are not abstractions, nor are the people impacted, but they are part of the lived realities of all of us within the classroom community. This is possible because the exercise asks participants to gather together in groups around specific systems of oppression and privilege that they experience. First, groups form around the system of oppression that they have personally experienced. Each group shares stories of their own experiences and then creates a listing on a large flipchart paper in response to the prompt, "I know I am in the presence of —— (the form of oppression chosen) when . . ." The groups then re-form around their membership in a group that is structurally privileged and dominant. In this group, they respond to the prompt, "What privileges do we get from being —— (a member of a dominant group)?" The lists on large flipchart paper are then placed around the room and class members take time to review each of the lists of everyday experiences of oppression and privilege. The group then gathers in circle for reflection.

This activity builds a more embodied awareness of the way these systems manifest for members of the class, including ourselves. It reveals that everyone in the room experiences and is impacted by these systems of oppression and privilege, that none of us is immune, and that these systems shape our relationships to one another. It sharpens our sense of compassion and accountability for ourselves and each other in the classroom, and the ways we are and may be in the future complicit with and/or participate in these systems. It also offers space to talk about how we can work together to challenge and/or disrupt the daily manifestations of these systems and stand in solidarity with those most impacted.

Listening, Brokenheartedness, and Accountability

As a teacher, one thing I have learned is that compassion and love are integral to teaching and social change. Over the years, I have faced a multitude of students who expressed defensiveness, anger, resistance, and hostility in response to my efforts to build critical consciousness about endemic oppression and violence. Sometimes I experience the dynamic as a battle I need to win, at other times I hope it will be a matter of offering more facts and critical analysis, and sometimes I just feel defeated. Sometimes it is just hard to reach people, and yet what I have also come to realize is that there is more to what is underlying their resistance. It is much more than intellectual, and is often tied to their own experiences of rejection, pain, and isolation. One of my first lessons to this effect came in the late 1980s when I taught a course on violence against women at MIT as an adjunct teacher. I had a young white man in my class who was relentless in his critique of feminism for not considering men's perspectives, and who spewed unrelenting venom against women survivors of sexual assault. As an adjunct teacher with little teaching experience, I did not know what to do. I was afraid to kick him out because of my precarious status at the university, and yet his behavior was more than hurtful against the other women students and myself. At the last session of the class, after he again berated me and the class content and focus, I asked him to stay after class to speak with me. My plan in the moment was to confront him about the harm that he had caused by his hostile attitude and words and to inquire as to why he even took the course (something I wish I had done much earlier).

He stayed after the class and began to pour out his anger at me, and at the broader world. I listened and did not interrupt him. I was not interested in another battle around our different realities. Within just a few minutes of him talking and me listening, we found ourselves sitting down. He shared his experiences of child sexual abuse, its impact, his anger at himself, and his inability to talk about it. He talked of the desire to commit suicide, of his self-hatred and painful despair. His story was heartbreaking, as was the story of our class. By the end of the conversation together, we were in a very different place from where we had begun. We now found ourselves talking about strategies to cope with self-hatred and despair (feelings I had had myself), and I shared a few resources in the area for male survivors of sexual abuse. This was quite a lesson in the power of active listening to transform a situation by getting to the conditions that underlay his hostility.

I am not excusing his behavior, and yet, through listening, an opportunity opened for a shift in the dynamics governing our relationship. I was able to hear more about the locus of his anger and hostility—the isolation, the pain, the self-blame he was carrying and for which he was seeking some relief—and he was able to see that I was not his enemy and that he had caused harm in our class. Through the conversation, I also came to recognize how I was, in part, implicated in the sources of his isolation, pain, and anger, given that I too had contributed to the invisibility of sexualized violence against men and its impact on all of our lives. I understood from this experience that I needed a different approach to harm—not one that would simply write him off as a misogynist, but rather one that would recognize the sources of his pain and anger while also insisting on a practice of mutual accountability—both his and mine—for the impasse of the class and his attacks on the members of the class, including myself.

Class participants, including professors, often do not have the skills to address these dynamics and to create, even on a small scale, the social transformation we envision. The problem is not the critical analysis or the anger at oppressive actions and structures; it is the dearth of skills to engage one another in the face of harmful words and actions that will lead to care and support for those harmed as well as support for the person who caused harm to take accountability. Both require acts of compassion, care, and community. Strengthening our skills in this sense has the potential to deepen relationships, rather than further fracture them. It allows us to learn more about how these systems are internalized into our identities and relationships and what it might take to transform. Active listening is essential in this process and a skill that I continue to practice, develop, and expand. It allows for ourselves and others to be seen, heard, and embraced, and in that process, to move toward healing and transformation.

PART II

Community Accountability and Transformative Justice

4

Shifting Paradigms to End Violence

We seek to build movements that not only end violence, but
that create a society based on radical freedom, mutual accountability, and passionate reciprocity. In this society, safety
and security will not be premised on violence or the threat
of violence; it will be based on a collective commitment to
guaranteeing the survival and care of all peoples.
—Incite and Critical Resistance, *Incite! Color of Violence*

Over the last seventeen-plus years, a newly inspired feminist antiviolence movement in the United States led by feminists of color has
been gaining momentum among activists, scholars, writers, and artists. Reignited and imagined by the visionary work of Incite! Women
of Color Against Violence—a national organization of radical women
of color—small and large groups across the country have worked to
shift feminist-informed antiviolence efforts from institutionalized
social services and legal advocacy to community-based mobilizing for
community accountability and transformative justice. At the center
of leadership initiating and developing these organizing communities
are collectives led by women of color and immigrant, queer, and trans
people of color.

This movement grew out of growing disillusionment and frustration
with both the realities of ongoing endemic violence and the limits of
institutionalized social services and criminal legal advocacy in making inroads to end it. While the feminist antiviolence movement in the
United States of the early 1970s began as a grassroots mobilization to
transform the social conditions that perpetuate, justify, and normalize
violence against women, over time it has congealed into social service
agencies (e.g., crisis support services, domestic violence shelters), legal
advocacy organizations, public policy initiatives, and community education focused on definitions and available resources.

As a result, most people in the United States continue to view sexual and gender-related harassment, abuse, and violence that occur in the United States as individual, private problems, rooted in personal and familial gender dynamics, and perpetrated by psychopaths. As leaders of the Seattle-based group Communities Against Rape and Abuse aptly suggest, "Sexual violence is often treated as a hyperdelicate issue that can only be addressed by trained professionals such as law enforcement or medical staff. Survivors are considered 'damaged,' pathologized beyond repair. Aggressors are perceived as 'animals,' unable to be redeemed or transformed. These extreme attitudes alienate everyday community members . . . from participating in the critical process of supporting survivors and holding aggressors accountable for abusive behavior."[1]

While support and advocacy agencies perform the urgent and necessary crisis work of supporting and advocating for thousands of individual survivors who live in a world where their experiences are mostly not validated or understood, their efforts are often not directed to transforming the historical social, economic, and political roots of violence, and so they often reproduce systemic oppression and violence. This is, in part, a result of the increased reliance for funding on the state and private foundations who then shape the structures, approaches, and agendas of the movement. For instance, many service and advocacy agencies support and rely on the Violence Against Women Act (VAWA) for funding. This state funding is primarily for law enforcement, policing, and incarceration strategies, some of it is for individualized social services, and a minuscule amount of money is earmarked for prevention, with none designated for community organizing. With neoliberal policies that mandate severe cuts to social services, including mental and physical health services and crisis intervention services, and with the simultaneous increase of funding for police and prisons, agencies increasingly focus on a narrowly defined image of "innocent" individual survivors of violence.[2]

No longer tied to the transformative goal to *end* violence through broad-based *social change*, much feminist antiviolence work became more desperately focused on *managing* pervasive violence by providing support for *individual survivors* of violence, stiffening and expanding criminal penalties, and increasing conviction rates for sexual assault and domestic violence.[3] This shift in the antiviolence movement coincided with the expansion of the prison industrial complex through mass incarceration of people struggling with poverty, mental health issues, homelessness, violence, and more. These policies, initiated in the 1980s under the rubric of public campaigns like the "war on drugs" and "get tough on crime," criminalize already-marginalized communities. They produce heightened surveillance, policing, and administrative violence against working-class and poor communities of color, queer and trans communities, and immigrant communities (particularly those from the global south). The mainstream antiviolence efforts around public policy, then, have contributed to the deepening of the structural roots of violence by contributing to the buildup of the prison nation and prison industrial complex.[4] The feminist antiviolence movement has not challenged the state's criminalization of communities marginalized by poverty, racism, xenophobia, homophobia, and transphobia or addressed in any significant way the devastating impact of these policies on these communities.

Annanya Bhattacharjee's signature report, *Whose Safety? Women of Color and the Violence of Law Enforcement*, published in 2001, made visible the systemic violence of law enforcement against women of color, including abuse and violence by police, immigration authorities, and prison guards; she also documented the criminalization of pregnancy and childbearing among women of color.[5] The interconnectedness of structures, systems, and practices of intimate, interpersonal, and institutional violence was drawn out in the landmark anthology by Incite! Women of Color Against Violence, *The Color of Violence*, followed by the group's call for shifting our paradigms outside of the restrictions of nonprofit social service and legal reform in *The Revolution Will Not Be Funded*.[6] Beth Richie's *Arrested Justice* shows how mainstream antiviolence efforts not only fail to address the systemic state, community, and interpersonal violence Black women face, but in many ways contribute to them. The narrow focus on particular forms of interpersonal sexual assault and domestic violence excludes many of the forms of violence poor Black women face. The "innocent victim" often is constructed within the narrow confines of white, middle-class, heteronormative gender prescriptions, which functions to not only marginalize poor Black women but criminalize them. The lack of attention to the way community and state violence interconnect with and compound interpersonal violence means that the layered and complex contexts of violence against poor Black women are not within the scope of most agencies. Instead, they uncritically rely on the criminal legal system that is simultaneously a major source of violence for poor Black women.[7] Andrea Ritchie's book *Invisible No More: Police Violence against Black Women and Women of Color* offers a powerful and significant analysis of the interlocking historical roots of policing and police violence against Black women and women of color, including colonialism, white supremacy, patriarchy, heteronormativity, and ableism. She tells the stories of hundreds of Black women and women of color, including trans women and gender-nonconforming people, in a multitude of circumstances across a range of identities and experiences, including women in the sex trade, women in prison, women with disabilities, and women defending themselves from violence, who have been injured and killed by the police. This is a vital contribution to our understandings of the connections between intimate and interpersonal violence, on the one hand, and police and state violence, on the other.[8]

These works, among many others, form the backdrop for the resurgence of radical feminist-of-color-led antiviolence projects rooted in the social realities of communities of color, queer and trans communities, and immigrant communities. These projects work to imagine, create, and practice community-based collective responses to incidents of violence that seek "safety and accountability without relying on alienation or punishment, including prison and policing."[9] The goal is to cultivate more intentional communities through the building of critical consciousness and skills for communal support and healing, for intervention and accountability, and for prevention and social transformation. This is the essence of community accountability and transformative justice.

In this chapter, I illustrate how community accountability and transformative justice approaches shift the focus and direction of antiviolence efforts from social services and legal advocacy to community-based movement building, from viewing violence as a problem of individual conflict to viewing it as one rooted in systems of oppression, from agency expertise to community-based knowledge and leadership, and from punishment to accountability. In the chapter, I draw from the work of many scholars, community organizers, and activists, as well as projects and organizations. This includes the work of the Women and Girls

Collective Action Network (WGCAN), a Chicago-based group that I actively participated in from 2005 to 2009. In 2007, we issued a report that I co-wrote with Melissa Spatz, founding director of WGCAN, called *Communities Engaged in Resisting Violence*. It was based on research and analysis developed by WGCAN, which had been convening Chicago-based groups to share ideas and strategies to increase community engagement and accountability for sexual and domestic violence. The report documents a number of projects in Chicago that were doing community-based organizing around intimate, interpersonal, and community violence. These projects created space for specific communities to build knowledge, skills, and strategies to address intimate and interpersonal oppression and violence, and each sought to shift out of a social service model to one that was more grounded in community organizing. I also draw on the work of organizations in Chicago and beyond that have since worked to build community accountability and transformative justice projects across the country. While some of these groups have officially folded, their work and many of the organizers who led and participated in these groups continue to shape current conversations. A few projects that have been instrumental to and inspired my own thinking include the Young Women's Empowerment Project, Young Women's Action Team, Project Nia, and Just Practice in Chicago, as well as Generation Five: Ending Child Sexual Abuse in Five Generations, Communities United Against Violence, Creative Interventions, the Storytelling and Organizing Project in the Bay Area, and the Audre Lorde Project's Safe Outside the System in New York, Ubuntu in North Carolina, and Southerners on New Ground, based in Atlanta.

I have chosen in this book to talk about community accountability and transformative justice together—as in CA/TJ—because the frameworks are interconnected, they have built upon one another, and many doing the work often use the words interchangeably. And yet the frameworks have their own histories that are important to recognize as well. The women-of-color-led shift to *community* accountability, first mobilized through Incite! Women of Color Against Violence and further developed through Creative Interventions, envisioned that rather than rely on external authorities—i.e., social service and legal advocacy professionals and agencies—to *manage* everyday violence and oppression—we needed to seek to engage community members in building the critical consciousness and tools so that we might turn to one another to create communal collective support, intervention, accountability, prevention, and transformation. At its most basic, community accountability envisions community members (e.g., friends, family, coworkers, peers, neighbors) collectively responding to violence by cultivating communal healing and accountability rather than punishment and shame. This may include developing communal support for those harmed, and/or intervening when we witness mistreatment and violence. It also may include engaging with those who have caused harm to take responsibility, to make things right, and to change and transform themselves and their actions. And it may include creating collective understanding of oppression and violence so that community members can engage in prevention and transformation of the roots of abuse and violence, and the underlying power relations and systems of oppression that sustain them. As Incite! writes, "Community accountability is not just a reaction—something that we do when someone behaves violently—it is also *proactive*—something that is ongoing and negotiated among everyone in the community. This better prepares us to address violence if and when it happens."[10]

Along with the work around community accountability, Generation Five, a visionary organization with goals of ending child sexual abuse in five generations, offered an initial framing of transformative justice in 2007 with its report *Toward Transformative Justice: A Liberatory Approach to Child Sexual Abuse and Other Forms of Intimate and Community Violence.* It suggested that transformative justice practices would open up paths for responding to child sexual abuse in particular in ways that draw upon and strengthen communal relationships rather than give in to the divisions and isolation created by violence. They write,

> This [approach] creates possibilities for those who have experienced violence to safely remain in relationships, families, and communities if they choose. This approach also creates possibilities for those who are abusive to maintain relationship with their community. Rather than removing for past behavior, transformation of future behavior is supported and enforced by those with whom they have invested relationships. It builds a network of support to build and maintain healthy, loving and non-violent families and communities. And it uses interventions in incidents to prevent future violence through broader community awareness, education and involvement.[11]

In order for such approaches to become realistic possibilities, community members must intentionally become invested in shaping their relationships and communities by cultivating the knowledge and skills necessary for support, intervention, and accountability, as well as committing to dismantling the social and political roots of abuse and violence. This means, in part, that we must shift from seeing ourselves solely as individuals with individual relationships to seeing ourselves as members of communities who are accountable to one another and responsible for the dynamics and patterns of the ways we relate to one another.

From Agency Expertise to Community Knowledge and Leadership

Heavily influenced by neoliberal ideology, most nonprofit service and advocacy organizations have professionalized staff and volunteers who respond to interpersonal violence at the level of the individual. The focus is on the immediate individuals involved, rather than their communities of relationship and belonging. This means that agencies are not set up to deeply engage community members to be actively involved in the processes of support, healing, or accountability.

Community accountability projects seek to build knowledge, skills, and leadership of community members to address abuse and violence. This shifts the expert-driven social service and advocacy framework to one that is community engaged. Social service and advocacy agencies are organized to serve communities, but are not necessarily community driven. Most are organized through a hierarchical "helper-helped" structure that separates experts from clients, and organizations from the communities they serve. The distinct hierarchical division between staff professionals and community members limits the community's depth of engagement in addressing community-based issues, concerns, and needs. Agency professionals tend to retain the knowledge, skills, and expertise, and community members then depend upon them for information, resources, and services that tend to be more generic. Community members are not seen as experts on their own lives, and do not necessarily have a say in what they need or want in addressing the very issues that are seriously impacting their lives. Instead, it is the agency boards and their accountability to the state and corporate funders who determine what is best.[12]

A community accountability approach means that community members intentionally build their critical consciousness and skills to increase our capacity to respond to oppression and violence as well as to work toward prevention and transformation. Rather than assume pregiven and static community formations, people engage in intentional and collective practices of *building community* in groups to which they are connected. The community may be small or large; for instance, it could be a neighborhood, a block, a friendship group, an organization, a nuclear, extended, and/or chosen family, a workplace, a hobby group, a musical community. As Generation Five offers, a community can be any "group of people in relationships based on common experience, identity, geography, values, beliefs and/or politics."[13] Within this framework, communities are also seen as works in progress, rather than as static entities, where our relationships to each other and to the whole can be remolded toward support, intervention, accountability, and justice—not from without, but from within. From this vantage point, a key practice in many CA and TJ groups is to create spaces for members to talk about what brings them together, what values they share, and what norms they agree upon to guide their relationships and activities over time. As Incite! envisions, "Networks of people can develop a community accountability *politic* by . . . building relationships based on values of safety, respect, and self determination, and nurturing a culture of collective responsibility, connection and liberation."[14]

Thus, community accountability and transformative justice projects often organize communities along different lines. For instance, the Northwest Network of bisexual, transgender, lesbian, and gay abuse survivors organized groups of friends as a "community" through their FAR Out (Friends Are Reaching Out) Program; Sista II Sista defined themselves as a group of young, working-class, Black and Latina women based in Brooklyn, New York, the Young Women's Empowerment Project (YWEP) in Chicago defined its community as "girls, including transgender girls, and young women, including trans women who trade sex for money, are trafficked or pimped and who are actively or formerly involved in the street economy. We are activists, artists, mothers, teachers, and visionaries—our vision for social justice is a world where we can be all of these things, all the time."[15] Females United for Action (FUFA) began as a group of young women of color, and as it grew, more queer women and gender queer youth became involved, and they shifted their identity.[16] Drawing from this model, in my classes on transformative justice, I encourage students to develop community accountability projects based in their own self-defined communities; for some, community means their family, for others their musical community, for others their friends, for others their racial, ethnic, sexual, or gender-identity community, for others their religious community. I also encourage students to see our class as a community to which we must each contribute and be responsible for each other's learning and well-being.

Rather than service organizations providing information about the existence of violence and the resources available to address it, CA and TJ projects often create space to build shared knowledge, expertise, and understanding among community members. In a radical shift from a social service model, YWEP in Chicago, for instance, led by young women impacted by the sex trade and street economy, built knowledge based on the experiences of those who made up the project. Their projects ran up against the controlling ideas of adult scholars, activists, and service providers about the sex trade and the youth involved in it; in fact, they described their community-initiated research project that guided their work as "a response to all of those researchers, doctors, government officials, social workers, therapists, journalists, foster care workers and every other adult who said we were too messed up or that we needed to be saved from ourselves."[17] Instead, they assert, "We recognize that girls have knowledge and expertise in matters relating to our own lives that no one else will have. *We are not the problem—we are the solution*."[18] Additionally, rather than seeing their project as another space that provides one-size-fits-all approaches to the multitude of experiences and issues the girls and young women may bring to the project, they say, "We don't tell girls what to do, we don't give advice, and adults don't take control of youth projects."[19]

YWEP created knowledge and strategies for resilience and resistance to violence grounded in their lived realities. They developed shared language around the "sex trade" and "street economy" to describe their experiences. Moving outside of the legalistic language of "prostitution" and "trafficking," they defined the sex trade as "any form of being sexual (or the idea of being sexual) in exchange for money, gifts, safety, drugs, hormones, or survival needs like housing, food, clothes, or immigration and documentation—whether we get to keep the money/goods/ service or someone else profits from these acts."[20] Grounded in the complexities of their own experience, they rejected the polarized language of choice versus coercion and of prostitution versus sex work. In their words, "Some of us have been forced to participate, some of us have chosen to participate in the sex trade, some of us have had both kinds of experiences. Others feel that the question of choice is irrelevant or more complicated than choice/no choice."[21] They further say they never use the word "prostitute" because they feel it dehumanizes them, and they do not use the phrase "sex work" because it does not include girls and young women who are forced or those who do not see what they are doing as "work."

While antiviolence educators and policy makers have sought to define experiences of "rape," "sexual harassment," and "domestic violence" in order to build public awareness as well as to help shape social policies to address them, the result is often narrow, generic, and legalistic definitions that require sharp lines of demarcation. This legalistic terminology makes it hard to talk about the everyday messy ways in which mistreatment and abuse live out in our minds, bodies, and hearts. In my experience with thousands of people who have experienced intimate, interpersonal, and community violence over the past thirty years, I find that mostly people are not sure if their experience qualifies as "violence" or if it meets the legal criteria. Many assume that verbal, psychological, and other nonphysical forms of violence do not add up to "domestic violence" or "sexual harassment" and so do not seek out resources, or that what they feel is a "bad experience" of forced and even violent sexual activity does not constitute rape. In Latoya Peterson's powerful essay, "The Not-Rape Epidemic," she explores the gulf between the legal definition of rape and young women's own experiences of rape; she writes, "Yes, we learned a lot about rape. What we were not prepared for was everything else. Rape was something we could identify, an act with a strict definition and two distinct scenarios. Not-rape was something else entirely."[22] She proceeds to tell many stories of "not-rape"—stories of violations, abuses, aggressions, and pressures that did not fit the definition.

Again, she writes, "My friends and I confided in one another, swapping stories, sharing our pain, while keeping it all hidden from the adults in our lives. After all, who could we tell? This wasn't rape—it didn't fit the definitions. This was not-rape. We should have known better. We were the ones who would take the blame."[23] Lynn Phillips's book *Flirting with Danger* explores this further through her analysis of interviews with college students who consistently did not name or recognize their experiences within the available definitions of rape, even when their experiences closely resembled these legal definitions.[24]

Additionally, because most agencies focus on heterosexual male violence, most educational materials and resources emanate from a heterosexist and heteronormative framework that does not resonate with LGBTQ experiences and communities, and so, as Lori Girshick's book, *Woman-to-Woman Sexual Violence: Does She Call It Rape?* demonstrates, it becomes quite hard to name and process our own experiences.[25] Even within the work around LGBTQ violence, there is a tendency to create one-size-fits-all models, rather than take into consideration the complexities and nuances of intimate and sexual violence. The book *Queering Sexual Violence* offers a powerful set of essays and stories about violence outside of gender and sexual binaries that has differential and complex impacts. Queering sexual violence means opening up space to talk about how people can abuse and be abused, how our experiences of sexual violence can and sometimes do impact our sexual and gender identities, and how healing is a long-term, complex, and multifaceted process. The generic approach does not create space for people to be able to address their everyday experiences of sexual violation, assault, and rape that do not look like what is presented as normative.

Community accountability projects open up the terms and meanings to community-specific conversations. The goal is to develop vocabulary and understandings of oppression and violence that attend to the specific identities, experiences, and contexts that are shaped by specific interlocking systems of oppression and privilege. Some projects create spaces to build shared language on what positive, loving, and caring relationships look and feel like, as well as those involving mistreatment, abuse, and violence. A multivocal vocabulary can help shift a community conversation from debating whether an experience is "bad enough" to constitute the legal definition of domestic violence, for example, to being able to address the multiple forms and dynamics of mistreatment and abuse within specific contexts and the power lines that shape them. This would create a context in which people would not have to wait until relational abuse fits the legal definition by escalating to a more threatening level for it to be addressed.

Generation Five and other CA and TJ projects approach harassment, abuse, and violence not as individual aberrations with roots in an individual's psyche but as social, community, and political problems with roots in the interconnected social systems of inequity and domination, including white supremacy, capitalism, patriarchy, heteronormativity, and colonialism, among others. In addition, they recognize that violence impacts people far beyond those immediately involved; it impacts all those in relationship with those harmed and those doing the harm as well as the broader community. Thus, as community members, we are in a position to become responsible for creating responses that promote communal healing, accountability, and broader social change. In building the skills of intervention, we must become more cognizant of how we are impacted as well as implicated within the violence surrounding us as well as how we may contribute to the harm in the ways that we respond or do not respond to any given incident. In this regard, both community accountability and transformative justice are embedded in broader social justice movements oriented toward social transformation.

By expanding the lens to include the impact of violence on community relationships, and the power lines and social dynamics that shape them, these approaches recognize that systems of oppression/privilege actively shape people's identities and relationships, and inform people's responses to each other's experiences of and/or involvement in violence. And so rather than presuming automatic "safety" or "equality" or "respect" on the basis of a shared identity or experience, CA and TJ compel communities to commit to creating a culture of accountability for power dynamics and abuses of power. As Emi Koyama envisions in the context of women's organizations, "[I]t would be more helpful to acknowledge that there are many power imbalances among women that are very difficult to eliminate than to hastily move to make them disappear. That way, we could hope to create structures that would actively counter the power relationships that already exist, that would hold ourselves accountable to each other."[26] Within this context, rather than assuming "we" are all the same in our victimization, survivorhood, or identity, we would be more attentive to the differences constructed by our experiences and relationships to these interconnected systems of power.

Moving beyond the Binary of "Victims" and "Perpetrators"

Mainstream feminist antiviolence discourse often constructs the categories of perpetrators and victim-survivors as inherently and essentially distinct groups—often along the lines of male/female; and even in same-gender relationships, there is an assumption that people fall within one category, not both. The us/them categorization schema freezes people into static identities as "perpetrators" or "victims," and their identities and experiences are constructed to fall in line with these categories. To talk about them as overlapping groups creates discomfort and has often meant that when people's experiences fall outside of this dichotomy, their experiences do not get addressed.

A consequence of this static divide is that socially constructed notions of *who* is a *legitimate and innocent victim* and *who* is a *real and always/already perpetrator* are often tied up in dominant power relations of race, gender, class, and sexuality. Innocence is most often tied to white, middle-class, heterosexual, cis-gendered, able-bodied femininity, and so the violence against women of color, lesbian, bisexual, queer, trans, and gender-nonconforming women, immigrant women, and women with disabilities, among others, is often minimized, rationalized, and the women themselves are blamed. Similarly, violence and criminality are projected onto people of color, lesbian, gay, bisexual, and transgender people, immigrants, people with disabilities, and other socially and economically marginalized groups, while white, middle-class men are rarely held accountable for their violence as their identities are not criminalized, there is a huge latitude for their behavior, and they are seen as always/already redeemable.[27] The result is that the interpretation and response to violence often solidifies these power lines and structural hierarchies.

In addition, the conflictual, binaristic process of naming the violence *within* a community often divides members who are enlisted to take one side *or* the other. Those who support the one harmed become invested in punishing, banishing, or criminalizing the person who did the harm, and those who support the person who did the harm become invested in defending that person and demonizing or blaming the one harmed. Addressing sexual assault and/or domestic violence within a community often feels, then, like a divisive, destructive, and irreparable process. The consequences of this binary are either that people deny, ignore, and/or minimize the mistreatment, abuse, and violence so as not to "take sides" or that people do take sides and the communities break apart along those divides. In either case, there is little opportunity for support, healing, accountability, or transformation within the community that would both support the person harmed *and* work with the one who created the harm to take accountability and commit to change.

Integral to transformative justice and community accountability is a belief in the inherent humanity of all people—the recognition that none of us is inherently "good" or "evil," that no one is born a rapist, sexual harasser, racist, or transphobe, and that no one is inherently a victim. As Generation Five suggests, "People that commit violence are not born that way; they are created by their histories and given permission by the inequitable practices and arrangements of power within the society in which we live."[28] Rather than pushing for punishment, incarceration, and banishment of the person who causes harm, or minimizing, denying, victim blaming, and abandoning the person who has been harmed, CA and TJ approaches lead us to rethink accountability and justice in ways that strive to build and deepen individual and community accountability in the face of violence. Ubuntu, an organization based in North Carolina, for instance, writes of their approach, "We are committed to thinking about justice in terms that do not instantly repolarize our community. We recognize that a stark division between 'us' and 'them'—'we survivors of violence' and 'they, the perpetrators of violence'—could not lead to a transformative healing of our community, but only to the continued fragmentation of it."[29] This follows from their name—"Ubuntu"—which connotes that "a person is a person through other people" so that a justice process that "dehumanizes or oppresses any of us does violence to us all."[30]

This approach seeks to make visible the multiple systems of oppression and privilege that create the power lines within and through our relationships. This means that we are all both impacted by and implicated within the inequitable systems that structure our relationships with one another. And so as we approach those who harm, or as we recognize the harms we ourselves are implicated in, we do not approach "them" as completely distinct from "us"; instead, we come to see the interconnectedness of our identities and actions in our shared historical, economic, social, and political contexts. As bell hooks so eloquently writes, "To the extent that I remain ever-mindful of the potential for me to be 'the enemy,' I am able to view my colleagues who maintain allegiance to dominator culture with compassion. When I demonize them or see them as only and always capable of being enemies, I become part of the problem and not part of the solution."[31]

Thus, within a group of survivors of violence, we might be compelled to consider not only our victimization but also our complicity in interpersonal and systemic violence and oppression. In a small Chicago-based survivor organization, FIRE, for instance, members committed themselves to talking with one another about "how we may perpetuate what we are working to end; so we ask ourselves—do we use/support ways of thinking about violence that allow it to continue? Does how we frame the issue of violence in our publication prop up systems of violence? We feel that these are important questions for us to ask."[32] Such a reflective community-building process was also built into the work of the Young Women's Empowerment Project. In describing their efforts to build community among themselves, they write, "We do this by helping girls find connections with each other, by looking closely at how we might play out sexism (like by calling girls 'ho's') and by creating a respectful, free of judgment space where girls can get information about how to change the world."[33] In addition, projects find ways to draw needed attention to how racism or ableism may be shaping the dynamics and relationships within their antiviolence efforts.[34]

The Broadway Youth Center (BYC), an organization in Chicago that works primarily with queer, gender queer, and trans youth of color, does not organize its services as solely for "survivors" of violence. In fact, no one has to identify as a victim or survivor to receive services, and those who have been involved in violence are not turned away. According to Lara Brooks, who was a key leader in building this intentional BYC space, the organization decided not to separate out "victims" from "perpetrators" because it recognized that multiple systems of oppression and privilege shape the experiences of the mostly poor youth of color who turn to BYC for support. Most, if not all, have been victimized by interpersonal violence, and many have perpetrated it, and they are all impacted by the violence of multiple institutions (families, schools, police, social service agencies). Rather than assume that BYC can offer "safe" space by excluding those identified as "perpetrators," BYC believes that safety is an ongoing negotiation that needs to be rebuilt when mistreatment, oppression, and/or violence occur within the space. According to Brooks, when faced with a situation of violence, BYC asks itself,

> How can we utilize our longstanding relationships to support the individual growth, resilience, and survival of these two individuals? What does safety mean within the context of this relationship? . . . In our space, we have the opportunity to use our relationships with young people to discuss and explore—using a pace that the young person defines—the intersection of personal, community, and state violence. For us, this is healing work.[35]

In 2009, the BYC created the Community Healing, Accountability, and Transformation Taskforce (CHAT) to create a model based in transformative justice and anti-oppression values that would offer strategies to "reduce harm and violence in our space through relationship building, popular education, and youth organizing," rather than punishment or banishment.[36] Recognizing the structural problem of working beyond capacity in the organization, they scaled back the number of youth served so staff could build stronger relationships with them and so that the staff could *collectively* reflect on and strategize responses to violence within the space. By creating approaches based in harm reduction and community accountability, they are less likely to permanently ban youth from their space. Instead, they work hard to keep youth connected to the space and/or to the resources that would best support their needs and goals. This reminded me of the powerful work of Roca, a youth organization outside of Boston, which centers its work in restorative justice values and practices, including unconditional love and peacemaking circles. Their use of circles within the organization with youth, staff, and community members is documented in Carolyn Boyes-Watson's book, *Peacemaking Circles and Urban Youth: Bringing Justice Home.*[37]

From One-Size-Fits-All to Community-Based Analyses and Strategies

The institutionalization of the antiviolence movement has meant that most organizations operate from a one-size-fits-all, gender-exclusive framework, with standardized gender-based definitions, options, and strategies.[38] These generic responses often do not "fit" the particulars of any community or multiple and interconnected forms of violence, and can, in some cases, be more dangerous than supportive. Normative ideals associated with white, middle-class, Judeo-Christian hetero-normativity often shape the goals and strategies of these mainstream organizations.[39] The impact of systemic racism, classism, homophobia, transphobia, ableism, and xenophobia in people's experiences of violence is mostly unaddressed. Because of this, the organizational responses to violence often reflect and reproduce these systemic structures.[40]

Alternatively, the Young Women's Empowerment Project created its own analysis and its own support system to address the particularities and nuances of its members' lived realities of being impacted by the sex trade and street economy. For instance, its research revealed that young women impacted by the sex trade in Chicago do not turn to the police for safety or accountability, because of their experiences of police surveillance, harassment, violence, and criminalization. The criminal legal system is not a realistic or safe option through which to address abuse and violence. Similarly, many of those interviewed reported avoiding social services because of mistreatment—including being turned over to the police, being called and stigmatized as "whores" and "sluts," and facing people who wanted to "save" them, who threatened to take their children away, who did not want to listen to them, and/or who would only provide services if the young women agreed to end their involvement in the sex trade or street economy. It was for these reasons that YWEP sought to build community among the young women toward support, healing, resistance, and accountability. As its report expresses, "This is about girls uniting. . . . We want to show that we are capable of helping ourselves without relying on the systems that sometimes harm and oppress us."[41] In order to build and expand this community, it created zines, fliers, and outreach grounded in its members' own experiences. The organization committed to a judgment-free, harm-reduction approach that honored young women's understanding of their own lives, that valued and supported their self-determination, that met them where they were, and that shared skills with which to reduce the harm and oppression in their lives. YWEP's research also became the basis for its organizing campaign Street Youth Rise Up, which protested the injustices youth face within these protective systems of social services, health services, and police, and which demanded changes in the system.

From Individual to Social Context

Social service approaches to support and advocacy focus on individual survivors and their immediate needs. The communal, institutional, or social contexts that shape and contribute to the violence may be visible, but muted in terms of how efforts are directed. Most agencies do not have the capacity to engage communities to address the issue or to push for institutional change. The structure and funding of these agencies ensures this focus on individual services, and this then reinforces the broader hegemonic system that individualizes social inequities, and makes systems invisible.

Community accountability and transformative justice frameworks bring into focus the social contexts in which violence takes place and highlight the role that legal, educational, religious, health, and social service institutions play in perpetuating violence. Expanding the lens from an individual one to a social and institutional one shifts the array of responses available, for instance, to harassment in the schools. Rather than creating policies to report and punish individual bullies, a CA/TJ approach examines how the school's climate, staff and teacher training, curriculum, as well as institutional practices related to policies contribute to harassment and bullying. Instead of pushing for better reporting, investigation, and adjudication of individual cases, transformative justice directs us to understand and challenge the institutional cultures and structural hierarchies that produce the entrenched environment of hostility and violence. This would lead to a critical examination of the institutionalized homophobia and heterosexism that are normative in the culture of the school, including among school teachers and administrators. We know that teacher preparation programs mostly do not focus specific attention on issues of sexual orientation and gender identity and the impact of institutions on them; for example, in 2012, the Illinois Safe Schools Alliance 2012 *Visibility Matters* report found that the vast majority of schools of education did not address gender identity in their conceptual frameworks, nor did they have university-wide nondiscrimination policies. They also found that Illinois continues to accredit schools that have explicit anti-LGBTQ lifestyle statements, covenants, or mission documents.[42]

From Criminal Legal System to Community Accountability

In general, the mainstream approach to addressing violence is through the criminal legal system; it is the primary option given to survivors to seek protection and/or accountability. This is despite the fact that most survivors are reluctant to use the system, and it often is not only oppressive and hurtful to those survivors who attempt to use it but also ineffective and highly discriminatory in achieving the goal of real accountability for violence and its impact. In the United States, only one in ten sexual assaults is reported, and of those reported very few end in conviction. Most survivors do not report their experiences to the police.

The criminal legal system, and the law enforcers who implement its policies and procedures, as noted earlier, are also often a major source of violence in communities marginalized by systems of oppression—communities of color, queer and trans communities, young women in the sex trade, immigrant communities, and people with disabilities, among others. As noted earlier, the works of Bhattacharjee, Ritchie, and Richie, among others, have documented, analyzed, and been used to address the way this systemic violence by police, INS officials, and prison guards, among others, is intricately interconnected with interpersonal and familial violence, as well as women's reproductive rights. Police, security, and immigration surveillance, harassment, brutality, and incarceration are daily realities for communities of color. And the push for greater police involvement and harsher sentences to address gender-based violence does not address the system's violence, and ultimately has contributed to "the proliferation of prisons which now lock up more people per capita in the United States than any other country."[43] Rather than being the bad behavior of a few individuals, the violence by police, healthcare institutions, or other institutions is systemic and institutionalized. And because the state, as a major funder of rape and domestic-violence crisis, service, and advocacy organizations, shapes their goals and mandates, these agencies are reluctant to critically challenge the sexism, racism, homophobia, transphobia, and xenophobia of these state institutions.

Moreover, the underlying logics of the state set the stage for the mistreatment, oppression, and violence of social services and healthcare institutions. These are the very institutions that are held up as the spaces of safety and support for those experiencing interpersonal violence, and yet this is not the case. For example, the Young Women's Empowerment Project research report, *Girls Do What They Have to Do to Survive*, found that a significant source of violence was institutional, rather than solely individual; as they write, YWEP wanted to "show the reality that we face: everyday girls are denied access to systems due to participation in the sex trade, being drug users, being lesbian, gay or transgender, or being undocumented."[44] They found that "girls face as much institutional violence (like from police or DCFS) as they do individual violence (like from parents, pimps, or boyfriends)"[45] and that institutional violence made the individual violence much worse.[46] In their follow-up 2012 research report on *Bad Encounters*, they found that police and healthcare institutions were the most frequently reported sources of mistreatment, including refusal to provide services as well as outright violence. The research also showed that a disproportionate amount of violence was directed against gender-nonconforming, gender queer, transgender, and intersex youth.[47]

Given that these institutions often fail the most marginalized and criminalized survivors, *and* are a major source of oppression and violence themselves, community accountability and transformative justice activists seek both prison abolition and the creation of alternative forms of responding to and creating accountability for violence. Morgan Bassichis describes that Communities United Against Violence in San Francisco and Oakland decided to shift its response to violence away from a reliance on the state: "[W]e recognized that state systems set up to address violence in fact exacerbate violence by traumatizing people who have been harmed, people who have been harmful, and their communities, and by extracting vital resources that could otherwise strengthen communities."[48]

Community accountability and transformative justice projects work to build knowledge as well as communication skills among community members so that they are able to collectively engage one another when they cause harm—to take responsibility for the harm(s), to respect and honor the needs of the person harmed, and to take steps toward their own healing, change, and transformation to prevent further violence. Organizations like Philly Stands Up have created support and accountability teams who can work with people to address sexual assault within their own communities. They support members to create a process for supporting the person harmed and for approaching the person who committed the assault to address his or her actions, the harm caused, and the personal and social roots of the problem. In these cases, the person causing the harm must, to some degree, admit that they caused the harm and be willing to take accountability. These efforts toward accountability are often complicated, difficult, and not always as successful as initially desired, and yet in most cases, they *are* important communal efforts to address the problem without relying on the violence of the state.

Compartmentalized Issues to Interconnected Realities

While the 1970s frame of "violence against women" emphasized the interconnectedness of the forms and contexts of violence, the process of institutionalization and funding led to scholars and activists creating services, advocacy, public policy, and research focused on specific forms of violence—i.e., rape, sexual assault, child sexual abuse, domestic violence, and sexual harassment. This has made it so that we understand types of violence to be separate and distinct from one another—that is, we talk about sexual harassment as separate and distinct from gender-based murder, as distinct from domestic violence as distinct from child sexual abuse as distinct from street harassment as distinct from rape in the context of war. Each type of violence has had its own trajectory of theories and research, public policies, organizational developments, and organizing initiatives, and the interconnections between them often are lost.

The result is that scholarship, public policy, and advocacy do not often consider how these forms of violence are interconnected—that sexual assault is integral to domestic violence, that child sexual violence is a form of domestic violence, and that sexual assault in the military is connected to US military violence against women in Afghanistan and Iraq. Moreover, this compartmentalization obscures the realities that most people experience more than one form of violence over the course of their lives, and that all forms of abuse and violence have roots in the multiple and interlocking systems of oppression, including heteronormative patriarchy, white supremacy, capitalism, imperialism, and ableism, among others.

One organization in Chicago that worked to build these connections was the GABRIELA Network of Chicago in the mid-2000s. It sought to build bridges between organizations focused on immigration or anticolonial struggles and those focused on sexual assault and/or homophobia. It worked to cultivate awareness among Filipinos in Chicago about the connections between the violence against women that is integral to US colonialism, imperialism, and global terrorism and the interpersonal sexual and domestic violence, as well as homophobia, within Filipina communities in Chicago.[49]

Bringing attention to the multidimensionality of both forms and contexts for violence creates opportunities for cross-movement organizing. Generation Five's *Transformative Justice Report* argues that pervasive child sexual abuse in this country has an impact on community-based organizing, but is rarely named or understood. The report suggests that child sexual abuse prevention could easily be integrated into "social movements and community organizing targeting intimate and state violence, economic and racial oppression, gender injustice, as well as age-based and cultural discrimination."[50] Such a strategy would ensure investment across issues by building a consciousness about how they are implicated in and connected to each other. Similarly, there has been increasing attention to the sexual harassment, abuse, and assault as well as dating and intimate partner violence within activist progressive communities and organizations. The book *Revolution Starts at Home* is an anthology of articles documenting both stories of violence within activist communities and CA and TJ projects seeking to address it.[51]

From Defending Innocence to Taking Accountability as Community Practice

Connie Burk of the Northwest Network argues that community account-ability cannot simply be about making individuals who cause egregious harm accountable. She suggests that a focus on individuals as if their behavior is aberrant within the community can lead to the same bina-ries of us/them and often leads to default responses of punishment and banishment, rather than deeper healing and change within the whole community. Instead, she suggests we might commit ourselves to creating accountable communities. Rather than thinking solely about "a collec-tive process for holding individuals accountable for their behavior," we might work to cultivate "individual and collective responsibility for building a community where robust accountability is possible, expected, and likely."[52] Burk approaches accountability as a skill, rather than an external process, a skill that "each of us must commit to developing as an internal resource for recognizing and redressing the harms we have caused to ourselves and others. Cultivating deep skills (and community investment) in personal accountability also better equips us to respect-fully request accountability from others and to be aware when someone is highly resistant to taking responsibility for their actions."[53] Inherent to building community in which accountability is integral must be the building of the interpersonal skills and practices that enable account-ability to flourish. Again Burk writes, "As more people develop these skills, the community becomes better able to expect and support ethical, organic accountability processes."[54]

Creating accountable communities necessitates the building of critical communication skills enabling members to talk openly about relational issues as well as difficulties, conflicts, and tensions within their relationships and within their communities. In my experience of feminist and queer activism, many groups have fallen apart over deep conflicts and divides, often connected to experiences of mistreatment, abuse, and violence. We often did not have the skills or understandings of how to shift the conflicts, and so often the group would become po-larized and divided. Given that so much in relationship building goes *unsaid*, when conflict arises, there is no basis for negotiating the con-flicts and tensions.

For instance, when we assume that our "private" lives are off limits and that it is inappropriate to ask one another questions, we may not ever say anything when we perceive problems, and so the issue often festers, builds, and gets worse. Or because there may be a tendency within a community to avoid conflict, we do not tell each other when we are upset with decisions or behavior, or when we witness minor or even major patterns of mistreatment, we may overlook them. But they continue to percolate underneath the group's activities, to undermine the group, and often escalate to greater conflicts and abuse.

If taking accountability for harm became a daily practice, rather than solely something that we demand of others in egregious situations, then taking accountability would be less fraught with guilt, shame, defensiveness, punishment, and retaliation. It would create more compassion for one another when we make mistakes, when we speak and act in harmful and oppressive ways (intentionally or unintentionally), and/or when we contribute to harm in some way. And it would make it easier to admit wrongdoing.

When I have hurt my friends and/or loved ones, I too have suffered and felt isolated. It helps immensely to have a space in which to talk with others to gain understanding and to figure out ways to make things right. There are few spaces in which to talk about the harms we have caused and the systems of oppression in which we have been complicit. Mostly it seems that when confronted, we try to prove that we are not responsible—to prove our "innocence." Or we try to blame others, or to claim that we are the real victims. Making it a practice to take accountability and to create supportive spaces where we can talk about our actions and/or complicity would go a long way toward creating more justice in our everyday interactions.

In the *Building Communities* project at DePaul University, we create spaces for people to explore and practice what it looks and feels like to address difficulties and conflicts in our communities. Rather than presume that our relationships will be conflict free, we practice creating shared values to guide our relationship building, and we practice skills of talking through the differences and conflicts that create tensions and potential divisions in the group. Making a commitment with people in our families, peer groups, and organizations to practice direct communication about everyday conflicts can create a solid ground for addressing more egregious behavior. Being open, honest, and direct about how we experience and witness one another's behavior can prevent the escalation of abusive power relations, and can create more just relationships within our communities. This is not an easy practice, and we often fail at it. And yet, it is through practice that we learn. We must return again and again to practice to learn to embrace the process, rather than to see ourselves as failures or to gloss over the conflicts.

CA and TJ as Living Practice

A core commitment of those doing the work in CA and TJ with whom I have worked and learned is that there are no easy answers or template solutions to building support, intervention, accountability, and broader social change. The practice is the walk and the mistakes are part of the process. A training collective in Chicago initiated by Shira Hassan calls itself Just Practice—and it is a great mantra for this work. Just Practice. It is in and through the commitment to practice that we see the possibilities for change and transformation for a different future to build with one another. We learn through practice, and we need to be willing to face, and even embrace, our mistakes, our failures, and our missteps as well as our successes and our transformations. Practice is the way toward endless and radical possibilities, but only if we embrace the process with humility, openness, curiosity, and hope.

5

Collective and Communal Support

Healing takes place in community, in the telling and the bearing witness, in the naming of trauma and in the grief and rage and defiance that follow.

It is part of our task as revolutionary people, people who want deep-rooted, radical change, to be as whole as it is possible for us to be. This can only be done if we face the reality of what oppression really means in our lives, not as abstract systems subject to analysis, but as an avalanche of traumas leaving a wake of devastation in the lives of real people who nevertheless remain human, unquenchable, complex and full of possibility.

—Aurora Levins Morales, *Medicine Stories*

In the dominant culture, we often place the burden of responsibility for addressing intimate and interpersonal violence on individual survivors. We expect survivors to be the ones to speak up, to officially report incidents, to seek accountability, to find safety, to solicit support, to resolve the situation, and then to "move on." Rape crisis and domestic violence service agencies work to provide the necessary support, advocacy, and educational resources so those who have experienced violence are not alone and are not isolated in addressing it. And this they do. These individualized services play a life-saving role in the lives of thousands and thousands of people who have experienced sexual assault and intimate partner violence.

And yet for many reasons, there are many, if not more, people who have experienced intimate, interpersonal, community, institutional, and state violence who do *not* access these services. Some do not seek services because they do not know about them, or they have had bad experiences with social services; some may not want to talk with strangers, some may perceive social services as hostile to their identities and /or communities, and some feel or know from experience that the agencies will not welcome and/or embrace who they are.[1] Some may not recognize their experience in the frameworks and definitions offered. Some may deeply appreciate the necessary support they receive from a counselor or advocate from an agency, but continue to be isolated in the experience when among their friends, families, and communities. The services may feel disconnected from and alien to their chosen communities, even as they provide support for individual healing.

Violence divides, harms, and hurts our relationships, and the possibilities for healing and change are dependent on how our close friends, family, and other people in our lives respond. Trauma impacts people's abilities to support and care for one another, particularly when support becomes an individual's responsibility to bear alone. While many people experiencing violence would prefer to talk with friends and family members, or sometimes, depending on the relationships, with neighbors, coworkers, or religious or spiritual leaders, most often they do not feel that they would receive the validation and support they need.[2] And their fears are often confirmed as the broader dominant culture feeds denial, minimization, and victim blaming and rarely provides critical awareness and understanding. While agencies offer crucial support to individuals in the midst of violence, because of the mandates of funders, most are not focused on building the knowledge and skills of the broader community of people with whom survivors are most deeply connected and who might best be able to offer support and care to their family, friends, coworkers, and peers. And because many survivors, and their family and friends, have not developed a collective critical consciousness about intimate and interpersonal violence, they are left with the defaults of victim blaming, minimization, discomfort, and/or distancing. These responses create further harm and isolation both for the one who has experienced violence and for all those impacted. As Timothy Colman describes,

> Survivors frequently encounter community members who distrust what we say, minimize our experiences, or insist that it couldn't have really happened that way. When people are confronted with someone they know openly recounting experiences of interpersonal violence, or exposing any violence previously invisible to them, it can shake them to the core, fracture their understanding of the world. Often they'd rather

just not deal with it. For community responses to be adequate, they must emerge from an understanding of how violence fractures and isolates, how it remaps spaces, how it lives in people and shapes their lives.[3]

Often when family and friends want to offer support, they feel inadequate to respond. Many do not feel they have the necessary understanding or skills, and/or feel confused, distraught, and upset themselves. Those who initially offer support may become so overwhelmed that they decide they need to distance themselves from the person and the situation. Because of this, many friends and family may assume that the best support comes from professionals. When the person experiencing violence does not seek out these services or does not follow their advice, friends and family are sometimes frustrated and give up on them. For instance, some people may wish their friend would simply leave an abusive relationship, or, alternatively, they might feel that their friend should work harder on the relationship. And yet, as pointed out in the blog of the FAR Out Project of the Northwest Network, "Neither set of responses acknowledges the complex dynamics of abusive relationships, nor the myriad factors informing a survivor's choice to maintain or leave a relationship." Survivors often stop seeking out support, feeling that their friends or family members do not understand what they are going through.[4]

As a result, many are left alone to deal with the aftermath of violence, which increases isolation and shame. As Alexis Pauline Gumbs says, "When violence is something that the person experiencing it has to manage all alone the cost is huge."[5] Many struggle with the mandate to "just get over it" and suffer isolation. The difficulty of "getting over it" is often seen as a failing of the person as an individual, rather than a failure of the community. And yet communal contexts and relationships are integral to people's ability to cope, to recover, and to heal from the destructive harms of violence—physically, emotionally, spiritually. Timothy Colman, reflecting on his own experience, writes, "Whereas before I had seen myself as broken, my isolation and alienation caused by some personal failing, I now saw survivors' isolation and alienation as a failure on the part of their communities."[6] TJ/CA seeks to cultivate the confidence, willingness, and support of friends, family, coworkers, peers, and others so that they can offer support, care, and space for those harmed to feel comforted, to process their experiences, and to heal. CA encourages community members to come together as a collective in developing support, rather than to respond solely individually. This is in part because community members are more likely to sustain support when they are not alone and because they are also impacted by the violence, and so the collective can offer a space for them to share their upset, concerns, and whole range of mixed feelings and responses.

This chapter examines the shift from individual to collective healing, and explores some concrete methodologies that activists, healers, artists, and educators, who are also friends and family members, use to create collective spaces for communal support and healing. These strategies shift the focus from individual support for individual survivors to collective support for survivors and their communities—it shifts the emphasis from "what can *I* do" to "what can *we* do" to support and heal together from the impact of everyday oppression and violence.

From Individual to Collective Support and Healing

What does it mean to shift from individual to collective healing? Most sexual and domestic violence agencies define support as listening and validating individuals who experience interpersonal violence. They provide this validation by active, affirmative listening and support, and by linking people to additional options and resources. They also explain options for how a survivor might address and seek justice for the violence (e.g., to report to police or not).

This service approach structures support as something we—as individuals, as experts—do *for* a survivor, not something we do *with* them. And agencies often encourage friends and family members to support a survivor in seeking out individual or group counseling, while also offering to be a supportive listener. They distribute "How to Support a Friend" guides that direct friends and family members to *provide support to the survivor* along *their* individual journey of healing, recovery, and restoration. The resources available mostly do not offer ideas on how to build *communal* support and healing. They mostly do not emphasize or explore the impact of the trauma on the friend or family member, nor do they recognize that supporters may also be struggling with their own experiences. A social service framework encourages those doing the supporting to stuff their own feelings and responses to the violence, and/or to seek individual support elsewhere. In the rape crisis trainings I have participated in, the trainers strongly discouraged us from sharing our own responses and/or experiences with survivors seeking our services. One of the most powerful messages in rape crisis training is that the role of the support person is to listen, offer options, and then respect a survivor's decisions, even when we may have stories to share or when we may want to engage in more reflection with someone about their choices. Rightfully, these directives reign in supporters who think they "know best" how to respond, and who do not necessarily respect survivor self-determination, and yet they may also cut off any possibility of a more caring connection.

Supporting survivor self-determination is important, and the goal of support should not be to control or mandate decisions *for* survivors. At the same time, these mandates lead to a "hands off" approach to support that can reinforce a survivor's sense of individual burden, isolation, and disconnection from friends and family as they try to deal with the trauma alone. It ultimately makes the violence their problem and no one else's, and makes it seem as if they must walk a particular path of healing and accountability and must do it on their own. In turn, this approach offers little to individual friends, family members, or other people related to the survivor who may also be experiencing the impact of the trauma on themselves and on their relationship with the survivor.

As a result, processing the experience of violence becomes very individualized, rather than collective, and often creates more isolation rather than interconnectedness. One consequence is that friends or family members often end up feeling burnt out, resentful, and even despairing about their supportive efforts, especially when the loved one's needs and emotions feel beyond their individual capacity, or when they do not respond in the ways they want them to respond. This is particularly true when supporters themselves have no support for processing the impact of the trauma on themselves. Many feel distraught and overwhelmed by the experience, with little practice in how to build support with and for each other in ways that might deepen, rather than strain, their relationships. The structure of support, then, often further separates family and friends from one another in a time when connection and bonding may be most important.

With a shift from individual to collective support, there are more people involved who can build support and meet the needs of the survivor as well as support one another in the process. The burden of violence becomes a collective responsibility rather than individual, and the possibilities for deepening relationship and accountability with and for one another in the face of violence grows rather than diminishes. Community accountability, with attention to the interconnected relationships of friends, family, and broader community, encourages community members (e.g., friends, family, coworkers) to gather to support the person directly experiencing the violence and to process, support, and heal from the violence together. The roles of community members are embedded within the situational responses, rather than positioned outside of them. Support becomes something you cultivate with one another collectively, rather than something you as an individual offer to another individual.

In my experience, it is in the sharing of stories that survivors and supporters feel less isolated and alone in the experience, as well as in the response. Through sharing stories in community, a person's experience becomes part of a broader collective set of stories and experiences. It is through this process of sharing that we have the potential to deepen our bond with the person harmed and with one another, as we have all been impacted by this trauma and many others across our lifespans. Such a collective process offers the opportunity to deepen people's understanding of how mistreatment, violence, and abuse, as well as the possibilities for support, healing, and resilience, are a part of all of our lives. The sharing of stories does not take away from the particular and immediate experience of the person who has been harmed; instead, when communal support is nurtured, individuals are less isolated, burdened, and alone in the experience, and this can create more room to initiate and create healthy, healing, and creative ways of responding to oppression and violence. Our experiences of violence are most profoundly shaped by the responses to it—having family and friends "be there" for survivors can make all the difference in the world.

Creating communal, collective, and sustainable support for those who have experienced oppression, abuse, and violence is integral to building community accountability. And yet this support cannot be presumed. As Andrea Smith of Incite! Women of Color Against Violence and many others have argued, the idea of "community" cannot be romanticized;

communities of support must be built, rather than assumed. This means that people who see themselves as part of a community must engage in an intentional process of building knowledge and critical consciousness among community members about violence, its root causes, and the cumulative trauma it creates in its wake. It requires that friends, family, and other members of a community engage in one another's lives and relationships, and, to some extent, have some shared understandings of what oppression and violence are. It requires intentional efforts to collectively share ideas for support and care that family and friends find most helpful, and to build the skills that would enable communities to respond in supportive and potentially transformative ways. Ultimately, it requires friends and family to build relationships with each other grounded in mutual care, compassion, and accountability. This creates a relational context in which people are in a better position to collectively provide support and to be able to offer communal spaces for healing, rejuvenation, and transformation.

Healing in Community

Projects across the country have been cultivating communal and collective forms of support and healing (e.g., Ubuntu, FAR Out). One of the visions of such initiatives is of communities—small and large—where some or many agree to participate together in building the knowledge, skills, and strategies to support survivors and each other. Ubuntu, a grassroots organization based in Durham, North Carolina, for instance, initially formed in 2006 to support the African American woman survivor in the Duke University rape case and to protest the university's and community's response of victim blaming, denial, and hostility directed toward the survivor. Ubuntu went on to develop community-based support for people in its communities experiencing sexual and domestic violence. It committed to building the critical consciousness and skills that would enable community members to really "be there" for survivor healing, resilience, and resistance. In an interview in *Make/Shift Magazine*, Alexis Pauline Gumbs, a founding member of Ubuntu, offers a story of how the Ubuntu community supported one of its members when she came to after a life-threatening incident of domestic violence against her. When the group first gathered with her for support, they brainstormed a plan to create safety for her and her children. As Gumbs described, "This included offering our homes as safer places to stay, staying at the community member's home, child care, researching legal options and community based alternatives and coming up with plans, back-up plans, and times and places to check in and shift the plan, and listening and listening and being ready to support."[7] According to Gumbs, rather than having a pregiven script, for Ubuntu, it is about coming together in the moment to figure out what needs to happen in the particular situation. And it requires people collectively committing to be responsive to intimate, interpersonal, and community violence. This is a commitment that emanates out of "the political education and collective healing work that we have done, and the building of relationships that strongly send the message . . . you can call me if you need something, or if you don't."[8]

Having support, knowledge, and expertise from within the community can change everything; as Ching-In Chen reflects in her introduction to the online zine *The Revolution Starts at Home: Confronting Partner Abuse in Activist Communities*, powerful community-based support has been very important for her. She writes that it "was to not have to feel alone and isolated, to be able to feel hopeful about the possibilities that there could be ways to figure out how to feel protected in whatever, whichever ways we needed to."[9] The intentional building of community makes community responses both possible and sustainable. Community building is about much more than responding to individual incidents of violence; as Gumbs says of Ubuntu, "[E]verything that we do to create community, from childcare to community gardening (our new project!), to community dinners, to film screenings, to political discussions helps to clarify how, why, and how deeply we are ready to be there for each other in times of violence and celebration."[10] Additionally, in the face of specific incidents of violence, Ubuntu cultivated relationships with service providers and other community resources that it can call upon when appropriate and necessary. As a result, someone experiencing violence and their community of friends and family have a broad set of options and skills as well as a deeper sense of accountability toward one another for ongoing support and healing. As importantly, when people come together in the face of violence, it simultaneously strengthens people's relationships and commitments to one another. This communal support lessens the potential for violence to create long-lasting isolation, division, and trauma among and between members of the community.

Building Knowledge and Skills for Support

> I am proposing that we create a world where so many people are walking around with the skills and knowledge to support one another that there is no longer the need for anonymous hotlines.[11]

The question then is how to build the skills and knowledge needed for collective responses that support healing, that break down isolation, and that strengthen people's connections and commitments to one another. The Northwest Network in Seattle, Washington, developed a project called FAR Out (Friends Are Reaching Out) for queer-identified survivors and their closest friends and family members. Their goal was "to create a community culture that values open and honest communication, and reinforces the importance of friendships in resisting domestic violence."[12] As Connie Burk, director of the Northwest Network, reports, FAR Out intentionally creates space for friends and social networks to have conversations about "relationship values and goals, how to get (and give) support without putting one's business in the street, what being responsible for one's own choices in context might look like, what agreements they wanted to make about open communication and resisting isolation, and how to respond when abuse occurs."[13] This requires a shift away from the reality that even among friends, intimate relationship dynamics are often not openly shared and discussed.

The FAR Out project offers a vision of friendship communities where it is a common practice to openly share the details of intimate relationships, rather than keep them private, and to develop shared agreements about how members would like one another to respond when mistreatment, abuse, or violence occurs. This allows friends to be much more willing to engage one another in the face of mistreatment and conflict, and allows one another to talk about negative and potentially abusive dynamics in intimate partner or friendship relationships. Being able to share the burden of difficult relationship dynamics, including abuse and violence, can deepen the commitments of friends to each other. Moreover, through these intentional conversations, people can gain "new tools for reaching out to loved ones who might be in difficult relationships and for supporting themselves and others in their efforts to live in congruence with their values."[14] As Nathaniel Shara writes, "One of the primary questions behind the FAR Out! project is always: 'What structures can we *proactively* put in place to meaningfully support ourselves and each other when hard things come up in our lives?'"[15] When friends take time to collectively explore what support might look like for themselves and each other, rather than to presume that they know, there is a stronger foundation of support when abuse and violence occur.

Support can also be much more than one person listening to another—it can mean sharing experiences, self-care strategies, and resistance stories; it can mean gathering together for collective distraction when everyone needs a break; it can mean listening to all the messiness of situations without judgment and without a compulsion to create an immediate solution. When people work together to create supportive dynamics within their own chosen community, rather than following a one-size-fits-all set of guidelines, support is potentially more organic, meaningful, and oriented to the present needs and situation. In this way, creating support becomes a practice that is not static or unidimensional, but rather shifts over time depending on the situation, who is involved, and people's individual needs.

FAR Out and Ubuntu both offer examples of what is possible, as well as what is necessary, to build supportive and accountable communities. The intentional building of consciousness and skills within relationships is essential. I can say without hesitation that despite my work within feminist antiviolence movements over the past thirty years, such intra-community or intra-organizational conversations are rare. Even within our organizing communities committed to support, healing, accountability, and transformation, there has been a tendency to still respond from within a more individualistic social service framework, albeit a feminist one, and to act as if the problem is external to ourselves. We have not always had the skills and capacity for support and healing when violence happens within our own groups and organizations. As Jen Curley, a Chicago-based healer and organizer, asks, "Do we know how to show up for each other when violence or other crises occur?"[16] And if not, how can we come to know and begin to practice this showing up? Showing up is foundational to community accountability.

Community accountability for support and care for those experiencing violence would also shift the prevalence of abuse and violence within our relationships. Shannon Perez-Darby, a FAR Out member, suggests that the rates of domestic violence would actually shift dramatically if we broke the isolation that so often accompanies it; she asks,

> [W]hat would it mean if every person who was surviving a pattern of power and control had friends and family showing up to support them through all of the ins and outs of their abusive relationship? How would rates of domestic violence change if every survivor could go stay at their mom's house to recuperate and get support and if every person who was battering someone had friends reflecting back to them the impact of their behaviors?[17]

The possibilities for ending violence feel so much more achievable when we commit to showing up and being accountable to supporting those who are experiencing violence rather than ignoring, minimizing, or normalizing the behavior and dynamics.

Community Support Circles

Restorative justice support circles are a powerful method of cultivating communal healing and transformation in response to violence.[18] Community support circles create spaces for people to collectively support those impacted by violence, to become accountable for building and maintaining support, as well as to celebrate people's resilience and resistance. Circles are different from feminist consciousness-raising (C-R) groups and survivor support groups, and yet their goals are interconnected. The feminist C-R method to address violence against women, commonly used in the 1970s, created powerful spaces for the collective sharing of experiences from which to develop political analysis and strategy. People's stories were used to decipher their commonalities, which would be the basis of cultivating a critical consciousness about the shared conditions of women's lives because of sexism and patriarchy. The C-R groups shifted to support groups in the late 1980s as the movement became more institutionalized and services were more oriented toward the support of individual survivors and less oriented toward political analysis. While support groups were mostly survivor led in the beginning, many are now run by therapists or certified counselors. While they provide much-needed support, their goals are primarily for individual healing, rather than collective liberation. Support groups may or may not be composed of members of the same community, most often they do not have a social or political purpose beyond personal support and healing, and their goal is not necessarily the building of critical consciousness. In other words, while support groups are often lifelines for people in their individual healing, they do not build collective support within people's communities. Their goal is to support individual healing, rather than collective liberation from social structural causes of endemic sexual, domestic, and other forms of violence.

Community support circles, on the other hand, build communal and collective support for those impacted by a specific experience of abuse and violence. When a support circle is brought together, the person harmed has an opportunity to process their experience, needs, goals, and strategies with a group of people they have chosen from their community (e.g., friends, family members, coworkers), who are also processing the experience. The structure and format of a circle is not a back-and-forth of listening and responding to the survivor, but rather a circular process wherein each member shares their feelings, stories, and perspectives with each other and in response to one another, thereby building a communal dialogue.[19] In support circles, no one person is designated the sole survivor, the sole expert, or the sole decision maker. In other words, no one person in the circle has to carry the full burden for the violence that occurred and for what happens next.

Circles are organized around questions that all participants are invited to speak to: Why have we come together in community? What has happened to our friend and/or family member, how are they feeling, what do they need? How has the violence impacted each of us? How have we coped with violence in our own lives? What have been our experiences with self-care, healing, coping? How might we each contribute to support and join with the survivor in dealing with the situation? What are our sources of resilience? What can we offer to the survivor and to members of the circle for ongoing support? The support circle process allows each member to contribute to the dialogue by sharing their experiences with the particular issues that the person is facing—abuse, immigration, healthcare, abortion, isolation, sleeplessness, etc.—and by offering support in addressing the needs of the survivor. Participants learn more about what each other brings to the circle, including our experiences, our struggles, our knowledge, our resources, our resilience, and our resistance. The sharing of experiences deepens the relationships among the community members, and the outcomes can be transformative.

In community support circles, those participating begin to journey together with the survivor as they make decisions about how to move forward in their life, and they begin to respond as a collective in meeting the needs of the survivor and all those in the circle. Through this process, we have the opportunity to experience the transformative power of healing in community by working together to build a response to abuse and violence. Outcomes of the circle are collective rather than individual, and so individual survivors are no longer the sole carrier of the violence and its aftermath nor solely responsible for how to respond; instead, the experience is something that each member now carries with them and that is held by the support circle participants as a whole. It can be transformative for those who are experiencing violence and/or are struggling in relationships, and for those who are members of the circle who may also be struggling with past or present violence.

I participated in an amazing support circle for a younger friend who had just learned she was pregnant. She was struggling with a boyfriend who was often disrespectful and abusive, and who had threatened harm if she chose to end the pregnancy. A group of friends and mentors came together in circle to offer support as she was deciding what to do about her pregnancy, her relationship, and her life. The circle was powerful in letting our friend know that we each deeply cared for her and that we were there for her as individuals and as a community. In the circle, each of us shared our own experiences with pregnancy and raising children—one of us had kids, a couple of us had had abortions, one of us had worked at a women's health clinic that provided abortions, some of us had never been pregnant. In addition, most of us had struggled with difficult, abusive, and/or violent relationships, and all of us had the experience of yearning for love, respect, and hope in our intimate relationships.

I was awed by the rich and abundant wealth of experiences, perspectives, concerns, and feelings that we each brought to the circle. These in turn provided her with a rich context from which to understand her experience. There was no pressure for her to make any particular decision, and yet the circle process was foundational to her making the decisions that made the most sense for her at the time. She knew that members of this supportive community would continue to be there for her as she moved forward. As circle participants, we each came to see our own lives in relation to hers and to each other's in a way that was much more fulfilling than getting together to offer her a set of options and resources she could use to make her own decision.

Support circles offer an opportunity to explore what it means to be there for one another in times of difficulty or crisis. Through my own experiences in circles with classes, friends, and organizations, I have come to discover that what kind of support people need can be vastly different across our identities and experiences. For some survivors of sexual assault, having a space to talk about it every day is most supportive, while for others, getting together with a friend and not talking about it at all is what is needed, and these needs may shift and reverse over time. Sometimes what can be most supportive is providing transportation or a place to stay, and for others, it might be text messaging without any face-to-face communication. In the process of communal storytelling, we not only learn more about what each other might need in times of difficulty, but it also deepens our understanding of and relationship with one another. And we come to understand that what support looks and feels like may shift and expand.

Additionally, through support circles, we have the opportunity to recognize the need for support within the group, not solely for the person directly impacted. It becomes apparent that everyone in the group needs each other's support in order to navigate the crises and divisions created by the abuse or violence as it wreaks havoc on people and all of their relationships. Creating support within the community for all involved shifts the burden of the situation to the group, rather than allowing it to fall solely onto the survivor or onto one or two people who are trying to provide direct support to the person immediately harmed. It also brings in many people surrounding the situation who may otherwise either not know about the situation or feel disengaged, powerless, and/or conflicted in response to it.

From Speak Out to Community Support Circles

For thirty-plus years I have attended speak outs and Take Back the Night (TBTN) marches, rallies, and gatherings across the United States. Over the past twenty-two years, I have participated in these events each year at DePaul University, where I teach and learn. Until 2011, it would take me days to recover from these events. Each year I would say that I would never go to one again. I felt that the traditional format of the TBTN speak out was not achieving the core goals of building a movement, creating communal support, and achieving a sense of justice. Yet, I also felt, and continue to feel, that it is important to be in community with others in the process of naming our experiences, seeking justice, raising consciousness, and building a movement to end violence, and this has been one of the few collective forums in which to do so.

On the one hand, as a public event, TBTN draws attention to the pervasiveness of sexual, domestic, and other forms of violence; it offers people a space to speak out about our experiences, to listen to one another's stories, to face the pain and harm of violence, to embrace one another, to fuel the anger needed to motivate change, and to invite people to join together in a broader struggle for justice. The speak outs are reminders that intimate, interpersonal, community, and state violence—so well hidden, minimized, and/or justified—continues and has lasting impacts on people's lives. For many a survivor, the speak out can be life changing because it offers an opportunity to tell stories in a space where we feel we will be believed, affirmed, and supported in the telling.

On the other hand, TBTN has not necessarily encouraged participants to recognize each other's resilience and resistance, to support ongoing healing in community, or to commit to working together to build a more broad-based movement to end violence. In actuality, the speak outs often feel isolating, depressing, hopeless, and even devastating, particularly when they are not situated in a broader community of support and/or social change. I often find it difficult to recover; some years, I have lost days to upset, despair, hypervigilance, and depression. And I know I am not alone. I often worry about the many survivors or witnesses who tell their stories in front of large and often silent audiences. I especially feel for those who show up alone, tell their stories for the first time, and then leave immediately, still alone. I wonder how they are feeling as they make their way to their next destination—a home, a bar, a long walk, or wherever they choose to go. I know how lonely I have felt when I would begin my journey home on the train—on edge, fearful, upset, sad, depressed, enraged . . . not knowing what to do with it all. Over the years I nurtured friendships so I would have someone to call, and I developed more self-care strategies to recover from the event. And still I worried a lot about those who might not have such support in their lives and might not have access to community support.

Given these concerns, coupled with my growing knowledge and experience of restorative justice support circles, in 2011, Michelle Emery and I, through the Building Communities, Ending Violence Project[20] at DePaul, transformed the individual speak out of Take Back the Night, with its large audience format, to creating support circles of ten to fifteen participants each to share stories of our lives related to violence. Our goal has shifted from providing people with a space to tell their own individual story of violence to creating a communal space for the collective sharing of experiences, resilience, and resourcefulness. We structure the circles toward cultivating a relationship among participants whether they know each other or not. The circles are organized around a set of questions that ask participants to share stories of inspiration, violence, community- and self-care, resilience, and resistance. This has become our TBTN tradition at DePaul, and it continues to come together with a public rally and march to protest sexual and other forms of violence and to demand accountability from the university.

TBTN support circles shift the dynamics of the speak out from a space where individuals share stories of pain and victimization with a silent and attentive audience to a collective sharing of our lives. We invite all participants to share and build upon each other's experiences, perspectives, and strategies. In any given circle, the participants may have multiple and different experiences of and relationships to violence—including survivors, witnesses, family and friends of survivors, and/or bystanders. Each has an opportunity to share their stories of healing, resistance, resilience, struggle, and transformation in response to the violence in their lives and in their communities. This process creates opportunities for participants to listen to each other's stories and to share their own—sometimes stories in response to others' stories, and sometimes not. The circles create a space to tell stories not only about our experiences of violence, including our witnessing of violence, but also stories of our strengths, of our resilience, and of our resistance. Participants share paths and strategies for healing and self-/community care. Each member offers insight, knowledge, and experience to the circle.

In our first year of offering circles, we gathered responses from the sponsoring student group, Feminist Front, to assess their experience of the change in format from individual to communal storytelling. We found that overwhelmingly students reported that they felt very supported, less traumatized, and more connected to each other and to the DePaul community. One student reflected, "We need to know each other's stories and know who we can trust. These peace circles teach us to trust and love once more." Another shared, "It allowed . . . members of my circle to truly get to know one another, not just hear one story about them." Another student wrote, "I could really feel the community and love in the peace circle and I think it was a safe space to share and begin the healing process." Another participant reflected, "[I]t gave me a chance to feel like I was a part of supporting someone through a healing process rather than being a passive observer."

Since 2011, we have found that more cis-gendered and gay men as well as queer, gender-nonconforming, and transgender students participate and share their experiences of violence than they had in the years previous, and that the kinds of violence included in the stories have also expanded beyond the more exclusive focus on sexual assault. In general, the event itself has become a space that cultivates a deeper and more expansive understanding of abuse and violence. For instance, in the circles that I have kept, students have told stories about the violence of transnational adoption, of bullying, of anti-Muslim bigotry, of child sexual abuse, of racial and sexual harassment, of sibling-to-sibling sexual violence, and more. By encouraging everyone to participate, the circle helps people come to see themselves in relationship to one another and part of a larger whole.

In addition, because we invite each member of the circle to share their story, whether they have been directly harmed or not, the distinctions between "survivors" and "nonsurvivors" become more blurred. This creates a space where participants who have witnessed violence, or have relatives, friends, and/or coworkers who have experienced violence, or live in communities experiencing ongoing oppression and violence are all able to share their experiences and the impact of violence on their lives and relationships. This enables all participants to hear one another's multiple and differential relationships to violence and their differential impacts. This in itself is transformative. In numerous circles, I have had seemingly heterosexual men share that initially they did not feel they had a "right" to speak because they had not been directly victimized. They had taken themselves out of the category of people who had "experienced" and/or been "impacted" by violence. Yet in the same breath they would share their own stories of experiencing and witnessing violence and of supporting family members or partners who had experienced violence. In one circle, a student told the story of a friend who had perpetrated violence and talked about his deep upset and confusion as to how to deal with him and the situation. Over the years, many people participating in the circles who do not identify as survivors come to realize that they are in fact deeply impacted by violence and have a stake in addressing it. Their stories deeply touch me and nudge me again to reflect on the barriers we have set up around who can speak to what issues, around what constitutes "experience" or who can claim to be a "survivor." I realize now how the speak-out format had served to individualize and isolate the people impacted by the violence, and to undercut the possibilities for communal healing and change. The circle process inevitably expands our understanding of who is impacted by violence, and, in so doing, opens up who can be invested in trying to change it.

When we understand violence as having to do only with the individuals who are directly harmed or those who cause the harm, we lose sight of the impact abuse and violence have on everyone connected to the people or situation immediately involved. When this collective impact is not acknowledged, then those not directly involved have no space to process their feelings and responses, they do not feel responsible for addressing the violence for themselves and their friends or family who have experienced it, and they often do not feel they have a right to speak about it. When we recognize the interconnectedness of the stories and the communal impacts of violence, we are more enabled to collectively contribute to and participate in healing, intervention, prevention, and transformation. Our response to violence becomes not just what we are doing for someone else but what we are doing with them and for ourselves as well.

After the small circles have shared stories at TBTN events, participants gather together into one large circle to reflect on the experience and to share their plan for taking care of themselves once they leave the space. We pass a bowl of stones around the circle. Each person chooses a stone as a reminder of the community we created that evening and of our commitments to self-/community care, healing, and transformation. Some of the common takeaways participants share each year include community, love for those gathered, gratitude for the stories, and appreciation of each other's resilience and strengths. It is a beautiful and powerful experience—listening to the love, affirmations, visions, and strategies offered for healing and transformation. In 2011, one of the students reflected back to me, "It completely transformed the meaning of the event for me. It wasn't so much watching people re-live horrible experiences as it was about giving people a space to heal & connect with others. That's something I think gets lost in the 'traditional' speak out format. The impact was just as great but we left feeling energized and hopeful."

Healing Justice and Building Movements

We see providing immediate support for individual survivors and longer-term social transformation as interrelated and mutually-strengthening types of work. To resist, we must heal; to heal, we must resist.[21]

Healing in community nourishes people's resilience and resistance and our capacity for active participation in social justice movement building. And yet feminist and social justice movements, structured toward political analysis and strategies for social and structural change, do not often prioritize healing. In part this is the case because support and healing are seen as individual processes related to our personal experience of trauma, rather than as deeply collective and communal needs. For the most part, community organizers do not often recognize the trauma of cumulative oppression across time and place nor the ways it impacts our everyday relationships and everything we do and say. There is more emphasis on end product, rather than the process and its relationship to the people involved. As a result, activists and community organizers have in the past tended to view self-care as personal, not social or political. And, in service and advocacy organizations, where the focus is on the individual, there is much less emphasis on the collective impact of trauma, including on those doing the work itself. Because of the division between professional/client and activist/community member, those of us who are supporters and/or advocates do not often attend to the emotional, physical, spiritual, and intellectual impact of listening to the stories and trying to support the needs of community members, nor to our own experiences of violence, and the relationship between the two. Here too agencies and organizations often approach the needs of those doing the advocacy and service work as personal and individual, outside of and disconnected from the work itself, and as a potential problem. Ultimately, this leads to a narrow and limited view of healing as a short-term process that will lead back to a "productive" life and/or involvement in movement organizing.

And yet, the impact of trauma is much deeper, particularly given the ways in which oppression and violence are so endemic to our social environments. Trauma shapes the structures and dynamics of our relationships, communities, and movements, whether we are addressing violence or not. It can diminish our capacities for love, compassion, trust, and connection, and in turn, informs the way we respond to difficulty, conflict, and stress produced by a context of oppression and violence. As Generation Five recognizes, "The impact can establish patterns of reactions based on traumatic experiences from the past, irrespective of whether the present actually reflects the same dangers or not. These typical reactions such as denial, paralysis, hopelessness, blame, rage, and shame play out in our interpersonal and organizational relationships. They are also present in the responses we may get from the communities and networks in which we live, organize and work."[22] These reactions can hurt and undermine the work of building supportive and accountable relationships and communities.[23]

Unless we create spaces for healing from oppression and violence within our justice work, these traumas will continue to impact our movement building. As Aurora Levins Morales suggests, "When the fight against oppression doesn't acknowledge the grief and fear and rage and wounded selfhood, the terrible burdens of internalized lies about who we are and what we're worth, then we become loose cannons, vulnerable to terrible mistakes of strategy, to mistreating each other in the name of liberation."[24] Alternatively, when we provide spaces for collective grief, mourning, and healing, we become much more able—individually as well as collectively—to be engaged in the collective struggles for change. As Generation Five writes,

> Many of us have experienced gross injustices that have deepened our commitment to understanding the world as it is and to creating new visions. This trauma can produce incredible forms of creativity and resilience, as well as limitations that keep us from actualizing those possibilities to our fullest potential. In dealing with our own experiences of oppression and violence and how they play out among us, we become increasingly more able to transform the conditions that allow that violence and oppression to occur, and to create the just world we seek and deserve.[25]

Creating space for communal healing and connection supports our deep-seated pockets of resilience. Generation Five defines resilience as "the ability to holistically (mind, body, spirit and relationship) respond to and renew ourselves during and after trauma. It is the ability to shift ourselves from automatic survival responses—some of which may be useful, some of which may have undesired consequences—to a more calm, connected and cohesive place."[26] Nurturing people's resilience is necessary to sustain our resistance and our movement work of cultivating support, intervention, accountability, and transformation.

The resistance to self-/community care within movements is slowly changing, in part through the work of activist healers committed to "healing justice." According to Cara Page, healing justice is a framework for "healing inside of liberation." Tanuja Jagernauth, Chicago-based healer/activist, says,

> Healing justice acknowledges and addresses the layers and layers of trauma and violence that we have been living with and fighting for generations. And, it asks us to bring collective practices for healing and transformation INTO our work. It recognizes that we HAVE bodies, minds, emotions, hearts, and it makes the connection that we cannot do this work of transforming society and our communities without bringing collective healing into our work.[27]

Building collective support and communal healing into movement building means we are collectively carving out paths for individual and social transformation that shape our work within the movement, not only outside of it. By collectively creating strategies for intra-community healing, accountability, prevention, and transformation within movement and organizational processes, we are able to heal and mend the ongoing trauma and its impact on our organizations and movement. We begin to practice the vision we are seeking to build together. The process of collectively creating knowledge, building communication skills, and intervening in oppression and violence through collective practice is transformative justice in the making. We begin to learn what it means to create more just relationships within and across our communities.

6

Everyday Responses to Everyday Violence

"Our friend's girlfriend was so possessive and controlling—talking for her, putting her down in front of us, obsessively texting her and wanting to know her whereabouts when she wasn't with her. I wanted to say something to her partner, but didn't know what to say."

"A group of us [students] from the class were walking by the grocery store and saw a man yelling at and pushing a woman around. Because of her uniform, we knew she was an employee of the store, but we didn't know what to do, so we kept walking."

"A student in a class said mean and derogatory things about women who work in the sex trade, and no one said anything, including the teacher."

"My good friends always use the word 'gay' in a homophobic way, but I've given up challenging them because we always end up in shouting matches."

These are all stories that friends, students, and colleagues have shared with me, and I could tell thousands of other stories from my own life as well as stories that others have told me or that I have read about or heard. The stories reflect common responses to witnessing—knowing that what is happening is wrong but not knowing what to do about it, feeling helpless, and yet also recognizing that by not responding we are in some sense colluding in it. According to Generation Five, "The most common response to violence is collusion—knowing violence is happening and allowing it to happen."[1] And yet when we hear stories of widespread abuse in an institution, or a family, we ask insistently, why didn't anyone intervene? Why didn't anyone stop the abuse? Developing the skills and confidence to address the everyday acts of oppression and violence we witness is one of the central goals of community account-ability and transformative justice.

There are many reasons why people do not intervene in everyday acts of oppression and violence, and the reasons are not necessarily that people do not care, or that they think the behavior is acceptable (as evidenced in the stories above). Instead, most people who might want to respond do not feel prepared or ready. As witnesses, we may not be sure of what to do, of our role, and/or of our understanding of the situation and thus what is called for. We may worry that whatever we do might escalate the oppression and violence, might prompt retaliatory physical, emotional, or verbal violence, and thus might put the person being harmed and/or ourselves in more danger. These fears and barriers to intervention are real, especially when we feel alone and responsible for any outcome of our response. We may fear that we might worsen the situation, particularly when responding would mean challenging people who have authority and/or power to escalate the violence or harm us. In all of these cases, the risks feel that much more intensified. And so we rely on the police or some other external authority, we pull ourselves away to avoid engagement with the situation, or we respond aggressively and often escalate the problem.

Kaethe Weingarten, in her book *Common Shock: Witnessing Violence Everyday*, suggests that people experience "common shock" in the face of everyday violations, and this shock shapes our (in)ability to respond. She writes, "Witnessing violence and violation is challenging, whether at the moment that an act of violence occurs or later, when the acute situation has passed. . . . We are physiologically primed to withdraw, react aggressively ourselves, or numb out, responses that correspond to flight, fight, or freeze."[2] When the context of the violence is familial or even institutional, in situations where we have deep and complex interpersonal relationships to those doing the harm, many more constraints come into play. Again, as Weingarten writes, "From children and adults who are bystanders to bullying, to communities who are bystanders to ethnic or racial discrimination, people often behave as if paralyzed. . . . as if they are physically frozen, psychologically afraid and helpless, caught in complex relationship dynamics that trap them into silence and inaction. Bystanders are often people who are overwhelmed by what they witness."[3]

We may find it more difficult to intervene or respond when the person is someone we know, respect, care about. We tend to think of people we care about as "good" and therefore incapable of abuse. We also may find it more difficult to intervene with family, friends, or coworkers because we are afraid of the impact doing so might have on our relationship with them. According to Stop It Now!—an organization that works toward intervention and prevention of child sexual abuse—"[W]e all want to view people that we know as 'good,' and to believe naively that we'll recognize the 'bad' ones. . . . [W]e're generally reluctant to recategorize someone we respect into the negative category without absolute proof."[4] We tend to think of those who sexually abuse and assault children as monsters, rather than as people who have a mixture of qualities, who may act in a variety of ways, and who may be people we know and love.[5]

In the face of abuse within a family, friendship, or workplace community, we may fear fracturing and/or destabilizing our relationships. According to Generation Five, it may be hard for people to intervene because of their own "histories and relationships of dependency, fear, or love of the people they allowed to sexually abuse children that they know."[6] Power dynamics of age and gender within families, and of gender, race, and rank within organizations, often constrain people's willingness and ability to directly address conflict and/or violence. For example, workers may fear being fired, or children may fear getting in more trouble, or students may fear failing grades if they report. When intervention only looks like reporting to the police, family members often opt to explain away or minimize the problem so they do not feel responsible for state intervention. This is not to excuse nonintervention, but rather to say that it is important to recognize the underlying dynamics that inhibit intervention so that we can work to navigate these complexities in the service of expanding the options available for the ways people respond beyond minimization and denial.

This chapter explores community accountability (CA) and transformative justice (TJ) ideas and strategies that build people's awareness and skills to intervene, interrupt, and/or disrupt everyday oppression and violence. Given that most people's core reactions to violence are often limited to fight, flight, or freeze, responses that are mostly ineffective in transforming situations of violence, we must expand our choices for intervening in everyday oppression and violence so as not to rely on external authorities, such as the police, that often reproduce rather than transform situations of oppression and violence. The chapter draws upon concrete approaches groups and individuals are using to build more effective interventions.

Expanding the Possibilities for Responding to Violence

Community accountability and transformative justice seek to increase people's critical awareness of everyday oppression and violence so that we can potentially shift and transform situations and/or prevent them altogether. As Grace Poore, human rights advocate and documentary filmmaker, suggests, "People are willing to take action and be socially responsible if their awareness is raised about how harmful and undeserved violence is, and if they are taught to recognize signs of violence and, most importantly, if they are trained how to make interventions before, during, and after violence occurs."[7] Without the critical consciousness and skills, people are much less likely to intervene, and the harm continues and often worsens. Weingarten suggests that people can learn to shift from our core reactive responses of fighting, fleeing, or freezing toward "compassionate witnessing." This would require us to be aware of the shock to our system in the face of everyday violation and to practice expanding our options of response.[8]

Given that our core reactions to violations are grounded in habits, not nature, then with practice, they can shift. Poore writes, "[B]ystanding is like breathing. We engage in it on the conscious and unconscious level. It's premeditated and also instant, instinctual. We can take big breaths, little breaths, or hold our breath. If we do any of these things often and long enough, they become a pattern."[9] With intentional practice we can shift our responses and expand our options for intervention. The key term here is "practice." With practice, we can shift from initial reactions of shock, fear, and helplessness to a space of being able to thoughtfully and compassionately respond. One practice is becoming aware of our breath and then to practice taking deep breaths to calm our nervous systems in the face of harm. Awareness slows us down and creates mental space where we can consider options that might interrupt and/or deescalate a situation, offer support to the person being harmed, and/or engage and redirect the person doing the harm. With more options available, we are less likely to avoid the situation or to escalate it by physically intervening or by calling the police or external authorities.

Mobilizing Bystanders

When people have an opportunity to think outside of the box, many more options emerge for taking an active role in responding to everyday violence. Because of the individualistic approach embedded in US culture, most people think of interventions as something for heroic individuals who act alone; this individualized approach makes the risks, the fears, and the barriers that much more resounding in the direction of nonintervention. Alternately, when we think more collectively, we are likely to see more options. As Weingarten writes, "Many of us can more easily see ourselves finding the courage to act with others than we can imagine ourselves responding to a problem all by ourselves."[10] In fact, the possibilities multiply when we shift from "What can I do?" to "What can *we* do?"

The potential for building collective responses was brought home to me years ago when, in a class, two students shared their experience of being harassed in their campus dormitory. They talked about two white, heterosexual, male students who were harassing people on the floor whom they perceived as "feminists" or "gay men," including the two students in my class. Class members advised the students either to ignore the behavior in the hope that it would go away or to ask the resident advisor to intervene, which would entail an official complaint report and process. The students who were being harassed thought that avoiding the behavior was the best solution for them. They did not want to cause trouble in their first quarter of being in college, they did not trust that the resident advisors would take their complaint seriously, and they were afraid that officially reporting it would escalate the situation.

As my class began to descend into feeling hopeless, I asked how many people lived on the dorm floor and if there were witnesses to the harassment. They responded that yes, there were about sixty residents on the floor, and a good number of them had observed and/or even encountered the behavior. To their knowledge, no one had intervened or reported the behavior, which, as I noted earlier, may have been connected to the fact that the students in this dorm were all in their first year of college. As a class, we began to generate more questions: Were other residents uncomfortable with the harassment? *Yes.* Might some be open to discussing it? *Maybe.* Might some be willing to intervene during or after an incident, if there were others who could join them? *Maybe, yes.* Might there be any students who knew those doing the harassing who might encourage them to stop? *Maybe.* What would it take for concerned students to speak up, to publicize their disagreement, to show public support for those being harmed? *Talk about it together, act together.* What might be the social norms of the dorm that make this behavior appear normative or acceptable, or that might make people less willing to intervene? *Fear, conflict avoidance, first-year hesitance.* What could concerned students do to shift these norms? *Lots of things.* What resources from the broader campus community might they enlist to address the harassment in an educational and accountable way? *The women's and gender studies program, LGBTQ Student Services.*

Exploring these questions led to a much livelier conversation and generated a broad array of strategies. These included reaching out to other people in the dorm who had experienced, observed, or heard about the behavior, were upset by it, and wanted it to stop. This group could meet and brainstorm ways to intervene—they might agree to post fliers on their dorm doors that support and celebrate queer, trans, bisexual, lesbian, and gay people and that affirm feminist perspectives and actions. Such support might crowd out the homophobia, antifeminism, racism, and other normative systems operating with affirmations and celebrations of marginalized identities. They could also initiate a forum to explore the impact of harassment on those harmed and to develop collective strategies to respond. They could offer floor discussions on sexism, racism, and homophobia as well as LGBTQ and feminist activism. They could use hall billboards to advertise events related to feminism, LGBTQ community, and/or about oppression, harassment, and violence. They could reach out to others being harassed and form a support group. They could make plans and build skills for direct interventions when the harassment was occurring. As a class, we also brainstormed direct ways people on the dorm floor could disrupt, interrupt, and/or distract the two white male heterosexual students whenever they witnessed the harassing behavior. Additionally, the class thought that if the men had friends or acquaintances who were also troubled by their behavior, these friends could talk with them about their behavior and its negative impact and encourage them to stop and to make an effort to mend the harm done.

While the class did not pursue these strategies, as it was the end of the term and the individuals most impacted did not feel ready to take on such a process, we were energized by the possibilities. The classroom strategy session created a space for us to think together about how such actions might bring about deeper and more lasting change in a dormitory than either ignoring the harassment or simply reporting it as an individual problem.

Public places where people are anonymous to one another are sometimes more difficult locations in which to generate a communal response to witnessing violations and violence. And yet, when one person makes the move toward intervention, it opens space for others to take the risk of joining. At a conference on white privilege a few years ago, an older white woman told the story of when she was traveling on a bus from the airline terminal to the airport parking lot. A group of young white men at the front of the bus began to racially taunt and harass the bus driver, an older African American man. At first, the group of other white passengers sat silently, looking ahead. Eventually, an older white man approached the young white men and told them to stop. After they ignored him, he persisted, and they told him to back off. He refused and continued to confront them; at one point, they started moving toward him, yelling and physically threatening him. At another point, the young white men started backing away and settling down. The older white man turned around and saw that the other white passengers, including the white woman storyteller, were finally standing right behind him. The young white men stopped when they saw that there was a group willing to take action. This story opens up possibilities for intervention. It is also important to recognize that this story may have had different outcomes had the intervener been African American, Latino, Asian American, Arab American, and/or a white woman or a queer or gender-nonconforming person, or if those doing the harassing were young men of color, or if the passengers were people of color. Any changes in the power lines might have shifted the dynamics of the situation and the potential for intervention. In any case, sharing such stories opens up the possibilities for intervention and for creating space for talking about how power systems impact any given situation.

In Shakti Butler's film *Cracking the Codes: The System of Racial Inequity*,[11] Joy DeGruy, author of *Post-Traumatic Slave Syndrome*,[12] tells a powerful story of when her light-skinned African American sister intervened when a white woman cashier racially profiled and mistreated DeGruy and her daughter. Immediately prior, this white woman cashier greeted DeGruy's light-skinned sister with a warm and happy welcome and, without a second's hesitation, accepted a check for the groceries, no identification required. When DeGruy proceeded through the checkout, the cashier's whole demeanor changed. She barely spoke with her, and when DeGruy wrote a check, the cashier asked for three forms of identification. When she presented her identification, the cashier began to search through her bad-check list. As her daughter teared up, DeGruy began to assess her options for responding, being mindful that she did not want to cause further humiliation to herself or her daughter. At this point, her lighter-skinned sister-in-law stepped up and asked the white cashier, "What are you doing?" When the white cashier claimed it was a policy to ask for identification, DeGruy's sister-in-law reminded the cashier that she had not asked her to provide an ID. The cashier then said that was the case because the light-skinned sister was familiar to her. The sister-in-law responded that it was actually Joy DeGruy who was a frequent shopper at the store, having lived there for years, while she herself had only recently moved to the area. Soon the white manager arrived to inquire as to what was happening. After the light-skinned sister-in-law got involved with the manager, two elderly white women joined in to question the cashier as well. For DeGruy, this experience illustrates the possibilities for those privileged with light/white skin to step up and speak up when we witness unfair and discriminatory treatment.

This story, like the other, is not without its complications—does her sister-in-law's intervention reinforce white privilege, or challenge it? Would it have been different if she had not known DeGruy? What if she had not been light skinned? All of these are good and important questions to consider as the particular identities of those involved and the power lines that shape the dynamics of any given situation always shape the outcomes. What these stories show is that speaking up and intervening have the potential to shift the situation for everyone involved.

Storytelling, Collective Interventions, and Community Organizing

Whether or not the outcomes are successful, nuanced, or contradictory, sharing everyday intervention stories and creating the space to critically explore the strategies for intervention are imperative. They make the spectrum of options available more imaginable, and they build the capacity and skills for implementing those options. As Weingarten writes, "We need examples of behavior *we* can emulate, that feel bite-size and doable. People who feel competent act more to help others. We need to create histories in our families, communities, and nations not just of heroic actions but of everyday ordinary actions that help."[13]

Creative Interventions, in Oakland, California, initiated the Storytelling and Organizing Project (STOP) just for this purpose. The mission of Creative Interventions, founded by Mimi Kim, was "to create community-based options for interventions to interpersonal violence," with a focus on developing "collective, creative, and flexible solutions, which take into account the realities and resources of each situation and community."[14] One of STOP's projects was to record and circulate stories of collective interventions wherein family members, friends, and/or community members intervened to disrupt or stop interpersonal violence: "from Korean and Latina mothers protecting their children from physical and sexual harm, youth standing up for a friend who had been sexually abused by someone in their neighborhood, a mother who taught her son not to rape, to a Maori family coming together to stop a father from beating his son."[15] The stories are of collective, community-based responses to violence that do not rely on external authorities (e.g., police, social services) for intervention. Rather than conceptualizing community accountability as "new," Kim argues that community-based interventions are happening all of the time across generations, particularly in communities of color; she writes, "Our failure of imagination was not rooted in a lack of examples, but rather in the devaluing of community-based actions."[16] Often the only community-based interventions publicized are those that involve violent vigilantism, and the impact of this publicity is to further dampen people's willingness to intervene; thus, people are even more reluctant to respond themselves and more likely to see the police as the only option. And yet the police themselves are often involved in active oppression and violence, particularly against low-income and poor people of color, including women and queer and trans people, and so many people do not see them as an option either.

The stories told through STOP are powerful illustrations of how family members and friends draw on their relationships, experiences, and knowledge and work together to prevent and/or respond to violence within their own lives and communities. They do not present the collected stories as *model* answers or as templates for future action. Instead, they encourage community activists and educators to use the stories as a stimulus for critical reflection, dialogue, inspiration, and imagination. One of the stories offered is by Phoebe and is about a collective response to racist neighborhood violence. Upon finding out that their friend, a Black woman, had been attacked by seven white men on a busy city street in Melbourne, Australia, fifteen friends gathered together to respond by raising awareness in the neighborhood. In the process, they found out that, on the night of the attack, a white supremacist group had been organizing in a local pub. They decided to create and distribute stickers that said "racism is not welcome here" and a pamphlet that encouraged people to speak up against racism when they witnessed it. They informed local businesses about the incident, and told them that while there were people around, no one did anything. They asked the business owners to display the stickers. They approached three hundred businesses and so had three hundred conversations, and a hundred of the businesses put up the signs. They also did some radio and media interviews about the racism and the white supremacist organizing in the area to create broader critical awareness in the neighborhood and in the city.[17]

In another story, Di Grennell, from Whangarei, Aotearoa-New Zealand, talks about a family intervention to protect a nephew who, with friends, had accidentally shattered the back window of his father's parked car while playing ball. Knowing that the father's upset would most likely result in violence against their son, his mother called on her extended family for help. As she says, "[B]efore he got home we burned up the phone lines—sister to sister, cousin to cousin, brother-in-law to sister-in-law, wife to husband, brother to brother. This was because my husband and his brother know that there are some lessons you are taught as a child that should not be passed on." Together they mobilized support and an intervention so that when the father arrived home to find out about his car window, he "was protected by our combined *aroha*, or *love*, and good humor, by the presence of a senior uncle, by invitations to decide how to get the window fixed in the shortest time for the least money."[18]

For STOP, storytelling about collective interventions offers a space for movement building.[19] As Di Grennell reflects, "This is only a small story that took place in an unknown valley, not marked on many maps. When these small stories are told and repeated so our lives join and connect, when we choose to embrace new learning and use our 'bigness' to heal not hurt, then we are growing grace and wisdom on the earth."[20] By bringing people together to share their stories of intervention, groups expand their repertoire of ideas, tools, and strategies that they can draw from for communal, collective interventions within their own communities.[21] Stories of community-based interventions that do not rely on external experts and authorities highlight the vast potential of everyday people to respond to abuse and violence. They speak to the potential of building the capacity for community members to collectively address the multitude of injustices shaping community relations. STOP writes, "A community that is able to support safety and self-determination for all of its members is one with the power to challenge the other injustices it faces."[22]

Expanding Imagination and Skills for Collective Interventions

Creating space to practice expansive options that shift our core and embedded default responses of fight, flight, or freeze is essential. Groups across the country have been creating such spaces. In the spring of 2010, I participated in my first "Safety Lab" offered by Communities United Against Violence and Generation Five, based in the San Francisco Bay area of California. In the workshops, participants learn to develop the skills for shifting from our core reactions to centered responsive interventions. These workshops, as described by Morgan Bassichis in the essay "Reclaiming Queer and Trans Safety" in *The Revolution Begins at Home*, begin "with a review of the common (often experienced as automatic, or 'knee-jerk') reactions to challenging or harmful situations:

minimization on one end (which can look like denial, silence, victim blaming), and retaliation on the other (which can look like punishment, isolation, shaming, vigilantism)." The point is not to shame any of us for having these responses; as Bassichis explains, "[T]hese are often survival strategies that can take care of us in the moment, but have long-term costs (such as damaged relationships, further harm, unchallenged community norms)."[23] The workshops provide space to imagine and practice a "middle path," what Bassichis describes as a "centered, grounded place we can call accountability, which is a practice of taking responsibility for our actions."[24]

In that first workshop I attended in 2010, we used scenarios from our lived experiences to explore our core default reactions to witnessing oppression and violence—avoidance or aggression. The facilitators encouraged us to use an experience with a mild, rather than high, threat level so as not to be retraumatized, and to begin to build the skills. I chose a painful falling out with a community-organizing friend with whom I had worked closely on many collaborative projects. Because of our failed attempts at reconciliation, we no longer worked together, our community was divided, and I dreaded running into her at events. My reactive strategy was to avoid running into her and exiting when I found myself in shared space—a flight response that just made me feel worse. In the workshop, they encouraged those of us with flight responses to practice responding with aggression as well. While this was not initially difficult, given my anger at what I felt to be her unwillingness to work toward a resolution, it did not feel transformative. Both reactions—flight and fight—left me feeling tense, holding both frustration and despair in my body and heart.

The trainers then asked us to imagine and then try out a middle-path response grounded in our core social justice values. For me, this called up my values of compassion, commitment, accountability, and love. From this place, I began to imagine a new path between us built on our previous work together and our hopes for a world without violence. From this place, it felt much more possible to acknowledge her presence, greet her with openness, and see beyond my frustration and despair. As I did this, I could feel my body and mind relaxing. I felt less entrenched in the immediacy of the conflict, and could feel the possibility of shifting the dynamic. While this engagement with her might not fix the impasse,

I was reminded that shifting my response allows for other possible futures in our relationship and work together.

Since then, I have been working with DePaul students, staff, and faculty as well as community organizations to offer skill-building workshops in community accountability and transformative justice through a DePaul-based project called Building Communities, Ending Violence (BCEV). Our goal is to create a space where people cultivate knowledge and skills for healing, intervention, accountability, and prevention within their communities, however they define them. Initially drawing upon my experiences with CUAV's "Safety Labs" and inspiration from the stories from the STOP project, BCEV offers collective strategy sessions[25] for people to brainstorm, imagine, strategize, and role play collective interventions into everyday oppression and violence that do not rely on external authorities (e.g., police) and do not involve shame and punishment. In the sessions, we practice shifting our energy in response to witnessing oppression and violence, finding what the CUAV trainers called a middle path, and developing strategies and skills for intervention. Each time, I witness myself with others finding a much broader range of what might disrupt, shift, and/or prevent violence.

We organize the strategy session workshops around stories of street harassment, dating violence, familial violence, sexual or racial harassment on campus, homophobia and transphobia, among other forms of violence. The workshops use the stories as a springboard to collectively create, imagine, and practice community-based responses. In strategizing around a particular story, participants collectively brainstorm a list of community members (e.g., family members, friends, public transit riders, coworkers) who may be connected to the situation and the individuals involved. Working in small groups, participants act as a group of community members who are coming together in order to collectively respond. The groups generate actions toward building collective support, immediate intervention, efforts to cultivate accountability for harm, and/or strategies to address underlying dynamics and root causes. The small groups brainstorm possible interventions, choose one to explore more deeply, and create a role play to simulate what it might look like to interrupt a situation of harassment or violence that they then present to the larger group.

The role play allows participants to practice the skills of intervention and to experience what it might feel like to enact them. Each person has an opportunity to embody the role of a community member working with others to intervene, or the role of the person harmed or the one doing the harm. They can potentially feel what it is like to offer support or to be supported, to challenge a friend or family member's behavior or to be challenged, and how it feels to create collective conversations about abuse and violence with others in their community. After the role plays are presented, the larger group discusses what it feels like to role play, the strengths and weaknesses of the intervention, and what we learn in the process about the possibilities for accountable community interventions.

The goal of the strategy sessions is not to come up with a perfect intervention; instead, it is to practice what interventions might look like and to reflect on the difficulties, risks, and possibilities that might arise for all involved. While one result of the strategy sessions can be that participants learn that the possibilities for community engagement are far greater than previously imagined, we also come to realize that our role-played interventions, like those in real life, are often quite messy, fraught, and complicated. Engaging in these strategy sessions, then, in addition to expanding possibilities, also cultivates more humility and compassion as we experience and/or witness the flawed and failed interventions around us.

The strategy sessions are also quite thought provoking as participants often reflect on how rare it is that they see themselves as members of a community, and how rarely they share their seemingly personal problems with friends and family members. Even for many of us who are deeply engaged in antiviolence work, it feels rare that we share our own experiences with one another and with our home communities (i.e., biological or chosen family and friends). I have been struck by the response of more than a few antiviolence activists who, after experiencing a strategy session, reflect back, "I couldn't even do this with my own group of friends." This response makes me aware of how difficult it is to sincerely build community with one another, a community that we might look to for support, a group of people who could collectively come together to address a situation. It reminds me, then, of how such community building has not necessarily been integral to much antiviolence work.

Many of us—despite much of the rhetoric of collectivity and *social movement*—continue to feel quite alone.[26]

The strategy sessions also offer space for reflecting on how difficult it is to shift from a "what can *I* do?" to a "what can *we* do?" response to violence. In the United States, people are programmed to be individuals, to act independently from others, and to be *self*-determining. The result of this is that when we experience and/or witness violence, we often feel that we have to address it by ourselves, as individuals, and we do not immediately think to gather others together. BCEV designs the strategy sessions to get people to begin thinking and acting as a collective, rather than solely as individuals. Witnessing the everyday violence in our lives and choosing to intervene as individuals can feel difficult to impossible, time consuming, upsetting. Without any support, most people may inevitably choose to turn away and/or to rely on the police or other external authorities. When people have the opportunity to imagine and practice collective responses, their vision of what is possible shifts. With a group, there is less isolation, less fear, less burden, and, as importantly, with a group there are more ideas, more options, and overall more energy for engaging in the situation. Shifting to a question of "what can *we* do?" changes everything.

Daily Practices to Interrupt Relationship and Familial Violence

In the context of relationship and familial abuse and violence, it is also hard to think collectively. In the United States, the defaults are to call the police, to get a restraining order, or to report to some other institutional authority. And yet, as documented over and over, most people do not call the police or make official reports except when the violence has escalated to the extreme; and when people do report "less extreme" violations, they often face authorities who minimize or trivialize their experiences. To some extent, witnesses to violence, including friends and family, rely on the police because they are afraid to intervene themselves—afraid of escalating the violence and/or being attacked themselves. Witnesses are also often not sure of their role, given ideas about individual and familial privacy. The result is that we often do not intervene until situations have escalated so far that people feel there is no choice but to call the police. Increasingly, though, antiviolence activists and community workers are experimenting with intervention models in which people in the community step up to interrupt violence in the moment in ways that do not escalate the violence.

Breakthrough, a global human rights organization that uses multimedia and popular culture to inspire people to act for justice, developed an international "Bell Bajao [Ring the Bell]" campaign. It calls specifically for "one million men, one million promises" to actively interrupt, challenge, and work to eliminate men's violence against women.[27] According to Mallika Dutt, founder and director of Breakthough, the organization first initiated the campaign in India. Many of the women with whom it had been working wanted men in their communities to be more actively responsive and accountable for addressing the violence within their families and communities. Breakthrough works in partnership with groups around the world to create powerful short videos demonstrating what "Ring the Bell" could look like—a group of young men in India interrupt their cricket game, a neighbor outside working on his car stops his work to "ring the bell," and more. They show men hearing and/or witnessing a man demeaning and/or abusing a woman, and then stepping up to interrupt by "ringing the bell." The campaign illustrates how an everyday act like ringing the doorbell can "shift silent complicity to active engagement."[28] Dutt says the campaign is about "bringing men and boys on as partners to end violence against women—to move beyond men as only perpetrators or bystanders, and become partners in creating solutions for change." Rather than asking, "What would you do if that were your mother, sister, or daughter?" Dutt suggests, we need to ask, "What would you do if that were your father, your brother, your son?"[29] The campaign has reached more than 140 million people in India, and has been adapted in many other countries, including Brazil, Malaysia, Sweden, and the United States. Breakthrough's successes show that "culture can change culture; men can be part of the solution to ending violence; and, specific concrete actions lead to greater engagement." As Dutt writes, "Our work is really about making human rights a very organic part of popular and public culture . . . I think it's about empowering individuals. To make them realize their contribution means something. A single act can go a long way, both in and of itself and to motivate others." This includes interrupting violence, challenging the disrespect of women on the Internet, and/or standing with women who have been abused.

In the creative collective strategy sessions of the BCEV project, often participants share stories of on-the-spot interventions that offer momentary interruptions of violence. While such interruptions may not necessarily prevent future violence, they interrupt it, and in so doing they communicate to those involved their awareness of what is happening, their willingness to interrupt it, and their unwillingness to accept it.

In one BCEV strategy session, a participant told a story of a time when she and her partner were bicycling down a neighborhood street in Chicago and saw a man pulling a woman down the street and yelling at her. Knowing they had to do something and quickly, they decided to find a way to disrupt/interrupt the violence, not by confronting the man's behavior (fear of escalation) but by diverting the two people's attention. They rode their bikes up to the two and simply asked, "Do you know where the nearest Chicago public library is located?" The man stopped yelling and pulling on the woman, and they both turned their attention to the two women on bicycles and to the question at hand. After talking a bit about the location of the library, one of the bicyclists looked straight at the woman, and asked if she was okay. She said yes, and the two women on the bikes continued on their way. While they knew that this was not the end of the story for the relationship violence they had witnessed, they knew that the interruption created a pause and deescalation of the conflict. By directly supporting the woman, they also let her know that they supported and cared for her well-being, and it communicated to him that they were well aware of his violence and that they wanted it to stop.

After some practice in strategy sessions we do as part of my transformative justice classes, a student was excited to share how the learning had enabled him to diffuse a fight in a local bar he frequented. He told us that his default response had always been to immediately leave whenever a fight would start. This time, as he started to leave, he thought about what we had been practicing in class. Instead of leaving, he turned back toward the fight and began to divert people's attention toward something on the television monitor. After a few moments, he had garnered everyone's attention, and the energy of the fight shifted to the television and a shared conversation about the sports event on the TV rather than the fight. He was amazed at how easy it was to divert the attention of those in the conflict, and while he recognized that it was not preventative of future fights, or might not always work, for him, in that moment, his response to distract people's attention did shift the energy and demonstrated the possibilities for the future. It also created an opportunity to share his strategies with his friends, and it opened up a conversation that they had not had previously.

Less Oppression, More Collective Liberation

The emphasis in these strategy sessions is on creating *collective* responses that do not rely on one system of oppression to address another system. In Patricia Williams's book, *Toward a Colorblind Future*, she tells the story of a young white woman who angrily responds to the sexism of a man by invoking her sense of superiority based on class; she writes about how easily the "impulse to antidiscrimination is defeated by the intrusion or substitution of a different object of enmity. This revolving door of revulsions is one of the trickiest mechanisms contributing to the enduring nature of prejudice; it is at heart, I suppose, a kind of traumatic reiteration of injurious encounters, preserving even as it transforms the overall history of rage."[30]

In "Standing by My Sister," critical race theorist Mari Matsuda suggests a practice of "asking the other question" as a way of building coalitional consciousness that could help prevent the invocation of one system of oppression in response to another.[31] It is a practice that makes visible the interlocking systems of oppression that shape any given incident of violence. For instance, when we think that a sexual assault is primarily being caused by sexism, we might ask, what does race or racism have to do with it? What does classism have to do with it? How does homophobia shape it? Asking additional questions encourages an exploration of how multiple structures of oppression work together to shape any given incident.

It is equally important to ask questions in relation to individual and/or institutional responses to violence. Questions might include the following: Does the response rely on or perpetuate sexism, racism, homophobia, classism, ableism, or any other system of oppression? Does it reinforce or undermine inequities? Does it lend itself toward prevention of future violence? Is the response oriented toward punishment or accountability? What kind of community does it envision and cultivate?

What kind of world does it posit? What kind of movement might it contribute to building?

It is often quite easy in a white supremacist society to mobilize white, middle-class communities in response to real and alleged interracial sexual violence committed by men of color against white women, and at the same time much more difficult to mobilize these same communities around white men's sexual violence against white women and women of color. Strategy sessions, then, must provide intentional reflection on the multiple and interlocking systems of oppression shaping our responses to violence. In one of BCEV's early strategy sessions on street harassment, for instance, my cofacilitator, Michelle Emery, and I felt that racism and white privilege shaped the white participants' clear critique of the interracial harassment against white women on public transportation, and their simultaneous minimization and victim blaming when it was white men harassing women of color. This experience was an important reminder that when we do this work, we must always cultivate a critical awareness of the power lines in any given situation. When we fail to do so, we may contribute to racism and white supremacy, for instance, in the name of addressing violence against white women.

In 2010, my partner, Francesca, and I experienced this first-hand when we moved into what initially felt like a close-knit block on the north side of Chicago. Like the neighborhood that surrounds it, our block has a mixture of white, Latino, Haitian, Nigerian immigrant, African American, Jewish, and gay and lesbian neighbors, with a good number of interracial couples and multiracial families. Soon after we moved in, a white gay man who lives on the block with his white partner sent an e-mail to neighbors on the block's listserv. He reported that two young Latinos, one of whom lived on the block and the other of whom was his friend, were verbally homophobic to him and his partner. He asked for ideas about what to do. Many responded with support, care, and concern, as well as upset at the harassment and at the young men who were doing it. Initially, the most vocal on the listserv suggested calling the cops and getting CAPS involved. The people advocating for a police response invoked the idea of zero tolerance for harassment and thought an aggressive response would be the most supportive of the gay men and the most clear-cut in punishing the young men who were doing the harassing behavior.

As the conversation continued, the responses became more racialized. Some began to attribute the homophobia to bad parenting and ignorance, which became linked, in the conversation, to their Latino identity, to the son's mother, and to speaking Spanish. No one from the Latino family was on the listserv, and no one on the listserv seemed to know the family, and so the default was to rely on stereotypes easily supplied by the broader culture. The other response initially vocalized was to minimize the problem and to attribute it to "boys will be boys"; those advocating this response felt that the incident might be isolated, and that if nothing else happened, it would resolve itself. Others, including my partner and I, began to offer some alternative framing—countering the stereotypes about Latinos, naming the homophobia and racism of the police, and raising concerns that police involvement was quite aggressive given the situation and its potential for further dividing the block and for criminalizing the young men.

As the two default options were weighed, a third approach emerged that was about engaging in a conversation with the two young men. One of the white gay men decided that this felt like a good and important first step. Soon after, he reported back that he had talked with one of the young men about his negative commentary and asked him to stop it. While he was glad to have talked with him, he did not feel that the conversation had had the impact he had desired. He reported that he wanted to talk with the mother, but was concerned that he did not know her nor did he know Spanish. Another neighbor who speaks Spanish stepped up to go with him to talk with the mother. They reported back that they had had a very good conversation with her that resulted in a deeper apology from her son. The conflict resolved, and in the process, it seemed that the relationships of those involved were strengthened, rather than further fractured. It was a great example of developing a community response to homophobic harassment that supported the gay men targeted, that did not rely on racism and the police, and that offered the possibility of building relationships within the community that had not been there previously.

Prevention as Intervention

In considering intervention, it is important to recognize that there are many opportunities to address situations before the violence has occurred and/or escalated, and before the urgency leads people to rely on the police, or step away from the situation. This is part of the mission of the organization Stop It Now! that draws on a public health model for intervention as prevention. It guides and supports efforts to prevent child sexual abuse by "mobilizing adults, families and communities to take actions that protect children before they are harmed."[32] Through its research with child sexual abuse survivors and those who are in relationship with them, it finds that the potential for preventative intervention is significant. If family, friends, neighbors, and other community members had the knowledge and skills to speak up as soon as they have a concern, rather than waiting for some kind of proof of abuse, much child sexual abuse could be prevented.

Some of the core guiding assumptions of Stop It Now! are that child sexual abuse is a family and community issue (i.e., that most people who abuse are known to children rather than strangers); that adults can prevent child sexual abuse before it occurs, rather than waiting for proof of its existence; that the burden of responsibility for intervention should be on adults, rather than children; that everyone has a role in prevention, including nonoffending adults as well as those who are at risk of abusing; and that treatment can play a role in prevention.[33] Through its work in numerous communities, it finds that "adults will act to prevent abuse if they have access to accurate information, practical tools, guidance and support; and communities will mobilize around prevention initiatives that address the complexities of abuse closer to home."[34] This goes back to the idea that people's willingness to intervene in the face of potential or actual abuse is connected to their knowledge, recognition of options, and skills. When people do not intervene, it may have less to do with lack of concern and more to do with their lack of confidence, clarity, and skills.

Stop It Now! is a leader in developing public campaigns with educational billboards, pamphlets, and tip sheets for early intervention and prevention of child sexual abuse. Its tip sheets, for instance, offer guidance on how to recognize potential child sexual abuse and what action steps community members might be able to take if they have concerns about someone's behavior toward children. In one tip sheet, "Don't Wait: Everyday Actions to Keep Children Safe," the organization encourages parents and caregivers to "set and respect family boundaries" and to model saying "no" and practice respecting children's right to say "no" with regard to hugging, kissing, and tickling. It suggests that adults should encourage children to be able to identify and name body parts without shame, to identify inappropriate behavior, and to understand the difference between "a secret and a surprise." Most significantly, it encourages adults to practice talking about these uncomfortable topics so that we might be more prepared if and when we need to talk about them with children. For instance, the tip sheet suggests, "Say the 'difficult' or 'embarrassing' words out loud so that you become more comfortable using those words, asking those questions, confronting those behaviors. Having stress-free conversations with both the adults and children in your life about difficult issues gets everyone in the habit of talking openly and honestly."[35] With practice talking about these topics among friends, family members, and peers, we are in a much better position to say something when we witness behavior that feels inappropriate, rather than avoiding it. Avoiding it does not stop it and contributes to its prevalence as well as its escalation.

In the mid-to-late 1990s through 2010, Stop It Now! worked with local, community-based organizations to develop social marketing campaigns around child sexual abuse, akin to public health campaigns for HIV/AIDS and cigarette smoking. These campaigns were directed toward urging people at risk of sexual abuse and adults who might be witnessing risky behavior to take action.[36] From its research with those who have sexually abused children, Stop It Now! argues that people at risk of sexual abuse "want to and will" seek out help if their behavior is addressed. The campaign was quite challenging in the communities within which the organization worked and drew a lot of attention. It required that communities be educated on the realities rather than the myths of child sexual abuse. A couple of the messages developed for the campaign in Minnesota targeted the "more challenging population— those having sexual thoughts and feelings about children, but who have not yet acted on them."[37] The organization crafted and tested messages based on focus groups of people in treatment for sexual abuse, and then also ran them by stakeholders, including sexual abuse survivors, media, law enforcement, and others, to solicit input, to refine the language and wording, and to make people aware of the campaign. For instance, one Minnesota billboard said, "Having Sexual Thoughts About Children? 1–888-PREVENT. Safe and Confidential Helpline. You Can STOP IT NOW.org." This campaign yielded an increase in the number of phone calls from people who were struggling with their sexual thoughts, feelings, and/or desires for children, and the hotline was able to provide people with resources and support as preventative measures.

The campaigns also targeted adults who might have concerns about another adult's behavior. For example, in Virginia, the Stop It Now! campaign "encourage[d] people to 'trust your gut feeling' if some behavior makes them uneasy."[38] One of the billboards boldly stated, "It doesn't feel right when I see them together. Call 1–888-PREVENT Child Sexual Abuse"—and it featured an adult and a child holding hands. The compelling argument of Stop It Now! is that rather than waiting for confirmation that sexual abuse has occurred, adults can take action by seeking out support and guidance for how to address their concerns. This campaign resulted in more phone calls by concerned adults to the hotline, which was able to assist people in making decisions about what next steps they might take toward prevention. Stop It Now! offers valuable next steps for adults who have a "gut feeling" that "something isn't right" about how an adult or adolescent is interacting with a child.[39] The steps include trusting the feeling and taking the steps to "learn what's happening around you." The organization offers many examples of behavior that might bring up questions. It encourages people to learn more about warning signs of child sexual abuse and to write down observations in order to keep track of the what, when, and where. It also encourages people to find another person with whom they can share their concerns, rather than carrying them alone. Working together would build more support in the process and help in decision making about next steps. Stop It Now! offers family, friends, and community members a range of resources and options for creating important conversations that could prevent and/or stop child sexual abuse, in a way that both protects children from sexual abuse and also seeks to build accountability with the person at risk for perpetrating sexual abuse. Most importantly, Stop It Now! offers concrete steps for adults to take action and responsibility for the prevention of child sexual abuse, and for creating stronger, healthier, and accountable relationships across generations.

Community Building, Everyday Interventions, and Social Change

Community building is integral to making real the possibilities for intervening in everyday violence; it is a cultural shift from "I" to "we" and a shift away from the binaristic framework of responding by either retreating or reacting with aggression and violence. Creating spaces for community members—family, friends, coworkers, activists, artists—to share and reflect on our everyday experiences with violation and violence, as well as to collectively strategize and practice alternative responses, is an important component to these necessary shifts. Rather than carrying the burden of response as individuals or relying on external authorities such as the police, CA and TJ direct our attention toward one another—the people in our communities—as potential allies, resources, and partners in responding to and healing from the everyday oppression and violence that shape our identities, lives, and experiences. By joining with others to address everyday violence, we shift the contexts in which violence takes place. If we build relationships and communities, small and large, where it is clear that people will support and affirm those who are targeted and will intervene to interrupt and stop any violation that occurs, aggression and violence will not have such a space to fester, grow, and do harm. Moreover, when harm occurs, people will be there to address the harm in ways that potentially shift and transform the situation toward accountability and healing, rather than more oppression and violence.

From Punishment to Accountability

Real justice comes through healthy communities wherein
members are accountable to one another and take one another seriously—not through police and prisons.
—Ubuntu, "Documents: About Ubuntu"

[A]n abolitionist perspective is a positive rather than a negative project. That is, rather than argue that all prisons should
be dismantled tomorrow, our task is to crowd out prisons
with other forms of justice-making that will eventually demonstrate both the ineffectiveness and the brutality of prisons.
—Andy Smith, quoted by Mariame Kaba in "Raping
Little Girls, Transformative Justice, and Community
Accountability"

When Incite! Women of Color Against Violence and Generation Five
began to organize around the frameworks of community accountability
and transformative justice (CA/TJ) in the early to mid-2000s at a more
national level, it was a collective breath of fresh air. They opened up
the possibilities for addressing and ending violence without relying on
oppressive and violent institutions and systems. They created space for
imagining, sharing, and practicing community-based collective responses
to violence that would cultivate healing, intervention, accountability, and
transformation. The approaches emerged out of years of critical analysis,
questions, and organizing by feminists of color and queer, transgender,
and antiracist feminists who experienced and witnessed the limits, inac-
cessibility, and violence of law enforcement and the criminal legal system,
particularly for communities of color marginalized and criminalized by
the state. The CA/TJ movement draws on the recognition that the roots
of abuse and violence are in the historic legacies of interlocking systems
of oppression and privilege that continue to produce deep and enduring

trauma, rather than in individual or "cultural" group psychology. Viewed through this lens, the responsibility for violence is much broader than the individual, while individual accountability for our actions and our contributions to these systemic injustices is still essential. Rather than rely on individualized punishment orchestrated by a violent state apparatus set up to maintain social and economic power systems, CA/TJ efforts cultivate individual and collective accountability for pervasive oppression and violence within and across communities.

In this chapter, I explore some of the central ideas and approaches community organizers are using to cultivate individual accountability for oppression and violence that do not rely on law enforcement and the criminal legal system. Drawing on feminist-of-color-led critique, I first briefly discuss why the default to the criminal legal system fails survivors on every level, and does nothing to contribute to real justice or accountability. The current system is not only ineffective, inaccessible, and not a viable source of support or justice for those experiencing harm, but law enforcement, the criminal legal system, and prisons themselves are deeply steeped in and perpetuate oppression and violence. I then introduce CA/TJ frameworks that approach justice through a lens of accountability, rather than punishment, and through community processes, rather than through individual adversarial adjudication. These approaches open up possibilities for addressing harm that seek to rebuild and transform relationships rather than further fracture and divide them.

For Most, the Criminal Legal System Is Not the Answer

The contemporary feminist antiviolence movement that mobilized in the late 1960s/early 1970s made significant contributions to naming the endemic violence of sexual harassment, rape, and battering as social and political problems, rather than personal problems. Grassroots radical, socialist, Black, Chicana, Puerto Rican, Asian American, Indigenous, and other antiracist feminists recognized that the historical and social roots of endemic violence against women lay in broader systems of oppression. And yet as the movement became more institutionalized, it increasingly became tied to legal advocacy approaches set up to address mostly individual incidents of violence from within a gender-exclusive framework. Feminist legal reform, rather than radical social change, became the most dominant voice and framework for addressing those causing harm, and oriented itself in alignment with the state.

The institutionalization of the movement served to significantly narrow what antiviolence advocates and activists have come to see as the only options for people to be able to address interpersonal and intimate violence. Calling the police and/or reporting to institutional authorities have become the default and often the only option for addressing incidents of violence. If we do not follow this mandate, we are told that there are no other options. And yet, despite this pressure to report, most people experiencing sexual and intimate partner violence do not and will not call the police (or other external authorities, such as university public safety offices), except in cases where the violence and threat of violence are escalating and the situation is life threatening, or sometimes when the person causing the harm is a stranger. This does not mean that survivors do not want justice or resolution; it is just that they do not see the legal system or authority structure as the place for it.

People experiencing sexual violence, intimate violence, or interpersonal violence do not rely on the police or report to the authorities for a wide variety of reasons. In my experience with thousands of survivors over the past thirty years (including myself), and from extensive research, I have discovered that many do not report because they are not sure their experience even qualifies as "violence" or if it meets the legal criteria for specific crimes (which are quite narrowly defined). As members of Ubuntu aptly describe in relation to sexual violence,

> Many of the injuries that accompany, perpetuate, foster, or stop just short of what is legally defined as sexual assault are not deemed as injuries in the eyes of the legal system of the United States. These injuries include psychological and emotional damages to survivors, to the survivors of all trauma, to the communities of which survivors are a part, and fear and intimidation stemming from even the threat of violence. The legal system is ill-prepared to work for actual justice, and it will never be an institution that can promote healing.[1]

The legal framework is narrow, and police officers, district attorneys, and judges continue to be skeptical of reported intimate and interpersonal violence, particularly when it falls outside of the narrow confines of "stranger" violence, most specifically interracial violence of men of color against white, middle-class women.

Many who experience sexual and intimate violence recognize the narrow confines of the law. Narrow legal definitions shape the broader culture's interpretations of sexual and intimate violence and often serve to minimize if not deny people's experiences. Many rightfully worry that the police as well as the broader community will stigmatize and blame them for the violence, and that people will not believe them and/or will minimize the harm, or will harm them in response to their efforts to address the harm. Many do not report because those doing the harm are family members, friends, love partners, coworkers, and acquaintances, and while they want the violence addressed, they do not want to involve the police, nor do they want the people incarcerated, nor do they want to go through a formal and adversarial process.

Many people of color, queer and transgender people, and immigrants from the global south do not report because they have witnessed and/or experienced criminal legal systems criminalizing, stigmatizing, marginalizing, and incarcerating them, their family and friends, and their home communities. And for immigrants, particularly undocumented immigrants, they fear that they, or the people who have harmed them who are also part of their families or communities, will be deported. As Annanya Bhattacharjee, Beth Richie, Andrea Ritchie, and others have documented and analyzed, the state is actually a major source of violence against many women, queer, and trans people of color.[2]

The criminal legal system is also not the answer for many who do report. For those few who report, the results are very mixed and sometimes lethal. Many survivors of intimate and sexual violence have terrible experiences in the criminal legal system, experiences that reflect many of the fears and concerns discussed above. Many rape survivors who go through the legal system refer to it as the "second rape" because of the negative treatment by the police, the defense attorneys, as well as the prosecutors.[3] The vast majority of the reports never make it to trial. The system is not set up to support and validate survivors or to create a space for healing or justice.

While I have not spent an extensive amount of time in domestic violence court, each time I have been there over the past twenty years, I have witnessed the isolation and cold realities of the system. Those

seeking restraining orders are often sitting alone, except for brief meetings with legal advocates, who while supportive are quite harried and
stressed given the enormity of what they need to do, and thus they often
focus on facts, not comfort. This isolation is compounded by the arbi-
trariness of the decisions by judges about whether they will warrant a
restraining order or not.[4] For example, in 2014, while accompanying a
friend to domestic violence court as she sought a last-resort restraining
order, I witnessed a young Latina seeking an order against a landlord
who was harassing and stalking her. The highly skeptical judge interrogated and then chastised the young woman. She insinuated that the
young woman was, more than likely, sending "mixed messages" to the
landlord. While the judge eventually approved the restraining order, the
judge's hostility was injurious in and of itself. That same day, when an
elderly African American woman came forward to seek one against her
son, the same judge scolded her for caring about her son. While she
approved the request, she took the liberty of mandating that the elderly
woman promise her that she would cut her son off for good. Appalled
by the judge's treatment of those seeking orders, I inquired afterward
with one of the court advocates and was told she was one of the most
sympathetic judges at that courthouse.

For Black women and women of color, in particular, turning to the
state can be brutal and sometimes lethal. Andrea Ritchie's book, *Invisible No More! Police Violence against Black Women and Women of Color*,
offers a powerful historical analysis of police brutality, sexual assault,
profiling, and lethal violence. In it, she makes visible the very real and
life-threatening police violence against Black women and women of
color, including violence against women seeking police protection in the
face of violence against them in the contexts of domestic violence, and
in the context of the sex trade, as well as police violence against women
with disabilities and women migrants and immigrants, among others.[5]
This is not unusual given that the state historically and in an ongoing
way criminalizes women of color, including queer, trans, and gender-
nonconforming women, in particular, for defending themselves from
violence, despite the realities that the police and criminal legal system
are hostile, not safe or protective.[6]

In sum, the reality is that most people do not turn to the police or
the legal system, and that for those who do, the experience produces

more harm. This means that when women and queer, trans, and gender-nonconforming people experience violence in relationships or within communities, and when they do not want to turn to the criminal legal system for very good reasons, they feel that there are no other options to seek justice. And this is what has to change and what CA/TJ strives to address.

What community accountability and transformative justice approaches and practices offer are paths toward justice, healing, and transformation that do not rely on the police or legal system that so many resist, and that take us beyond prisons and punishment as answers to preventing and stopping violence. These are frameworks grounded in imagination, creativity, and a yearning for real justice, even as the practices and on-the-ground efforts are often messy, contradictory, and not always "successful" in the traditional sense. In the rest of the chapter, we will visit some of the key concepts and practices.

Punishment Is Not Accountability Is Not Justice

The "get tough on crime" logic that carceral feminism accepts is that vengeance, criminalization, and retribution are what justice means for most people. And yet, this is not always, or even often, the case. Many do not want the state to incarcerate, punish, and/or murder those who have done harm. For many who experience intimate and interpersonal violence (including myself), often, what they want most is for the person to stop their violence, to acknowledge the harm, to apologize, to feel remorseful, to take accountability, and to be willing to change themselves and their behavior. Vengeance, hatred, and more violence are incapable of offering any of these outcomes. This is certainly true for the many of us who have been harassed, abused, or assaulted by members of our families, intimate partners, dates, friends, and coworkers, among others. In my own experiences of sexual violence, I could not imagine going to the police to report my father, a graduate professor, a good friend, a lover, or even an acquaintance, for many of the reasons given above. I also did not turn to law enforcement because I knew from growing up with violence in my family that punishment does not change or transform a person's behavior, it does not lead to understanding, nor does it erase the harm.

In the current system, often accountability is conflated with punishment. When we say we want someone to be held accountable, we often mean that we want them to be punished, penalized, excluded, abandoned, or hurt in some way. CA/TJ give us an opportunity to rethink what we mean by accountability and what taking accountability might look like in response to the harms of oppression and violence. Rather than punishment as the definitive response, the process of taking accountability becomes the goal. Boyes-Watson captures the distinction when she writes, "[G]enuine accountability is an active experience, not a passive one. It is something we do, not something done to us."[7] In my classes on transformative justice, we often spend time sorting out the differences between punishment and accountability. When we talk about punishment, the words that we most associate with it include "dehumanization," "isolation," "pain," "torture," and "cruelty." We reflect on how punishment offers no space for second chances, for change, no space to reflect on the roots of violence, and no space to develop self-awareness and responsibility for the impact of our words and actions on others. In other words, with punishment, there is little to no potential for a person to address the harm caused, to make amends, or to commit to a process of change and transformation. Alternatively, when we talk about accountability, the words and phrases that come up include "understanding," "responsibility," "making amends," "offering apologies," and "admission of harm." We reflect on how a process of taking accountability creates space for deeper understanding of individual and social motivations for oppression and violence, for taking responsibility for the impact of our behavior, as well as an opportunity to commit to a process of self-awareness and change. Taking accountability, in other words, creates an opportunity for someone to understand the "why," not just the "what" of an act, to cultivate more self-awareness about our acts and their impact. Taking accountability offers those of us who have harmed the chance to take responsibility, to respect the needs and desires of the person harmed, and to make a commitment to change, and it offers the person harmed and others in the community more understanding and, potentially, healing.

The process of taking accountability offers space to think about why we did what we did, to understand the individual and social roots of our actions. In the current punitive and zero-tolerance atmosphere, there is a lot of resistance to seeking to understand why someone perpetrates violence; when some of us do seek those answers, there is resistance. Some claim that we are giving those who harm "excuses," "letting them off the hook," and not holding them accountable for their behavior. This logic conflates the act with the actor; it assumes that the person causing harm is simply evil, that they are acting of their own individual psychopathic volition, that the conditions of their lives do not matter and are of no consequence with respect to their violent behavior, that they themselves are irredeemable. Moreover, this logic of disposability assumes that we are not related to the person causing the harm—that we do not care about them or their future.

And yet, not asking why leaves us with no place to go with our questions, disappointment, hurt, and upset, beyond revenge and punishment. CA/TJ opens up these questions; as Adrienne Maree Brown writes, "To transform the conditions of the 'wrongdoing,' we have to ask ourselves and each other 'Why?' In my mediations, 'Why?' is often the game changing, possibility opening question. That's because the answers rehumanize those we feel are perpetrating against us. 'Why?' often leads us to grief, abuse, trauma, mental illness, difference, socialization, childhood, scarcity, loneliness."[8] And here again, this does not mean that someone is "off the hook," but instead, it does mean that the person is a full human being who, like us, has made mistakes, committed harm, and been harmed, and has the potential to take accountability for his or her behavior and its impact.

Within the system of retributive justice, we are discouraged from taking responsibility for the harms we ourselves commit because we do not want to be seen or treated like those we have deemed expendable, unworthy, and less than human. As Aurora Levins Morales writes, "If we are willing to say that some people don't matter, that some people are unaffordable for the planet, then what forgiveness is there for any of us, if we commit errors, even crimes? If we agree to accept limits on who is included in humanity, then we will become more and more like those we oppose." Again Morales writes, "I am holding out for a radical refusal to compromise on the possibility of any one of us to heal, make new moral choices, make amends and reclaim kinship with those we have harmed."[9]

We Are All Implicated in Violence

Grounded in the same system we are committed to opposing, punishment focuses solely on the person doing the harm, and does not encourage us to consider our own or the broader community's complicity in, let alone capacity for, violence nor our relationship to the conditions that underlie such violence; instead the focus on individual perpetrators encourages everyone else to see ourselves as wholly outside of violence, as innocent, as distinct from those "others" we determine to be criminals. Morales suggests that this is key to this form of justice, where there is little room to reflect on the connections between the self-identities of those doing the punishing and the self-identities of those being punished; she writes, "The urge to punish, to execute, to wipe them out is the refusal to consider what we ourselves might be capable of."[10] If we think that there is a group called "perpetrators" and that "they" are distinctly different from "us" (the good ones), then it makes it much more difficult for "us" to see how we ourselves can and do cause harm to others or how we are complicit with the violence of others. As Morales so eloquently puts it, "I believe part of what makes it so hard to consider perpetrators as part of our constituency is that we cannot bear to examine the ways in which we resemble them."[11]

Transformative justice and community accountability offer a lens of interconnectedness, mutuality, and community. They challenge us to recognize ourselves in others' behavior and to understand the roots of our interconnectedness, rather than to distance and disconnect from those doing harm. A story Thich Nhat Hanh tells in *Being Peace*, for me, captures the essence of this lens.[12] In talking about the many boat people who are refugees fleeing Vietnam, who are facing death while striving to arrive at the shores of Southeast Asia, he references the rape of many young girls and women by sea pirates. In telling the story of one twelve-year-old girl who "jumped into the ocean and drowned herself" after being raped by a sea pirate, he recognizes that we may be inclined only to take the side of the young girl, and only want to kill or take revenge on the sea pirates. He challenges us to broaden our lens:

> If you take the side of the little girl, then it is easy. You only have to take a
> gun and shoot the pirate. But we cannot do that. In my meditation I saw

that if I had been born in the village of the pirate and raised in the same conditions as he was, I am now the pirate. There is a great likelihood that I would become a pirate. I cannot condemn myself so easily. . . . If you or I were born today in those fishing villages, we might become sea pirates in 25 years. If you take a gun and shoot the pirate, you shoot all of us, because all of us are to some extent responsible for this state of affairs.[13]

Hanh reminds us that if we want to build peace with justice, we must seek to understand the life circumstances, identities, and experiences of those committing violence in the hopes that we see how we might be implicated in the violence and to commit to changing the conditions that produce it. No one is born a rapist or a murderer. The question we must consider, then, is how do people come to commit these acts? And how might we be implicated in the cultures, structures, and practices that underlie them? This does not mean taking away responsibility from the person or persons who have perpetrated the violence; it does mean widening the scope of accountability. Through asking these questions, we come to recognize the necessity for change and transformation within the broader community so that oppression, rape, and violence may be prevented.

From a transformative justice perspective, we understand that violence is not an aberration in our society, but is endemic. As Ana Clarissa Rojas Durazo writes, "We live, breathe, exist in, and help to create communities that are saturated with rape and violence. We are all affected and learn, model, ignore, and advance violence either consciously or unconsciously, even while we are simultaneously surviving it. . . . Enunciated in, for, and through structures and relations of dominance, violence is the architect of the social, inescapably constituting even love and intimacy."[14] When we bring together the seemingly personal violence with the institutional and historical legacies of violence, the lens for understanding and responding to interpersonal violence is widened. In the face of violence, community members have an "opportunity to dismantle institutionalized oppression and bring the group closer to social and economic justice."[15] As Durazo writes, "As teachers, survivors of violence, and people committed to healing, transforming, and ending violence, we ask: How and where can violence be undone? Where are the places/spaces of healing and transformation for survivors, for those responsible for their suffering, and for the society that created them? How do we create and maintain these spaces?"[16] Thus, accountability for abuse and violence is expanded to include the person who enacted the harm, the people and community connected to and impacted by the violence, and the institutions that produced the oppression and violence within them.

Community Support toward Accountability

Since the 2000s, organizations and communities have begun to create CA/TJ processes to address sexual and intimate partner violence. Organizational leaders in this work have included Bay Area Transformative Justice Collective, Creative Interventions, Generation Five, Just Practice, Philly Stands Up, and Project Nia, among others. Creative Interventions created and distributed a toolkit with ideas, guidelines, practices, and processes based in their experience of community accountability processes.[17] And *The Revolution Starts at Home: Confronting Intimate Violence within Activist Communities*, edited by Ching-In Chen, Jai Dulani, and Leah Lakshmi-Piepzna Samarasinha, offers a range of stories and practices being used across the country in a variety of contexts. The processes themselves are organic, meaning that each one is unique and different, as they emerge within a specific situation and a particular community. There is no template model for accountability processes, and they are often messy and complicated with varied outcomes.

Rather than legalistic adversarial processes resulting in punitive responses, CA and TJ processes enlist community members to create contexts and processes to support and care for those harmed (see chapter 5), as well as to support those who have done harm toward taking accountability and committing to change and transformation. The community—be it a group of friends, an organization, a neighborhood group, or a family—approaches each situation differently, depending on the needs of the person harmed as well as the context of the situation. An accountability process is not a coercive process, and if it is, it is no longer a transformative justice process. Community members might invite a person who has harmed into accountability and offer the person support toward that end, or a person who has harmed may recognize their wrongdoing and look to a group for support toward accountability.

Drawing from Generation Five's *Toward Transformative Justice* report, Esteban Lance Kelly describes the broad goals of accountability of the group Philly Stands Up; he suggests that they are to support a person who has caused harm to "(1) [r]ecognize the harm they have done, even if it was not intentional; (2) [a]cknowledge that harm's impact on individuals and the community; (3) [m]ake appropriate restitution to the individual and community; (4) [d]evelop solid skills toward transforming attitudes and behavior to prevent further harm and make contributions toward liberation."[18] The specific meaning of accountability will vary across situations, and is often connected with the realistic needs and hopes of the person who has been harmed.

These are not simple or easy processes, and they are not always successful. Sometimes people are willing to own their responsibility, address the harm, make amends, meet the needs of the person harmed, and seek personal transformation, and at other times, people refuse to take responsibility, engage in victim blaming, deny and/or minimize their behavior, and/or organize their community against the survivor and their allies.[19] And sometimes the person's willingness to take accountability fluctuates over time. Sometimes the people involved, including the person harmed, the person who did the harm, and all those around them, do not know what accountability means or how to approach situations outside of a framework of revenge and punishment, on the one hand, or support with no accountability, on the other.

Rather than seeing these complexities, mistakes, and event failures as insurmountable problems, those who have led such processes— Mariame Kaba (Project Nia), Mimi Kim (Creative Interventions), Shira Hassan (Just Practice)—remind us that we are in a process of learning, that there is no one answer, and that resistance is also integral to any process. Part of the problem with the current legal system is that it pretends to be seamless, cut and dry, and objective, and yet that is not what violence, resistance, change, healing, and transformation look like in real life. Life is much more complicated, nuanced, contradictory, and messy, and situations involving oppressive and violent behavior and acts are that much more complicated.

In Incite!'s anthology, *Color of Violence*, members of Communities Against Rape and Abuse (CARA), based in Seattle, offer a set of principles to help guide community accountability processes that will inevitably differ across communities and contexts. These core principles that guide their accountability processes include recognizing the "humanity of everyone involved" (including the person who has caused the harm), prioritizing survivor self-determination; safety planning and support for the survivor and involved community members; careful consideration of the potential consequences of the strategy; organizing collectively; ensuring shared political analysis of sexual violence; making clear and specific the requirements for aggressor accountability; communicating analysis and demands directly to the aggressor; soliciting assistance from the aggressor's community; and preparing for the long haul.[20] They suggest that an approach to accountability "must be creative and flexible enough to be a good fit for the uniqueness of each community's needs, while also being disciplined enough to incorporate some critical guidelines as the framework for its strategy."[21]

In the context of dating violence, for instance, taking accountability might mean understanding and seeking to meet the needs of the one harmed. Depending on the needs and wants of the person harmed, this could include making a direct and reflective apology that acknowledges the harm and its impact on the individual(s) or an apology made privately to the survivor, to the community, and/or to a broader public. It could mean agreements to not be in community spaces or to not participate in the same organizations, or to not be in any communication with the survivor. It could mean agreeing to move out of a shared living space. It could mean agreeing to seek out individual counseling, to actively address issues of addiction, and/or to participate in an anti-oppression group. It could mean paying for the survivor's medical bills associated with physical and/or mental health services. It could mean checking in regularly with one or more designated community members about the concrete efforts they are making to repair the harm and to transform their attitudes and behavior. It would most definitely mean accepting the self-determination of the person harmed and making every effort to meet their needs for safety and a space for healing and rejuvenation.

Focusing on Impact

The potential for a person to take accountability for harm within the context of a community is in part connected to the values and practices of a community in relationship to accountability. This is why so much of the work of community accountability has emerged within some radical women-of-color, queer, transgender, punk, and anarchist movement communities. These are communities committed to social change and justice and so they have created shared values, language, and frameworks around issues of oppression and violence. They have sought to create cultures that encourage their members to step up into accountability, rather than claiming innocence. A key stumbling block to taking accountability for participation and/or complicity in oppression and violence is the default defense of individual intentions as the lens for evaluating our behavior and its impacts. In the dominant culture, the claim that we did not intend to harm often outweighs attention to the impact of the behavior; that is, many think that if someone did not mean to hurt you, then they do not have to take responsibility for the hurt caused. This results in "I'm sorry you feel that I hurt you because I didn't mean to" instead of "I'm sorry that I hurt you." The claim of un-intention is a form of claiming innocence, evading accountability, particularly for harm produced by normative systems of oppression and violence. While those of us within feminist social justice circles may understand this, because of our avowed stances against injustice, we often exempt ourselves from this same scrutiny. This is in part what needs to change (see chapter 1).

Along these lines, I appreciated a story Terrence Crowley shared in his essay "The Lie of Entitlement." In it, Crowley, a white, middle-class, heterosexual man, describes how he shifted from defending his intentions to owning up to the impact of his behavior, and how this shift transformed his work on domestic violence. It was at a Men and Masculinity conference in 1990, when he heard Kathleen Carlin (then executive director of Men Stopping Violence), who challenged him with the idea that "intentions are not necessarily what gives my actions their moral value but rather their effects on others—specifically their effects on those people who are disenfranchised by my privilege, marginalized by my sense of entitlement . . . [and] rather than I, they were the ones to name those effects. What's more, they got to say what I needed to do to redress the damage."[22]

He goes on to reflect on his defensiveness when a batterer-intervention program told him he had to go through a year of training before he could begin to work with men who batter. From his perspective, he already had the credentials. Walking into the training, he saw himself as the "good guy," not the guy who was sexist and racist. On the first day of the training, though, the first check-in was to talk about his "worst incident of abuse to women."[23] He writes,

> Each week, I struggled with the principle of intentions versus effects while I identified my abusiveness and listed its effects on those I had silenced. Each week, I sat with those intense feelings of vulnerability, fear, and confusion as the reality of women was brought into the room. . . . Yet each week, I used my theological, psychological, social, and political training to concoct new ruses that would allow me to jump outside that system of accountability.[24]

After struggling with his own accountability, he came to recognize that the training was "not about helping *those guys*; it was about confronting my own abusive and controlling behaviors. My world shifted 180 degrees: I was going to be held accountable in a new way, accountable to women."[25]

As discussed earlier, in an environment saturated with the logics of retributive justice, claims of harm are often met with defenses of innocence, "good intentions," upstanding moral fibers. We do not want to be saddled with the label or designation of being a rapist, a sexist, a bigot, a racist. And so we deflect attention away from our behavior, or the behavior of those we love, and respond by projecting negativity onto those harmed, by denying the harm, by minimizing it, by victim blaming. This is a constant in antiracist work, where the accusation of racism itself is perceived as the more egregious harm, or potential harm, rather than the impact of the words or behaviors enacted.[26]

CA/TJ projects create spaces for people to develop the consciousness and skills that make people's recognition, acknowledgment, and ownership over our participation in oppression and violence more possible; such spaces invite us to accept responsibility for our behavior and its impact. As Morales writes, "Deciding that we are in fact accountable frees us to act."[27] It shifts us out of shame and blame, and moves us toward an openness to our own humanity, our vulnerabilities, and our flaws, which in turn enables us to be more open to building more just relationships with those we love and care about, those we know, as well as those we do not know.

Philly Stands Up, a transformative justice organization based in Philadelphia, distributes a pamphlet offering guidance for when people tell us we have harmed them. The pamphlet title boldly reaches out with an invitation to reflection: "What to do when someone tells you that you've violated their boundaries, made them feel uncomfortable, or committed assault."[28] The pamphlet offers a path toward accountability. Rather than taking the default response of defending our innocence by denying and minimizing harm and/or participating in victim blaming, the pamphlet encourages the reader to consider the harmful impact of our behavior. The path offered has the potential of healing the harm and division created by our actions; it challenges the behavior, not our personhood. And it asks us to deeply consider the impact of our words and actions, and to do something about them. In fact, it says that if we have crossed a boundary, created discomfort, or committed an assault, then it is incumbent upon us to "Take Responsibility for [Our] Actions." This means to reflect on our behavior and the impact on the person involved, to find out about and meet the needs of the person harmed, and to seek out resources and support to take accountability, to heal, and to make the changes necessary for future prevention. According to the pamphlet, it is best to recognize that our behavior has had an impact regardless of our intentions, and that our interpretation of what transpired may be different from the other person's. Ultimately, we must recognize that we caused harm and are responsible for the impact of our actions, even if we initially had a different interpretation of what transpired.

Recognizing that harm has occurred is an essential step in any accountability process. It is not about shame and blame, but a recognition and affirmation of a person's experience of harm. Moreover, if we are unsure that we understand what is being stated about our behavior, the pamphlet encourages curiosity, rather than simply defending ourselves and assuming we are in the right. As the pamphlet writer envisions,

Being called out is a gift.
It is an opportunity to grow.
Embrace that.
Assault is cowardly.
Owning up to it is brave.[29]

Support and Accountability

An important aspect of community accountability includes the idea that people in the community connected to the person causing the harm should support their efforts to take accountability for their actions and the impact of them and also to find ways to address the issues that they are also struggling with. As Generation Five describes, "Accountability in relationships means we are willing to interrupt problematic behaviors or dynamics and then support a process for transforming those behaviors."[30] Esteban Lance Kelly shares how Philly Stands Up engages with those who have harmed; he writes,

> Rather than shunt [those who cause harm] off as pariahs, we recognize them as complex, connected members of our community who are thus worth keeping around. In part, this reconceptualization popularizes the idea that when sexual violence takes place, everyone is affected. Therefore, all of us must heal from the incident. All of us have a role to play in holding the person who triggered the harm accountable, and in rebuilding the trust we lost in them due to their behavior.[31]

At the same time, such a shift in approach is not without its complexities and risks, such as the tendency to minimize the harm and evade the need for them to take accountability for the harm, and/or to get caught up in that person's defenses, rationales, excuses, and/or victim blaming. Ana Clarissa Rojas Durazo explores these complexities through a story of a community accountability process that took place when a student in a class admitted to having sexually assaulted another student (not in the class). While the student he assaulted was not present, friends of hers were in the class and understood its devastating impact on her and their community. In response to his disclosure, the class agreed to engage in a community accountability process wherein they "invited participants to find a balanced, joint commitment to the aggressor's humanity, while centering and respecting the survivor's experience of suffering engendered through the aggressor's actions."[32] As the process ensued, it became more complicated as classmates began to engage with the full humanity, struggles, and needs of the person who had committed the sexual assault. For instance, he shared with them his own experiences of oppression and struggle, and as Durazo reflects, sometimes it felt as though he was doing so to "evade responsibility, deter introspection, and deny the survivor's experiences" and in so doing moved the process "away from the possibility of accountability."[33]

Humanizing the person causing harm does not mean stepping back from their accountability; as Durazo writes, "[T]he presence of colonial violence or past traumas does not mean that we should forgive and forget when someone in our community commits an act of violence without seeking resolution for the survivor and for the larger community."[34] The class members had to remind him (and themselves) multiple times throughout the process, for instance, that his pain did not cancel out the harm he caused, and that his disclosure of pain did not minimize "the violence of his transgression . . . and [y]et [at the same time] we affirmed his disclosure by inviting him to continue the work begun in class and suggested that he spend time reviewing all the principles."[35]

Peace Circles and Community Accountability

Peace circles are restorative justice practices that foster community and accountability in response to the hurt and traumatic impact of violence.[36] The circle process builds deeper relationships in the face of conflicts and violence, rather than reinforcing entrenched divisions. Kay Pranis, Barry Stuart, and Mark Wedge, leaders in restorative justice efforts in the United States, suggest that circles shift our default responses from "coercion to healing, from solely individual to individual *and* collective accountability; from primary dependence on the state to greater self-reliance within the community; and from justice as 'getting even' to justice as 'getting well.'"[37] They are based on a belief in the "power of people and communities to connect positively, to confront harms, to address deeper causes, and to seek transformation."[38] In contrast to retributive justice, which focuses on what laws have been violated and therefore what punishment is appropriate, restorative justice asks first who has been hurt and what are their needs? And then, "How can we move toward healing? What can be done to repair the immediate harm and to prevent further harm? What wounds and circumstances—past and present—prevent us from having healthy relationships, both with ourselves and with others? What steps can we take to understand these wounds and to aid healing?"[39]

As a communal practice, circles can offer space for community members to explore the "collective dimensions of accountability." As Pranis, Stuart, and Wedge suggest, they can share their experiences vis-à-vis the questions, "[H]ave we ignored how social, cultural, racial, and economic conditions give rise to crime? Are we tolerating patterns that isolate individuals and lead to destructive behavior? Do our attitudes in some way create tensions within communities or polarize people into opposing factions? In other words, are we functioning in our families and communities in ways that contribute to the imbalances, misunderstandings, and inequities that culminate in crime?"[40] Restorative justice approaches crime and violence from within the values of interconnectedness, mutuality, and community. And thus circles, as Pranis, Stuart, and Wedge reflect, encourage us to consider how we "have an obligation to help make things right, including helping those who caused harm to assume their responsibility. We are all in some sense accountable to each other."[41]

Roca is an organization in Chelsea, Massachusetts, that works to "help disengaged and disenfranchised young people move out of violence and poverty."[42] Carolyn Boyes-Watson, in *Peacemaking Circles and Urban Youth*, shares Roca's powerful work of using peacemaking circles as a communal way to embrace, support, and actively engage youth in their communities. Roca approaches conflicts, including abuse and/or violence, as opportunities to explore breakdowns in relationships as well as oppressive dynamics within communities. Peace circles are their way of bringing people in the organization together to share the burden of a conflict and/or incident of harm and to determine collectively how to create support, accountability, and healing within a community. Boyes-Watson writes, "Circles invite us to engage in conflicts differently from the default stance of either avoiding a fight or bracing for one."[43] Indeed, she writes, "If we respond with a process that encourages us to be respectful, honest, open, and compassionate, conflicts can bring about personal growth, deepening our connection to others and helping us value our differences."[44]

Roca's approach to accountability, then, is something that is cultivated within a caring community.[45] Through circles, adults and youth come to know each other as whole human beings—as neither perfect nor flawed, but as a mix of both and in between. When youth make choices that create harm, the "[c]ircles weave mutual caring with mutual accountability, so that people are held in a good way. This gives them the inner strength to step forward and take responsibility for a healing journey."[46] Roca's circles encourage its members to share the responsibility of addressing and navigating conflicts and harm.[47] Conflicts then become the collective's responsibility, rather than one individual's, and people come to support each other in addressing issues, rather than seeing them as belonging only to some and not others. Boyes-Watson writes, "When the 'they's' go away and the 'we' shows up, people's awareness and capabilities change."[48]

Most importantly, for Roca, circles are not a singular method used only in response to incidents of violence, but rather they are a daily practice of building community within the organization—among and between youth and staff. The circles became a space for daily check-ins, for storytelling, for sharing accomplishments, for developing agreement around the meaning of shared values, and more. Thus, when conflicts and/or harms occur among members of Roca or by Roca youth within the broader community, Roca gathers youth and staff together in circle to process and understand the breach caused by conflict and harm. When people gather, because of the depth of relationship formed by circles as daily practice, they begin from a space of care and connection to one another in facing whatever the difficulty is.

Success Is in the Process and the Practice, Not Always the Outcome

While one of the key goals of a CA/TJ process is for a person to take accountability for the harm they have caused and its impact, success does not have to be gauged solely on whether they do, in fact, take accountability for their actions. Rather than seeing resistance as evidence of failure, we should recognize that resistance is essentially a part of the process of change. Creative Interventions, an organization that was "established as a resource center to create and promote *community-based responses to interpersonal violence*," created a two-year pilot study in which the group documented its work with communities to develop intervention and accountability skills and strategies. Mimi Kim, founding director of Creative Interventions, reflects on how the organization came to "expect resistance, without succumbing to it or accepting that the usual tactics of denial, minimization, blaming, and manipulation condemned an intervention to failure. A central question we hoped to answer was how we could anticipate, contain, and shift resistance toward accountability."[49] Resistance is not necessarily surprising if we do honest reflection on our own stories of harm when people have asked us to be accountable. As Kim writes, "Understanding the commonality of this dynamic flowed from our own reactions when being confronted about our harmful attitudes and actions."[50] Thus the question becomes, "How can community processes embrace resistance as part of an intervention rather than as evidence of failure?"[51]

As noted earlier, such processes are not seamless or linear; they are messy, complicated, and can shift forward and backward over time. This is important to recognize, as the recognition helps anyone engaged in a process to be able to grapple with those times that feel as though there is no accountability in sight, when it seems like things are moving forward, and then something happens that makes it seem that we are back at square one. As Bench Ansfield and Jenna Peters-Golden remind us, we need to rethink success in relation to our efforts toward accountability; they write, "Entailing frequent roundabouts, U-turns, and abrupt stops, they [accountability processes] must be adaptable and strong. Where a success model might seek to push through the disappointments, convolutions, and complexities intrinsic to this work, our approach aspires to hold a transformative process in its messy entirety."[52] These are not easy or simple processes, and they do not erase the harm that has occurred; as Mariame Kaba writes, "There is nothing 'soft' or 'easy' about this. CA processes test everyone and can be some of the most difficult physical and emotional work that we can undertake. Healing requires an acknowledgment that there are wounds. Healing requires parties who actually want to heal."[53]

CA/TJ processes of community accountability have become more common within social justice communities, some more public than others. We can learn so much from these stories. One process shared more broadly concerned an incident of sexual assault within BYP 100 in Chicago (the Black Youth Project, which focuses on justice and freedom through a Black queer feminist lens). In the context of organizing in Chicago, a young woman named Kyra publicly shared a story of sexual harm by one of the leaders of BYP 100 (Malcolm London) in November 2015. The organization responded by building support for Kyra and offering the possibility of engaging in an accountability process with Malcolm. Both agreed to participate in the process, which was developed through the guidance of Mariame Kaba (Project Nia), who is a national leader in restorative/transformative justice processes. The process included a support team for Kyra and an accountability team for Malcolm. In February 2016, after working with their individualized teams, the two met in a circle process to address the harm, which was a main goal set by Kyra early on in the process. In a report issued publicly, Kyra, Malcolm, and some members of the process talked about the experience and outcomes. For Kyra, the process was difficult, and yet she felt the support and care from the support team and from the broader community. She says the "process allowed me not only to hold Malcolm accountable for his actions but to also reeducate him so that he hopefully won't harm anyone else in the future. That was important to me." For Malcolm, the hardest part was coming to terms with contradictions between his politics and his actions. As he says,

> [I]t took me so long to wrestle with my ego. That I wasn't exempt. It took me awhile to even name the harm. I saw myself become the narratives I shamed other men for creating. . . . I had to decide to take responsibility for the harm or avoid responsibility. I am grateful for the community around me that guided me to a place of growth. To see myself not only in theory but in practice.[54]

While the processes of healing and accountability will continue as the official community accountability process has come to a close, this is a story of possibility and change. It reminds me, in the midst of such skepticism around working outside of the police and law enforcement, that change is possible, that people who do harm, including myself, have the possibility of taking accountability, being remorseful, caring about the person harmed, and engaging in a process of change.

At the same time, I believe that the process of engaging with someone on their behavior and its impact can shift the dynamics of a situation of violence, whether the person who has caused harm is willing to become accountable or not. When community members speak up and make their concerns public, they communicate to the person causing the harm that their behavior is no longer private, that it is not acceptable, and that members of their community are prepared to have conversations with them about it. With collective support and intervention, community members are letting people know that they know what happened, that they believe the survivor, that the survivor is not alone. As importantly, CA/TJ guides community members to support, rather than shame and/or abandon, the person. Support can mean encouraging them to take accountability, to share their own stories of accountability, to work with them to make the changes necessary to prevent further or future harm, and in doing so, to be able to continue being a member of the community. If the person who caused the harm wants to remain a member of the community, then they have the opportunity to do so by engaging in a conversation and making efforts to be accountable in the manner specified. Accountability efforts communicate to others in the community, including those participating in the collective process, that such behavior will be talked about, taken seriously, and addressed by the community. When nobody in the community publicly supports the survivor or names and addresses the oppressive behavior, it appears that it is acceptable, inevitable, and/or justifiable. Steps toward such critical consciousness building are necessary for community accountability processes to be able to offer any possibility toward healing or accountability

Feminists working to address interpersonal, relational, and familial abuse and violence have rightly been skeptical of restorative justice given the reality that families and communities of friends, coworkers, etc., often do not recognize and understand mistreatment, harassment, and abuse as wrong or harmful since it is so embedded in the culture. Our communities cannot be relied upon to support those harmed and to take accountability for our complicity in harm. More often than not, in the case of sexual violence and intimate partner or dating violence, our friends, family members, coworkers, and religious or social communities blame the victim, minimize and/or deny the abuse, and defend or prioritize the perspectives and needs of the person who has caused the harm, particularly men in the case of men's violence against women, and particularly men who are members of that same community. And thus the skepticism is not without grounding.

If community members—be they family, friends, coworkers, peers—do not have a critical consciousness about sexual violence and the power lines it often reinforces, then they may easily participate in blaming rather than supporting the person who has been harmed. Given this, a significant part of the work of transformative justice is to build critical consciousness and action that makes more visible the power lines and power dynamics that fuel violence and that creates communal commitment to transforming these lines as well. Peace circles can be used to create a space for critical consciousness building about the social roots of violence in patriarchal, racist, homophobic, etc., structures that produce not only the violence but the normativity of it and/or the common frameworks that justify it by victim blaming.

The process of building collective critical and compassionate consciousness around harmful behavior, abuse, and violence is essential given that so much of it is normative, rather than aberrant behavior. In order for a community to become accountable to one another around these issues, there must be ongoing efforts to build the consciousness and skills to be able to recognize, name, and understand the everyday violence that we are all steeped in, to instill a recognition of how we are all implicated within these structures of power that produce the harms, and to practice accountability every day rather than only in relation to more egregious harms.

Communities Take Accountability

Because CA/TJ recognizes that the roots of individual harm are not individual, but social, it calls upon community members (or organizations, or programs) to recognize the ways in which we may be contributing to the oppression and violence that we are also facing. It provides us with an opportunity to take stock of how the everyday norms and practices in our communities may have contributed to the violence. And thus, CA/TJ projects call for community-based engagement around an analysis and reflection on how the community itself must change if the goal is prevention and transformation.

An inspirational example of a community organizing response to sexual assault was that developed by a Chicago-based social justice performance group, Mango Tribe, along with the GABRIELA Network in 2006. They initiated a series of town hall discussions in response to "reports of rape and sexual misconduct by respected adult male members/ leaders in the Asian American community involving female youths, 15–18 years old." Some of the main goals of the town hall meetings were to create mechanisms of support for those experiencing and being impacted by sexual violence, including mechanisms to hold those doing the assault accountable, to examine the social conditions that allowed the rapes to occur, and to create prevention strategies that addressed those conditions. They identified the following factors as contributing to the rape culture of the organizations in which the violence took place: (a) a lack of critical consciousness about sexual harassment, assault, abuse; (b) a lack of mechanisms for addressing mistreatment and/ or violence within the organizations; (c) a culture of shame, secrecy, and victim blaming in the face of sexual violence; (d) a lack of resources and skills; (e) a lack of connection to feminist antiviolence work, and support services and advocacy. These were all areas of concrete action that GABRIELA and other organizations could take towards the prevention of future violence. One of its action steps was to circulate an open letter to social justice organizations calling for them to commit to building critical consciousness and to creating transparent processes of dealing with sexual assault within their organizations. The goal was to strengthen their coalition work in ways that would also work toward the prevention of sexual assault.[55]

More recently, as described earlier in this chapter, I was moved by the response of BYP 100 to learning of an incident of sexual harm of a young woman by a leader within the organization. In addition to developing a community accountability process to address the incident, BYP 100 developed a national Healing and Safety Council responsible for generating safety and accountability guidelines and processes to address harm occurring within the organization. The organization also developed "Stay Woke, Stay Whole: Black Activist Manual" as a guide toward the intervention and prevention of harm, and a consent training workshop that will be required of all active members in the organization. The young woman herself became a leader in developing the curriculum.

These organizational responses are significant in working toward creating a culture of accountability within an organization with the aim of prevention and transformation around sexual harm. They recognize that the organization and its members are also in process of learning and growing, and that there is not an end goal. Rather than responding to harm as if it is an isolated incident related to one person, these projects recognize and take accountability for not only how best to respond to harm when it occurs but also how to build consciousness and skills toward more collective accountability by shifting the organizational cultures to reduce and prevent future harm.

Conclusion

The practices, processes, and containers being created around community accountability and transformative justice are at the heart of prison abolition. If we recognize that police and prisons do not create healing, safety, or accountability, that they do not reduce violence, and that they are engaged in historically based and ongoing violence against people of color, people with disabilities, and queer, trans, and gender-nonconforming people, as well as immigrants from the global south, we must stop saying that the answers to intimate and interpersonal violence are police and prisons. It is for these reasons, among many others, that I am a police and prison abolitionist. As an abolitionist, I am committed to working with others to develop collective and communal responses that cultivate safety, support, and accountability and that build the grounds for broad social and structural change and transformation. As Angela Davis and many others have argued, abolition is not simply a movement to do away with prisons, as it is also fundamentally about cultivating and building love, care, accountability, and justice into our everyday relationships, communities, and organizations.

What we need is to build collective values and practices to address oppression and violence, in an effort to begin to build toward a future without prisons, without police, without vengeance and retribution as the default responses to violence. This is at the heart of the imagination and practice so integral to the projects of CA/TJ. As Bench Ansfield and Timothy Colman write, "What would happen if our responses to sexual assault came from a vision of the world we want to live in?"[56] These are projects in process, with no absolutes, no guarantees, no mandates, and yet full of possibility if we commit to practicing, learning from our mistakes, taking risks, and finding ways to be there for one another through the difficult, conflictual, and messy times. I will end with a quotation from Alexis Pauline Gumbs's essay "Freedom Seeds," which has been a source of inspiration in my work and in my teaching. She writes,

> What if abolition isn't a shattering thing, not a crashing thing, not a wrecking ball event? What if abolition is something that sprouts out of the wet places in our eyes, the broken places in our skin, the waiting places in our palms, the tremble holding in my mouth when I turn to you? What if abolition is something that grows? What if abolishing the prison industrial complex is the fruit of our diligent gardening, building and deepening of a movement to respond to the violence of the state and the violence of our communities with sustainable, transformative love.[57]

PART III

(Re)Imagining Feminist Solidarity

Disentangling US Feminism from US Imperialism

Since the US invasion of Afghanistan in 2001, most news reports tend
to attribute any gains in women's human rights or living conditions in
Afghanistan to the US-led invasion and occupation. In addition, as seen
in the two excerpts below, the reporters allude to fears about potential
US military withdrawal from the region:

> Though Afghan women have made gains since the collapse of the austere
> Taliban regime in 2001, violence against them remains widespread. There
> are fears the gains made could be lost when most foreign forces leave by
> the end of next year.[1]

> Women in Afghanistan have won back many of the rights they lost dur-
> ing Taliban rule from 1996 to 2001, when the Islamic movement was
> ousted by an American invasion following the Sept. 11 attacks against the
> United States. . . . There are fears that many of those freedoms may shrink
> as foreign forces depart by the end of this year and much of the interna-
> tional aid and assistance they brought to Afghanistan goes with them.[2]

At the same time, when the reports are about the pervasiveness of violence against women in Afghanistan, reporters often put the blame
on the Taliban, Afghan culture, and Islamic tradition. Both storylines
are grounded in a logic that places the United States in a position of
"saving" Afghan women and harks back to the initial arguments made
by the United States for the invasion. As we know, in the wake of 9/11,
the Bush administration, with its deeply antifeminist platform and
policies in the United States, justified its "war on terrorism," first in
Afghanistan (and then later in Iraq) on the grounds that the United
States must act in order to "save Afghan women" and to support wom-
en's human rights. This created a moralistic humanitarian justification
for what might otherwise be seen as a brutal invasion of a sovereign

country in retaliation for harboring those seen as responsible for the terrorist attacks of 2001.

US liberal feminist discourses and politics addressing women's issues under the Taliban contribute to these storylines. The Feminist Majority Foundation (FMF), a liberal feminist organization based in the United States, has had a public campaign against what the group constructed as "gender apartheid" in Afghanistan since the 1990s. It gained wide public engagement in its effort to bring attention to Taliban policies of gender segregation, forced veiling, and violence and brutality against women who did not follow the rules. Thus, in the context of 9/11, the FMF supported US military intervention that led to the installation of the Northern Alliance. Since its campaign did not account for the US role in fueling the rise of Islamic fundamentalist warlords and dictators in Afghanistan, it could uncritically welcome US intervention. In its efforts, it did not account for the role of the United States in the ongoing wars and civil and political unrest since the 1970s and their impact on the changing gender dynamics, structures, and relationships within families, communities, and social institutions. Nor did it account for the ways Afghan women's bodies were being used by the United States for its policy agenda, with little concern for the impact of the invasion and occupation on women's lives. As in mainstream media, many of the reports around violence against women in Afghanistan became evidence of the need for more US militarism and war. This is what brings together US liberal feminism and US militarism in the service of US imperialism.

This chapter explores strategies to disrupt these imperial hegemonic logics of US liberal feminism through a transnational feminist approach guided by the values of mutuality and accountability. A transnational feminist lens refuses the imperial logic of "saving," with all of its attendant assumptions of western superiority and righteousness. Through a transnational lens, we are able to recognize how US state intervention in Afghanistan, historically and in the present, directly contributes to the endemic intimate, community, and state violence against women. And looking through a lens of interconnected struggles, we further recognize the interconnections between the dynamics of gender violence in Afghanistan and those in the United States, with a specific focus on oppression and violence against women and queer and trans people in Muslim communities as well as in immigrant and refugee communities.

I begin the chapter with a brief discussion of how US liberal feminist discourses on women in Afghanistan are entangled with US imperialism. I offer the example of the FMF's "Stop Gender Apartheid" campaign, as it helped to garner public support for the US invasion and ongoing militarized occupation of Afghanistan.[3] I turn from this hegemonic framing to a transnational one that situates oppression and violence against women in Afghanistan within the entangled history of colonization, war, and violence in which the United States is a key player. Drawing on this framework, I explore how US-based feminism is often implicated in the endemic violence in Afghanistan, rather than being an outsider to it. To illustrate, I shed light on how the insular US liberal feminist focus on the *burqa* as a symbol of "other" women's oppression contributes to violence against women who veil in the United States and those who do not in Afghanistan. In a further effort to disrupt the imperialist "us/them" binary, I offer some ways to interconnect the endemic intimate, community, and state violence against women, queer, and trans people of color in the United States and those in Afghanistan. From this perspective, I lift up the resistance of Afghan women and communities, who are often silenced through this "savior" narrative.

Drawing on the work of transnational feminists, this chapter offers an approach to solidarity based in a praxis of accountability. I draw specifically on Sherene Razack's notion of accountability as

> a process that begins with a recognition that we are each implicated in systems of oppression that profoundly structure our understanding of one another. . . . Tracing our complicity in these systems requires that we shed notions of mastering differences, abandoning the idea that differences are pre-given, knowable and existing in a social and historical vacuum. Instead, we invest our energies in exploring the histories, social relations, and conditions that structure groups unequally in relation to one another and *that shape what can be known, thought, and said.*[4]

An accountability approach shifts US feminist efforts from an imperial "helping" of others whom we understand and define as "different" or "less fortunate" to a solidarity envisioned by Chandra Talpade Mohanty that emphasizes "relations of mutuality, co-responsibility, and common interests."[5] This is an approach predicated on a critical analysis of empire with a political praxis that disrupts rather than reproduces relations of domination.[6] A key step to such solidarity is one that recognizes the ways we are interrelated within and across power lines shaped by histories of colonialism and imperialism. As Mohanty writes, this "requires understanding the historical and experiential connections between women from different national, racial, and cultural communities."[7] In other words, rather than emphasizing the idea that there are distinctive and isolated differences between local and global communities that we need to "know" and "understand," between an "us" and a "them," a transnational approach of accountability attends to "the interweaving of the histories of these communities."[8] In building a narrative of the interconnectedness between the United States and Afghanistan, we recognize how the United States and US feminisms have been and continue to be implicated in the transnational struggles of Afghan women specifically, and Muslim women more generally.

US Feminism and Imperialism

Transnational, anti-imperialist, and antiracist feminists have exposed and challenged the imperialist roots of feminist theories and movements generated out of the so-called West since the nineteenth century.[9] In the context of the 2001 invasion and occupation of Afghanistan, many of us critically engaged and pushed back against the hegemony of the FMF, which had been the most prominent and visible US feminist voice on Afghanistan. The FMF, in conjunction with many other feminist and human rights organizations in the United States, spearheaded the "Stop Gender Apartheid in Afghanistan" campaign in the 1990s. As noted earlier, by 2001, this campaign had popularized the FMF's ahistorical and western-based understanding of the gender-segregated and brutal conditions of women's lives in Afghanistan under the regime of the Taliban. This popularization was dependent on erasing the role of the United States in the rise of the Taliban. The FMF saw the post-9/11 US "war on terrorism" as a political opportunity to fulfill its stated goals of ending "gender apartheid" and "restoring" women's human rights in Afghanistan, and its campaign helped to lay the groundwork for the public's acceptance of invasion and occupation as a solution to the denial of women's human rights and to the 9/11 attacks.

This framework became embedded in US foreign policy under the Obama administration, most specifically with Hillary Clinton's agenda in her tenure as secretary of state (2009–2013). Corinne Mason describes what has been called the "Hillary Doctrine" as a "women's rights" approach that "maintains that global violence against women is a national security issue by suggesting that a nation's instability is causally related to both underdevelopment and gender inequality. Moreover, countries where violence against women is rampant are understood as fragile states and, thus, the breeding grounds for terrorism."[10] This agenda of "women's rights" began to be used to justify military interventions, similar to earlier justifications for colonialism. In 2010, as noted by Mason, the release of the Quadrennial Diplomacy and Development Review (QDDR) revealed the alliance between the US State Department and the United States Agency for International Development (USAID).[11] It became policy to integrate the issue of violence against women into both development and security agendas integral to foreign policy. Soon thereafter, the International Violence Against Women Act (I-VAWA) was introduced to Congress; this act would define violence against women as an issue of national security *and* development. Mason argues that "[t]he Hillary Doctrine and I-VAWA both allow for the 'genderwashing' of imperial justifications, and I-VAWA in particular supports an investment in police, military, and peacekeeping to prevent and respond to gendered violence abroad."[12] In general, as Cyra Akila Choudhury notes, "[H]umanitarian armed intervention is increasingly seen as a necessity and not a last measure for preventing violence towards women and children; however, the devastating therapeutic violence of intervention itself is obscured and decoupled from human rights activism on behalf of third-world women."[13] In other words, those arguing for military intervention do not account for the insecurities and violence caused by the imperialist militaristic interventions, and instead provide more justification for them.

The stakes for challenging this agenda are more than significant as it becomes incorporated into white-supremacist, Islamophobic, and imperialist policymaking under the Trump administration. And I believe it is our responsibility to challenge and shift mainstream liberal feminism's projects, which assume that "we" are in the best position to "save" Afghan women, while refusing accountability for our contributions and complicities in creating past and current crises. Critically engaging these projects is important because this is a place of significant impact in terms of shaping public opinion and influencing foreign policy. The success, we must recognize, is related to the ways in which these feminist imperialist and orientalist logics are historically entrenched in US culture and politics more broadly. The public's embrace of the FMF campaign and the US government's cooptation of it occurred because the campaign does not challenge what "we" (the US public) think we know about "them" (Afghan people) nor what "we" think about "us." A public that is otherwise either antifeminist or disinterested in feminism in the United States accepts the arguments because the narrative reproduces rather than challenges these hegemonic ideas. The situation of women in Afghanistan is understood through a lens of cultural "otherness" that constructs Afghanistan's gender relations as "backward" in comparison to those in the US-dominant, white, middle-class culture constructed as "modern." It locates the roots of "their" women's oppression exclusively in patriarchal cultural and religious Islamic traditions, usually thought to be premodern, rather than in histories of colonization and resistance.

As Evelyn Alsultany demonstrates in her analysis of post-9/11 mainstream US media, the construct of the "oppressed Muslim woman" has become a central explanatory framework to justify US military interventions. These representational narratives about Afghan women's oppression, Alsultany suggests, mostly manifest as "active iterations of benevolent emotions—pity and outrage. . . . Pity makes outrage easy; feeling sorrow for someone's distress easily morphs into anger at the circumstances that caused the distress and thus outrage at the men, the culture, and the religion."[14] The combination of these emotions is key to US justifications for militarism, for exclusionary policies, and for criminalization; as Alsultany writes, it is in this "paradigm that combating terrorism requires 'liberating' Muslim women and punishing those responsible: namely, Muslim men or a 'barbaric' Islamic culture more generally."[15]

Given that "saving" is the common response to "pity," Sherene Razack asks, "How do we move from pity to respect, where we acknowledge our complicity in oppressing others and consider how to take responsibility for the oppressive systems in which we as women are differently and hierarchically placed?"[16] Transnational accountability-based feminist approaches answer this by shifting to a logic of accountability, respect, and reciprocity. Scholars and activists, including Lila Abu-Lughod, Sherene Razack, Zillah Eisenstein, Jasmin Zine, Cyra Akila Choudhury, Sonali Kolhaktar, Kevin Ayotte, and Mary Husain, to name a few, have all addressed the post-9/11 US feminist entanglements with Afghanistan, challenged orientalist and Islamophobic thinking, and argued for a radical rethinking of feminist engagements around Afghanistan and Islam, fundamentalism, and the "war on terror" more broadly.[17] They urge US feminists, like myself, to ask different questions. These include the following: How are our ideas and politics bound up with the discourses and logics of US imperialism? How do the stories feminists tell about the Taliban's brutal violence against women, and about Afghan men's violence against women more generally, solidify the public's support for the US invasion and military occupation of Afghanistan? How might our feminist scholarship and activism fuel the racist, xenophobic, and Islamophobic policies and practices within the United States? How can we begin to take accountability for our participation in and complicity with structural, political, and community violence within Afghanistan and its devastating consequences?

These questions lead us to more of a consideration of how we are complicit with, and how we contribute to, the social, political, economic, and cultural conditions in Afghanistan as well as within the United States. They force us to reckon with our relationship to the broader context by making more visible the interconnected geopolitical roots of violence that lie in capitalism, imperialism, and heteropatriarchy. Such an approach shifts US feminists to think more critically about our own contributions to this context and to US participation in it, including our scholarship and/or activism as "western" feminists. This approach makes it much more difficult for us to position ourselves as superior outsiders and saviors to Afghan society, or to anyone.

The Geopolitical Roots of "Gender Apartheid"

A transnational approach requires us to situate the contemporary context of violence against women in Afghanistan in the context of the interlocking systems of global capitalism, imperialism, and patriarchy, rather than solely within the internal gender dynamics of Islam and Afghan culture, which are often portrayed as monolithic, traditional, and ancient.[18] Through a lens of accountability, US feminists center the impact of US foreign policy, imperialism, and militarism on the evolving and ever-shifting gendered policies, ideologies, and dynamics within Afghanistan. This includes recognizing the role of the United States in the emergence of the Taliban and other extremist forces through its geopolitical Cold War strategy against the Soviet Union, which had invaded and occupied Afghanistan in the 1970s. The United States provided billions of dollars of weapons and military training to Mujahideen warlords and networks, including those currently in power, with no political or financial support for secular and democratic movements in Afghanistan. The United States supported these groups because they believed that the religious fervor of their organized base would be most effective in mobilizing against the Soviet Union. In other words, given the US goal to eliminate Soviet influence, not necessarily to support a democratic Afghanistan, the United States focused on those who would fight this war because of a collective and loyal adherence to a politicized Islam.

This US-fueled war against the Soviets had devastating consequences for the whole of Afghanistan—as Kolhakter and Ingalls write, "When the Soviets finally withdrew in February 1989, 1.5 million Afghans were dead, 5 million were disabled, and another 5 million were refugees."[19] Once the Soviets were removed, instead of supporting efforts toward reconstruction, the United States continued to support these Mujahideen resistance fighters to deter any further Soviet influence, with little concern about the emergence of a civil war in its aftermath.[20] Viewing these actions through a lens of accountability, US feminists must consider that it was from within these networks—built with substantial US military aid—that the Taliban, Osama bin Laden, and other extremist groups emerged; they did not emerge from Afghan culture or from Islam itself.[21] Moreover, even in the invasion and occupation after 9/11, the United States supported another of these extremist networks—the Northern Alliance. This group of warlords had actually been responsible for some of the worst atrocities against the people of Afghanistan during the civil war. Malalai Joya's book, *A Woman among Warlords*, and the book by Sonali Kolhaktar and James Ingalls, *Bleeding Afghanistan: Washington, Warlords, and the Propaganda of Silence*, both offer in-depth analysis and perspective on these historical developments.[22]

Given this broader geopolitical context, when US feminists want to stand in solidarity around the specific structures and forces impacting women in Afghanistan, we must account for how deeply "we" in the United States are implicated in these very structures and forces. We would have to consider where we were/are in relation to the rise of the Taliban and the current and ongoing crisis. We would have to recognize that US, Soviet, and other foreign intervention and occupation of Afghanistan are, in part, what give form and meaning to the evolution, development, and implementation of the gender-based restrictions and violations implemented by the Taliban. We might also consider how US gender-exclusive feminist research and advocacy actually contribute to the ways in which gender and Afghan women's bodies continue to be integral to the political mobilizations on all sides of the ongoing wars in Afghanistan—including the US and allied forces war against the Taliban and al Qaeda (to "save Afghan women") as well as the resistance to the US and allied forces invasion and occupation. Jasmin Zine draws our attention to how, "[i]n the 'war on terror,' Muslim women operate as pawns manipulated to corroborate the moral righteousness of the political and economic goals of U.S. imperial intervention in Muslim societies executed on their behalf as a campaign delivering their 'liberation.' On the other hand, they also operate as guardians of faith and honour in Islamic fundamentalist conceptions that must be safeguarded from the seduction and encroachment of Western moral corruptions."[23] As the organization of gender becomes a central site of difference used on the many sides of the struggle, including in US calls to ongoing war and occupation, we must look at the role of US feminist ideas and politics. In other words, we must think critically about how the particular forms of US feminist engagement may actually contribute to the crisis and to the endemic violence against Afghan and Muslim women, in Afghanistan as well as in the United States, rather than contributing to a process of addressing and ending it.

With a transnational feminist emphasis on the historical and geopolitical rise of fundamentalist movements in Afghanistan, our engagement begins from the location of our political accountability rather than from a place that assumes we are outside of the situation and that we are in the best position to know best how to improve the situation for women in Afghanistan. From this place of accountability, we also recognize that the problem is not solely Islam or gender apartheid per se, but is connected to a broad array of forces, including the United States and US feminism. The work of accountability, then, is more directed around our own complicity and participation, rather than our superiority. For me, it means that we ally against US foreign policies, military interventions, and imperial logics, rather than in support of them. This might include showing that US militarism does not significantly improve girls' and women's lives, or Afghan people's lives more generally. Most significantly, it means that we must critically challenge the entrenchment of Islamophobia and orientalism within the US military and US culture, including within feminist discourses and politics. We must disrupt the logics and discourses that project sexism and/or misogyny onto Islam and "other" cultures who are viewed as wholly isolated, different, and worse than our own.[24] We must recognize how these ideas fuel Islamophobic actions, policies, and movements within the United States and around the world.

US Militarism and Violence against Women in Afghanistan

As noted above, gender-myopic and decontextualized narratives obscure the role of the United States, including the hegemonic US feminist discourses and efforts, in the geopolitical and social roots of this violence and thus our relationship to these *and many other* human rights violations.[25] A first step toward accountability is to understand how the ongoing crisis in Afghanistan, developed through more than forty years of invasion, occupation, and civil war, contributes to the particular forms of violence in women's lives. This crisis has many roots that are interconnected with gender but not reducible to gender dynamics. The devastating social, economic, and political conditions are what continue to fuel violence generally, and violence against women more specifically. These US-fueled wars result in massive displacement (creating millions of refugees), rape, abduction, forced prostitution, poverty, extremely high maternal mortality rates, unequal access to resources, etc. When we center these conditions, we also come to recognize that they impact men and boys in Afghanistan, as well as women and girls, including sexual violence against boys and young men. This also means that feminists must, of necessity, not isolate the experiences of women and girls as if they were inherently distinct from men's and boys', nor reduce the problem to male supremacy. This does not mean that gender is not important; rather, it means that we must not isolate and decontextualize patriarchy as the sole force operating in women's lives. Instead we must recognize the multitude of interconnected forces and structures shaping people's lives in Afghanistan, including endemic sexual violence.

At the very least, it means we must consider the consequences of the US invasion that are often left out of the picture when we in the United States are only looking at a decontextualized structuring of gender in women's lives in Afghanistan. When I first started shifting my own understanding of Afghanistan outside of the lens of "gender apartheid," I came to learn that Afghanistan was, and continues to be, one of the most land-mined countries in the world.[26] According to the *Landmine Monitor Report* of 2009, there have been "at least 12,069 casualties from mines and explosive remnants of war (ERW) between 1999 and 2008. . . . The overwhelming majority of recorded casualties were civilians."[27] I also learned that these landmines have been connected to US involvement in Afghanistan since the 1970s. More recently, despite the condemnation of human rights groups worldwide, after 9/11, the United States began dropping cluster bombs; as Kolhakter and Ingalls report, "Between October 2001 and March 2002, the US dropped 1,228 cluster bombs containing 248,056 bomblets over Afghanistan."[28] These bombs scatter over large areas, making many citizens vulnerable, and they leave behind "unexploded bomblets killing civilians long after the attacks are over."[29] And so this invasion—justified in part by a call for women's rights— resulted in many more thousands of people who died in the midst of "massive dislocation, cold, disease, and a cutoff in aid supplies."[30] While exact numbers of deaths from starvation and disease are unknown, estimates range from ten to twenty thousand Afghans in that first year. The refugee crisis and displacement of many Afghans has continued since 2001; while many Afghans returned after the fall of the Taliban, most have not been settled. The UNHCR reports over five hundred thousand internally displaced Afghans in 2012.[31] These realities must be at the center of our understanding of the conditions of women's lives within the context of their particular communities and geopolitical locations.

As US feminists, we must be vigilantly critical of the imperial logic that claims that women's lives have "improved" under US occupation. In 2011, 213 women's rights advocates from around the world voted Afghanistan as the worst place in the world to be a woman.[32] A 2011 Amnesty International report states,

> Women in today's Afghanistan daily face a host of threats, from insurgent violence; attacks on schoolgirls and working women for daring to venture out into the public sphere; high levels of rape and domestic violence, as well as widespread physical and sexual abuse by state forces; forced and child marriage; and honor killings. 87% of Afghan women are illiterate, while 70–80% face forced marriage, many before the age of 16.[33]

The rates of domestic violence have reached epidemic proportions in Afghanistan; Soraya Sobhrang, of the Afghan Independent Human Rights Commission (AIHRC), reported that the AIHRC received "4,000 incidents in April–October, 1,000 more than in the same period last year."[34] The AIHRC attributes this increase to the overall lack of security in the country, not to cultural tradition. As Clementina Cantoni, a Pakistan-based aid worker with ECHO (the European Commission's humanitarian aid department), attributes these realities to the "[o]ngoing conflict, NATO airstrikes and cultural practices" that "combined make Afghanistan a very dangerous place for women."[35]

Fariba Nawa is one of the few writers for the US-based *Women's E-news* who critically challenges the cultural framework that the media, including *Women's E-News*, relies upon. She draws our attention to the code words embedded in US news reports, such as "[c]orrupt, tribal, medieval, misogynist" that are so misleading and wrong. She suggests a reframing of the violence against women and women's resistance to it. She writes,

> These women are fighting not just patriarchy but 30 years of what war does to a country. War has demoralized Afghan men, living with no jobs, no legs and no dignity. Some turn on their women as a result. It has created one million war widows, some who are forced to become prostitutes. Families in debt and afraid of being killed by drug smugglers barter and force their daughters into marriages. The daughters rebel and some are killed.[36]

She goes on to remind readers that women are not only victims but also perpetrators, and that for every man who is violent, there is another man who supports, advocates for, and stands with women in his family and/or community. Men's active support for women's resistance and resilience is well documented in Anne Brodsky's book, *With All Our Strength*, as well as in Malalai Joya's book, *A Woman among Warlords*.

Disrupting the narrative of weak and passive Afghan women, Nawa frames the violence against women as a response to women's *resistance* to gendered restrictions and discriminatory practices. She talks about women's active and daily resistance for survival as well as for change. Lifting up stories of resistance significantly undercuts the imperialist frame of Afghan women's weakness and powerlessness. In her own resistance to these hegemonic narratives, rather than a static photo of a woman in a *burqa*, Nawa purposefully chose a photo to accompany her article that captures a group of three Afghan men, with one holding a baby. As she notes, this image is a striking contrast to 99.9 percent of the images of Afghan men in *Women's E-News* and US media.

The US Military Role in Violence against Women in Afghanistan

When we take into account the broader context of war and occupation, and our own government's contribution to it, we can no longer understand violence in exclusively individual-personal-cultural terms. Instead, we must name the militia and state forces, trained and backed by the United States, and the US military as key contributors to the high rates of sexual violence against both women and men and for pervasive violence more generally. It is more difficult to find these stories circulating in the US media, and so this invisibility contributes to the imperial story of "saving Afghan women." Moving the United States into the frame of violence against women is essential in disrupting this story. One significant way in which the United States is directly involved in the violence is through its role in establishing and maintaining the Afghan Local Police (ALP) force. The United States provides the ALP with "military weaponry, training, and salaries."[37] This police force continues to be implicated in numerous cases of sexual violence and murder. The local Afghans view the ALP as another local militia that they have to navigate under great danger and duress. While the Afghan government and the United States argue that the ALP was created for security, Human Rights Watch (HRW) reports, "When militias engage in rape, murder, theft, and intimidation, and when there is little or no recourse to justice for victims, the creation of militias doesn't decrease insecurity, it creates it."[38] In their investigation, they found numerous abuses enacted with impunity by these forces in multiple areas. The HRW report documents that "[t]he crimes attributable to ALP members include cases of sexual abuse, unauthorized raids, land grabbing, extrajudicial killings, and an enforced disappearance."[39] One story is of an eighteen-year-old woman, Lal Bibi, who spoke out about being sexually assaulted and beaten by a group of men, including the US-trained ALP. While the US military insisted that the ALP were not involved, four were found guilty in November of 2012.[40]

The US and NATO forces also abuse, rape, and murder Afghan women. In 2005, Cherif Boussiani's UN special report argued that the involvement of US soldiers in the rape of women in Afghanistan must be included in any discussion of women's human rights. And yet these stories are even more difficult to find in mainstream US media, including in feminist media. One report in early December 2012, published on PressTV, an Iranian news outlet, carries the headline, "US Forces Rape Women in Northern Afghanistan";[41] according to veteran Gordon Duff, who framed and republished the article in *Veterans Today*, such rapes are common, but rarely reported on in the US media.[42] In March 2012, Stephen Lendman reported on US forces who murdered sixteen Afghan women and men and nine sleeping children in southern Kandahar province, with at least two of the women raped before being murdered.[43]

Because of the gender-myopic framework, combined with orientalism, that shapes reports about violence against women, the US military role in contributing to this violence and the context in which it is taking place is invisible. This is what must change. When we name the US role in this violence, it makes it less possible for the US government, media, and public to present ourselves as the benevolent "saviors" and "protectors" of Afghan women against Afghan men's violence. Instead, we would have to come to terms with how the United States—and, by connection, how we—are active participants in and supporters of the pervasive violence and conditions that produce it. If US-based feminists begin with the devastation, insecurity, and violence brought on by a US-led war and military occupation, our approach to support and solidarity would be significantly different. It would be less about "saving" and more about developing strategies grounded in accountability, responsibility, and mutuality.

A thread of interconnectedness that would serve the disruption of US claims to "superiority" might be one that links our critique of the US military's role in sexual violence in Afghanistan with the sexual violence that is also endemic within the institution itself. Not only is the US military *not* "saving" Afghan women, it is known for its own endemic racial, sexual, and gender-based harassment and violence. According to the Department of Defense, one in three women in the military experience sexual assault, and approximately 80 percent of women experience sexual harassment.[44] And women are not the only ones experiencing pervasive sexual harassment and assault; in a Pentagon report, it was estimated that of the twenty-six thousand cases of unwanted sexual contact in the military in 2012, 53 percent of these were cases of sexual violence against men.[45] Moreover, discrimination, harassment, and violence against lesbian, gay, bisexual, and transgender people in the military is rampant.[46] US military culture is one that demands silence, impunity for those accused, and retaliation for those who try to address the violence. While more awareness has been developed to address these issues, the framework for understanding it is focused on violence as an aberrant, rather than pervasive and systemic, behavior, and therefore the solutions rarely have to do with the roots of the violence.

US Feminism, the Veil, and Islamophobia

Viewing this situation through a lens of accountability, I have also come to critically reflect on how the US feminist obsession with "the veil" contributes both to justifications for the US invasion and occupation of Afghanistan *and* to discrimination, harassment, and violence against Muslim women in the United States and beyond. It serves to solidify the logic of Islamophobia that is so integral to US geopolitics under the guise of "saving" Afghan women. The western-produced images of Afghan women covered by the *burqa* have come to serve as *the* visual metaphor for violence against Afghan women and Muslim women all over the world.[47] These images accompany most US stories of women in Afghanistan, including in feminist media. They call up static images of oppression, powerlessness, and marginalization, not women's agency and lived experiences. Few stories focus on Afghan women's active, everyday, individual, and collective modes of survival, resilience, and resistance. This speaks to the hegemonic assumptions that US middle-class dress culture is a universal signature of freedom, individuality, and self-determination, whereas "other" cultures, by way of contrast, are not and so "their" dress marks "them" as inferior. This in turn contributes to the mistreatment, discrimination, harassment, and violence against Muslim women and other groups of women who veil. The images call forth an imperialist paternalism on the one hand and a fear-based xeno-phobia and "otherness" linked to discrimination and violence on the other hand. As Razack describes, "A message of Southern cultural infe-riority and dysfunction is so widely disseminated that when we in the North see a veiled woman, we can only retrieve from our store of infor-mation that she is a victim of her patriarchal culture or religion."[48] The veiled woman is a spectacle of "otherness" as well as "backwardness," and stands in contrast to the so-called freedom of fashion here. The images mark the need for US military intervention, control, and direction as the media simultaneously link these images as evidence of what they deem a culture of antiwestern terrorism. The discursive link between these images of the *burqa* and the idea that Islam is the basis for a ter-rorist threat to the United States, as Alsultany points out, "conceals how conditions of war, militarization, and starvation are harming women."[49]

Many US feminists have internalized and propagated the systemic "othering" of Muslim women that is embedded in US imperial history and its logics. A good many struggle to respect Muslim women who choose to wear the veil and who do not define the veil as the focus of their oppression. Afghan feminist mobilizing efforts against the atroci-ties of the Taliban regime never singularly focused on the *burqa*. While the Revolutionary Association of Women in Afghanistan (RAWA), an organization formed in the 1970s, drew needed attention to the Taliban's abuses of women, including the *forced imposition* of the *burqa* and the exclusion of women from the public sphere, its goal was never solely to protest veiling, and its analysis did not root the Taliban in Afghan cul-ture or in Islam as a religion. Instead, it consistently situates its struggle against the Taliban's patriarchal gender politics within a larger political struggle and history of war and occupation, including a struggle against the United States and other imperialist and militarist interventions in

Afghanistan's history.[50] Following RAWA's lead, rather than exercising judgment and speaking on behalf of others, Abu-Lughod argues that US feminists must do the "hard work involved in recognizing and respecting differences—precisely as products of different histories, as expressions of different circumstances, and as manifestations of differently structured desires. We may want justice for women, but can we accept that there might be different ideas about justice and that different women might want, or choose, different futures from what we envision as best?"[51]

A recognition of and respect for differences, while important, is not enough. As US feminists, we must take accountability for how the myopic focus of US feminists on the "veil" and the mass circulation of images of veiled women fuels Islamophobic and xenophobic fear-based harassment and violence against Muslim communities, including against veiled Muslim women, in the United States and beyond. As Alsultany suggests, "Stories of Muslim women who are victims of a barbaric culture and religion and the emotions that accompany it are used to rationalize the need to expel Muslims from the political community, deny them human rights, and justify detentions, deportations, racial profiling, and prisoner abuse."[52] These have escalated since 2001. Women who veil in the United States—the so-called *free* West—continue to face persistent discriminatory harassment and violence, although they are often invisible in the discussion of racial profiling and hate-based crimes.[53] In July of 2017, the Council on American-Islamic Relations (CAIR) reported a dramatic increase in bias incidents, harassment, and hate crimes for the first half of the year; the council found that "the most prevalent trigger of anti-Muslim bias incidents in 2017 remains the victim's ethnicity or national origin, accounting for 32 percent of the total. Twenty percent of incidents occurred because of an individual being perceived as Muslim. A Muslim woman's headscarf was a trigger in 15 percent of incidents."[54] Overall, women have had the *hijab* pulled off their heads and lit on fire, they have faced insults, intimidation, and threats of violence, and they have been physically attacked.[55] In 2008, the ACLU provided a glimpse into the institutionalized discrimination and harassment against Muslim women who veil; they reported, "Muslim women have been prohibited from wearing their headcoverings in a number of contexts. They have been harassed, fired from jobs, denied access to public places, and otherwise discriminated against because they wear hijab."⁵⁶ The contexts for this discriminatory treatment include workplaces, schools, law enforcement contexts, and public places such as public buildings and shopping malls.

In the fall of 2016, three women wearing the *hijab* were attacked; Christina Cauterucci reported, "One, a physical assault on two young women pushing strollers in Brooklyn, was perpetrated by a woman [Emirjeta Xhelili] who yelled 'You don't belong here!' and populated her social media feeds with insults to Allah. The third Muslim woman, a 36-year-old Scottish tourist, was assaulted by a man who tried to set her shirt on fire on Fifth Avenue in Manhattan."⁵⁷ Cauterucci notes that these attacks "illuminate the misogynist underpinnings" of Islamophobia. She writes, "Xhelili's specific naming of Muslim women in hijabs as her targets fits into the violent intersection of persistent efforts to regulate the bodies of both Muslims and women. It's a logical outcome of decades of Islamophobes framing their religious bigotry around women who wear their beliefs for the world to see."

While Arab and Muslim organizations, such as CAIR, and civil rights organizations, such as the ACLU, address this discrimination and harassment, US feminist groups, for the most part, have been silent. In my experience, while many feminists are quick to speak about the oppressiveness of forced veiling in Afghanistan, many seem hard-pressed to speak out against the harassment of and discrimination against women who veil in the United States. This is what needs to change.

For feminists in the United States, we need to consider how *our* focus on the dress of Muslim women contributes to this rampant Islamophobia. Recognizing how US feminisms are implicated in discrimination, harassment, and violence against Muslim women in the United States, we can take actions toward accountability and change. This includes deepening our understanding of the geopolitical context of the meanings of gender and Islam, in the United States, in Afghanistan, and beyond, and taking more active stands in solidarity against Islamophobia as it is being fomented here in US culture, in the US military, and in foreign policy. I appreciate the collaborative research project initiated by the European Network against Racism that brought together feminist and antiracist movements with a focus on Islamophobia and Muslim women. In 2016, the group issued a report through the European Network against Racism entitled "Forgotten Women: The Impact of Islamophobia on Muslim Women."[58] Spanning Belgium, Denmark, France, Germany, Italy, the Netherlands, Sweden, and the United Kingdom, the organization found that Muslim women's experiences of discrimination and violence were connected to the intersecting forces of gender, ethnicity, and religion. As in the United States, they found that the *hijab* and other clothing associated with being Muslim were what was most often associated with discrimination, harassment, and violence against Muslim women.[59] The report offers a set of recommendations for change, including specific directives to feminist and antiracist organizations. One key recommendation is to "avoid reproducing dominant power divisions. Integrate an anti-racism and anti-Islamophobia stance in the fight against patriarchy and gender-based oppression."[60] US feminists can take accountability by persistently challenging and transforming our feminist discourse so we are no longer feeding and nurturing the Islamophobia responsible for this widespread harassment and violence against Muslim people and all those identified as Muslim (even when they are not). Jasmin Zine argues that we need to be vigilant in recognizing and challenging how "the politics of representation acts in service of neo-imperialistic goals and global militarization as well as xenophobia and policies of racial profiling and exclusion."[61]

Making antiracism and anti-Islamophobia cornerstones of US feminisms would be an important shift in feminism's relationship to the larger geopolitical context. For one thing, it would disrupt and transform the assumptions that make Islam and feminism polar opposites. This polarization contributes to the dilemma Muslim women face, given Islamophobia on the one hand and patriarchal sexism on the other. In the context of addressing sexual violence by Muslim men against Muslim women, for instance, Mona Eltahowy writes, "[W]e Muslim women are caught between a rock and a hard place. . . . The rock is an Islamophobic right wing in other cultures that is all too eager to demonize Muslim men. . . . The hard place is a community within our own faith that is all too eager to defend Muslim men against all accusations."[62] As she notes, we have a US president (Donald Trump) who brags about his own sexism and sexual harassment but who simultaneously "has used so-called honor crimes and misogyny (which he ascribes to Muslim men) to justify his efforts to ban travel to the United States from several Muslim-majority countries." She then relays the exhaustion resulting from the way "Muslim women's voices and our bodies are reduced to proxy battlefields by the demonizers and defenders of Muslim men. Neither side cares about women. They are concerned only with one another."[63]

Policing of Gender Binaries in the United States

Just as the pervasive images in the media that consistently portray Afghan women as singularly poor, vulnerable, and victimized by "their" culture and religion, and thus in need of being "saved," are distorted, so are the images that present US women as "liberated" and "superior" and the United States as a space of gender equality, freedom, and democracy. As Mohanty points out, much scholarly research and many media reports on women in the third world are grounded in a constructed binary where western women are presented "as educated, as modern, as having control over their own bodies and sexualities, and the freedom to make their own decisions."[64]

Franks suggests that "the rigid assertion of Western cultural and moral superiority insulates countries such as America against self-critique in a way that is both dangerous and hypocritical."[65] She suggests, in contrast, an analysis that compares the constructions of "women" in both Afghanistan and the United States—constructions that obscure the realities of women's lives. She writes, "In both Afghanistan and in the United States the fantasy of women reigns supreme; a constructed and artificial femininity is everywhere on display while the facts of violence and exploitation remain hidden."[66] For instance, images of white, western, heteronormative, gender-conforming women's bodies are used for nationalist/imperialist purposes, at the same time that issues of discrimination, harassment, abuse, and violence are marginalized, minimized, and distorted within the United States. The image of the "liberated west" falls apart in the face of Christian fundamentalist and repressive state forces in this country that perpetuate interpersonal, community, and state gendered violence. Law enforcement and state violence against women—particularly those who are women of color or undocumented immigrants, those living with disabilities, those with physical and mental health conditions, those who are queer, trans, and gender nonconforming—in US prisons, schools, medical institutions, and public spaces is at an all-time high.

In deconstructing our orientalist/imperialist gaze as a method of approaching transnational solidarity, US feminists might also take accountability for how the dominant culture in the United States, including within US feminisms, is also entrenched in gender binaries with accompanying restrictive gender norms and regulations. Many of those who exist and act outside of these binaries are met with punishment, violence, incarceration, and murder, particularly if they are transgender, queer, and gender-nonconforming people of color. Joey Mogul, Andrea Ritchie, and Kay Whitlock's book, *Queer (In)Justice*, documents the criminalization of gender and sexual nonconformity in the United States, including its foundation in colonial conquest and the institution of slavery. Gender policing by families, schools, and corporate and criminal legal institutions is enforced through discrimination, violence, and brutality against all those identified as queer and gender nonconforming. This mistreatment and violence is often justified and rationalized by the archetypal conflation of queerness and gender nonconformity with pathology and criminality that is constructed through the lenses of white supremacy and colonialism; and it is policed through dress and other forms of gender presentation.[67] Andrea Ritchie's book, *Invisible No More! Police Violence against Black Women and Women of Color*, documents systemic and brutal police violence and murder of Black women and women of color; she illuminates this reality's historical and social roots in interlocking systems of white supremacy, colonialism, heteronormativity, capitalism, and ableism. Her incisive analysis of the multiple systems that shape the violence reveal the interlocking normative logics that frame its invisibility. The book is a call to action to antiviolence feminists, racial justice activists, and police and prison abolitionists to make this violence visible, to recognize its multiple and interlocking roots, and to use that as a vantage point for coalitional movement organizing.

Such a call is necessary because feminists have not been on the front lines of actively resisting or challenging the racialized policing and punishment of gender nonconformity, and often participate in marginalizing and criminalizing gender-nonconforming and transgender individuals and communities of color. This is evidenced in the predominant focus on "women" as a more or less homogeneous category defined by biology, in the ongoing ways that transwomen are not in-

206 | DISENTANGLING US FEMINISM FROM US IMPERIALISM

cluded in work around "women's issues," and in the feminist resistance
to the recognition of trans women as women. In the most visible and
mainstream feminist work that addresses gender inequality and discrimination, there is little to no critique of the institutionalized and endemic policing of gender nonconformity in schools, hospitals, families,
prisons, criminal legal systems, and media. These are often considered
LGBTQ or racial-justice issues, not women's/feminist issues. Feminists,
by and large, have also not addressed interpersonal and state violence
against gender-nonconforming and trans people, many of whom identify as women. At the same time, there is a growing movement within
feminism that seeks to change this gender-exclusive and binaristic lens.
Feminist scholars and activists—such as Andrea Ritchie, Beth Richie,
Mariame Kaba, Dean Spade, Morgan Bassichis, and Joey Mogul—who
are living and working within queer and trans communities of color are
at the forefront of transforming feminist politics and practices. In this
work, it is understood that (white, middle-class, able-bodied) gender
essentialism, binaries, and normativities are integral to oppression and
violence, and are working to make publicly visible this oppression and
violence in order to challenge and transform it.

A framework grounded in mutuality as well as accountability compels us to name and address the interconnectedness of these struggles
around gender normativity and violence in the United States with that
in Afghanistan and beyond. Doing this in a consistent public way disrupts the "us/them" dichotomies that operate in mainstream discourse
about gender in "other" countries, cultures, and religions. This is not to
return to a framing of sameness; instead, it is to recognize the highly
regulated and disciplined interlocking systems of gender, race, class,
sexuality, ability, and citizenship in the United States that produce
punishment and violence against those who do not conform, including against Muslim women who veil, or people who wear clothing tied
to their (non-Christian) religious identities. It is important to insist as
well as concretely demonstrate that the United States is quite decidedly
not a space of gender freedom and self-determination. While those who
are normatively *cis*-gendered, white, middle- and upper-middle-class
women and men, including those who identify as lesbian, gay, or bisexual, may experience a feeling of "freedom" in terms of "choice," they
do so only because they are adhering to a rigid gender regime structured

around a male/female binary. Transgender and gender-nonconforming individuals and communities, on the other hand, suffer from pervasive socially sanctioned discrimination, harassment, and violence, both interpersonal and state, based on gender- and sexual-identity presentation and dress and individual style.[68] In this sense, there are some pathways of interconnectedness with the ways gender normativity and disciplinary apparatuses operate within Afghanistan, while also having different but interconnected roots.

Afghan Women's Organized Resistance

Integral to the imperial logic of "saving" is one that presumes Afghan women are weak and passive as opposed to resilient, strong, and active. This abstract binary is problematic on many levels. To simply respond that Afghan women are the opposite of "weak" and "passive" also buys into the hierarchy of this logic. As we have seen, US feminists are implicated within the interlocking structures and systems that have produced the endemic crisis, and Afghan women, and people more broadly, individually and collectively, continue to find ways to live, to build community, to challenge the multiple systems and powers operating, and to transform the crisis into a more just and peaceful context. Within this context, I appreciate the work of J. Fluri, who reminds those of us in the United States who do not know that while we often talk about "Afghan women," there is no homogenous category of women in Afghanistan. As Fluri writes, "Afghan women's placement, position, and status at the household and community scale vary considerably by ethnic group, location, religious belief, socioeconomic status, education level, and also vary household to household when the former list of social indices are similar; rather, the social, cultural, historical conditions of women's lives vary across urban and rural contexts."[69] These differences translate into different politics, perspectives, and strategies of resistance and resilience in the contexts of ongoing conflict and war. In all areas of Afghanistan, women are engaged in varied daily acts of resistance—from working to address the daily needs of their families and communities to organizing underground schools and media networks to participating in local and national government bodies.

US feminists must engage and learn from Afghan women's individual and collective resistance in connection to decades of war, forced dislocations, and violence that has been ongoing and multifaceted. When I first engaged with the frame of "gender apartheid," I had no conception of the living histories of women or people more generally in Afghanistan. This framing occluded not only the US role but also a vibrant history of debates, discussions, advocacy, and activism among Afghan and Muslim feminists, intellectuals, and activists in Afghanistan, regarding gender and many other issues. These were histories that I mostly did not know about, which might have led me to understand more deeply the extent to which our histories are interconnected and intertwined.

Through my engagement with Afghan and transnational feminist scholars and activists, I have come to learn that women's rights, women's activism, and women's active involvement in the history of Afghanistan are much more complex and variable over time. I have found a variety of articles and books about women's lives and activism in Afghanistan that for me have been invaluable. Like many feminists in the United States, I was initially most acquainted with RAWA, particularly its organizational website and blog. It is this group's revolutionary transnational political analysis and its on-the-ground news reporting that have helped me to more deeply understand the confluence of national and international forces impacting the people, institutions, and communities in Afghanistan. It was through reading RAWA's website that I witnessed the significant disconnect between its framing of the issues and that of the Feminist Majority Foundation, even though the two groups had also worked together prior to 9/11.[70]

I also have deeply appreciated Malalai Joya's book *A Woman among Warlords*. She offers many powerful stories of the daily resilience and resistance of Afghan women and men who she shows have never uncritically accepted the dictates, laws, and violence of the Soviet Union, the Taliban, the Northern Alliance, or the US military. She shares her life experiences as a member of the Organization for Promoting Afghan Women's Capabilities beginning in the late 1990s and as the youngest member elected to the Afghan Parliament. She illuminates the everyday lives of the many people she works with and comes into contact with through her activism; it is deeply moving to learn about the persistent efforts of herself and many others to critically challenge the stranglehold of American-backed warlords who are responsible for the endemic violence, chaos, displacement, and lack of security in Afghanistan. While the book is her story, it is also the story of many others, and it serves as an important counternarrative to the dominant one that mostly circulates in the United States.

I have often taught Joya's book with the documentary film, directed by Meena Nanji, *View from a Grain of Sand* (2006). This film offers a contemporary history of Afghanistan through the lenses of three women—a teacher, a women's rights activist, and a doctor—who are currently living and working in refugee camps in Pakistan. The film highlights the intersecting forces, including the United States, that led to the rise of the Taliban and the consequences for thousands of people who had to flee their homeland. The differences between the three women's experiences, ideas, and perspectives are as powerful as their similarities, and the historical backdrop that also centers the impact of Soviet and US invasions and occupations and their relationship to the rise of the Taliban counters the imperialist narrative so entrenched in US discourse.[71] To provide further context for my classes when I show the film, I have also encouraged them to read Nilofaur Pourzand's article, "Afghan Refugee Women's Organizations in Pakistan (1980–2001): Struggles in Adversity." She provides a good overview of grassroots women's organizing in refugee camps since the Soviet invasion and occupation followed by the US-led invasion and ensuing civil war against the Soviets, and then the rise of the Taliban. This provides an important counternarrative to the idea of Afghan women's passivity; as she writes, "Even during the worst days, many Afghan women were involved in efforts to challenge the root causes of war, patriarchy and Islamic dogma. One manifestation of this struggle—Afghan refugee women's efforts and organizations in Pakistan—is one of the indicators of gains made by at least some Afghan women over the many years of conflict, though as a result of a collective tragedy and at great personal cost."[72] The article describes the many projects, organizations, and schools initiated and developed by Afghan women refugees that have served Afghan communities from the 1970s on, including those with a focus on women and girls. The war against the Soviets in the 1980s and through the 1990s with the establishment of the Northern Alliance in Afghanistan created a context where more restrictions were placed on women. There was no support for Afghan women's rights and education, and it was very dangerous for women to be actively involved in public. And yet refugee women actively supported their families and communities, and some sought out educational opportunities in Pakistan. Afghan women built numerous projects and organizations around health, education, income generation, and more.[73] During the same period, an Islamic Women's University welcomed women to study in the areas of medicine, literature, and Islamic studies, and the Afghan Women's Media Center provided "video and journalism training for Afghan refugee women."[74] These projects were under constant threat. During the Taliban's rule, 1995–2001, Pourzand notes, many Afghans in Afghanistan and in the refugee camps were opposed to the restrictive and oppressive regulations and policies; in this context, "Afghan refugee women were ready to take more upon themselves and their organizations in the international arena. They also realized more and more that their voices mattered and they had the potential to influence others."[75]

Another good source on the breadth of women's organizing comes from the feminist magazine *Herizons*. It published an overview of Afghan women's organizations in 2006; in its contextualization, it recognized that

> Afghan women . . . formed the backbone of a relentless civil society that provided the only threads of hope available to women trapped helplessly under the auspices of the Taliban. They operated healthcare clinics and underground schools. They funneled information out of the country, challenging the rest of the world to help their voices be heard as they struggled to secure and protect their own basic human rights. They established and administered women's organizations, resource centres and shelters.[76]

The magazine also made note of the Afghan Women's Network that was initiated in Pakistan in 1995 from the energy of the UN Women's World Conference in Beijing, with a similar network begun in Kabul.

Pourzand is also quick to remind (US) readers—given the tendency to generalize and homogenize—that just like anywhere else in the world, Afghan women's organizations represent a whole multitude of perspectives and activities with no one set agenda, and sometimes conflicting ones. As Pourzand describes,

> [O]verall RAWA is no doubt on the radical end of the spectrum, with organizations like AWN [Afghan Women's Network] somewhere in the

centre, and the women's organizations affiliated to the Islamic Parties to the right. . . . [T]he reality is even more complex, with each group including members who have a range of personal and political views, as well as ethnic, religious, tribal, class and other affiliations which influence their views and actions in a changing manner.[77]

Disrupting the Binary: Accountability and Muslim Feminisms

In Jasmin Zine's article "Between Orientalism and Feminism," she writes about the dilemma of Muslim feminists who must address the "dual oppressions of 'gendered Islamophobia,' that has re-vitalized Orientalist tropes and representations of backward, oppressed and politically immature women in need of liberation and rescue through imperialist interventions as well as the challenge of religious extremism and puritan discourses that authorize equally limiting narratives of Islamic womanhood and compromise their human rights and liberty."[78] Drawing on Miriam Cook's *Women Claim Islam*, she argues that when Muslim feminists engage critique from these multiple vantage points, they are able to shift "the binaries that lock critical engagements into polemical dialectics on to a space of multiplicity where various types of contestations can be addressed simultaneously."[79] Zine looks at the commonalities as well as divergences among Muslim feminists of both secular and religious perspectives in order to explore more opportunities for transnational solidarity.

Zine's work reminds me of how US feminist discourse is also implicated in the manifestation of this polarized dilemma Muslim women face, given the US feminist tendency to focus on Islam and patriarchy, and not to give critical attention to Islamophobia. It offers another place for accountability where we can take responsibility for being proactively and critically aware of how our feminist theorizing, research, and activism contribute to these dilemmas and binaries. From an accountability perspective, it means actively disentangling US feminist work from Islamophobia and US militarist and imperialist projects and following the lead of Muslim feminist efforts to address the multitude of forces and issues shaping people's lives, rather than reducing them to a singular one.

In addition, it means a deeper recognition that the default logic of liberal feminism—that shapes most feminisms in the United States whether they are identified as liberal or not—is embedded in colonial and imperial logics and visions. This is apparent, according to Cyra Akila Choudhury, in feminist presumptions about "progress" and "flourishing" and the ways in which many feminists accept Islamophobic logics that see any form of Islam as incompatible with feminism. This has led to paternalistic and dismissive understandings of Muslim women's continued adherence to their religion and culture, attributing it to "ignorance or brainwashing." Instead, Choudhury calls for a recognition that Islam plays complex and multifaceted roles in people's lives and that for Muslim women, their religion is not necessarily incompatible with their feminism. For Choudhury,

> To acknowledge this alternative view is not to say that Muslim women do not live in systemic patriarchy, that Islam is not patriarchal, and that gender subordination sometimes reflected in "traditional" arrangements ought not to be challenged. Rather, it is to say that opinions about how it is challenged, by whom, and what priorities are established can legitimately differ among women and are mediated by local contexts. It is also to acknowledge that Islam is not fixed and can be interpreted in a number of ways and that religion must be engaged by feminists if they seriously seek to support the full liberation and flourishing of women in the Muslim world.[80]

This argument leads to Choudhury's suggestion that rather than grounding our solidarity in international human rights or liberal feminist conceptions of progress, we cultivate "more support for local practices of human rights and liberation that are being engaged in by ordinary Muslim women and men in the global South . . . , even if we disagree with their definitions of liberation and human flourishing. This would require us to accept these women as fully capable humans and their commitments to their religion and culture as valid expressions of 'freedom.'"[81]

Conclusion

In this chapter, I have explored what a transnational accountability approach to solidarity for US feminists like myself might look like in relationship to Afghanistan. What I conclude is that it is incumbent upon us as US feminists to take accountability for how feminism has been implicated within our interconnected history as a step toward solidarity. Rather than seeing ourselves as outsiders with a benevolent interest in supporting or "saving Afghan women," we must recognize how we have contributed to the issues and struggles they are facing. Along these lines, we must become more diligent in disentangling our US feminist logics from US empire by undermining *orientalist* frameworks. As Nayak suggests, "in order for feminism to have resistance potential, it must acknowledge its own participation in Orientalism and its self-referential activism during colonialism, conflicts and the War on Terror."[82] This would be a feminism that articulates how it is also implicated in the systems in terms of both oppression and domination. We must take into account our own history and contextual relationships with the people of Afghanistan, to recognize the interconnectedness between "us" and "them," and "here" and "there." Along these lines, we must build a critical consciousness within our feminist organizations, projects, and communities about the relationship between the United States and Afghanistan to cultivate accountability for our role and relationship for endemic violence within Afghanistan. Most significantly, we must take accountability for how our feminist frameworks contribute to the imperial justification for US-led war and occupation and to the ongoing discrimination, violence, and banning of all those identified as Muslim and Arab in this country. We must make it a priority to disrupt, shift, and transform these frameworks on a much broader scale. In other words, we must cultivate accountability for the ways in which imperialist feminisms have contributed to and impacted US militarism, war, and occupation, including the violence against women perpetrated by US military forces as well the conditions of war that fundamentally fuel interpersonal, communal, and state violence against women perpetrated by Afghan men, women, and children. Finally, we must find ways to learn from and connect to the collective resistance of Afghan women throughout the world to build relationships of solidarity, rather than "saving."

9

Resisting the "Savior" Complex

We need to ask: Where am I in this picture? Am I positioning myself as the saviour of less fortunate peoples? As the progressive one? As more subordinated? As innocent? These are moves of superiority and we need to reach beyond them. . . . Accountability begins with tracing relations of privilege and penalty. It cannot proceed unless we examine our complicity. Only then can we ask questions about how we are understanding differences and for what purpose.
—Sherene Razack, *Looking White People in the Eye: Gender, Race, and Culture in Courtrooms and Classrooms*

In a context where it seems feminist social movements are barely visible in the so-called postfeminist context, Nicholas D. Kristof and Sheryl WuDunn, journalists and authors of *Half the Sky: Turning Oppression into Opportunity for Women Worldwide*, in 2009, began to garner broad-based enthusiasm in the United States around building an "incipient movement" to "save" the world's women. In their words, "We hope to recruit you to join an incipient movement to emancipate women and fight global poverty by unlocking women's power as economic catalysts. That is the process under way—not a drama of victimization but of empowerment, the kind that transforms bubbly teenage girls from brothel slaves into successful businesswomen."[1] Finding the book compelling, Oprah invited the authors onto her show twice in the fall of 2009, and they appeared on numerous talk shows in 2009 and 2010. The *New York Times* devoted one of its Sunday magazine issues to "Saving the World's Women" with the lead article by Kristof and WuDunn, and related articles, including one by then secretary of state Hillary Clinton on women's human rights, another on global philanthropy, and yet another on the successes of a girls' school in Afghanistan. On March 4, 2010, CARE, an organization featured prominently in the book, sponsored a national event hosted in nearly five hundred cities across the United States, to further mobilize the US public's interest in supporting philanthropic projects focused on women and girls. The events featured the premiere of a CARE-sponsored film project codirected by Lisa Leone and actress Marisa Tomei, called *Woinshet*, that tells the story of an Ethiopian woman who overcomes poverty and oppression.[2]

Inspired by the response to the book, a Half the Sky Movement website was launched, which includes links to the four-hour PBS and international broadcast documentary television series that premiered in October of 2012.[3] The documentary series "introduces women and girls who are living under some of the most difficult circumstances imaginable—and fighting bravely to change them." The film follows Nicholas Kristof with accompanying "celebrity advocates" America Ferrera, Diane Lane, Eva Mendes, Meg Ryan, Gabrielle Union, and Olivia Wilde, covering ten countries: Cambodia, Kenya, India, Sierra Leone, Somaliland, Vietnam, Afghanistan, Pakistan, Liberia, and the United States. According to the *Half the Sky Movement* website, "[T]he film reflects viable and sustainable options for empowerment and offers an actionable blueprint for transformation."[4] In addition, the project includes more videos, websites, video games, and links to partner organizations formed to support the empowerment of women and girls. The book and film have been celebrated by many mainstream liberal feminist organizations in the United States—including the Feminist Majority and *Women's E-News*, among many others.

Half the Sky seems to inspire passionate engagement across the conservative and liberal spectrum. Many people who might never identify themselves with feminism per se seem suddenly interested in talking about women, gender, poverty, and violence. They say they are compelled more than ever to "help" the cause of women. Upon the book's publication and all of the publicity surrounding it, I noticed a distinct change in public engagement on violence against women—the issues were more readily brought up in an array of conversations, where previously they may have been avoided or evaded. When the book first came out, a white gay male friend of mine earnestly brought it up at a dinner party to bring a more women-centered perspective into a largely gay male conversation; at numerous social gatherings people brought it up as a way of creating connections and bridging interests. And many students began to reference it as an important book that sheds light on women's lives.

Another group of feminists, myself included, did not share the enthusiastic engagement, and in fact felt the book continued a colonial and imperialist legacy that has shaped US engagement in women's human rights in the global south. For one thing, it was striking that the compelling interest in issues of violence seemed decidedly dependent on talking about "other" women, women located outside of the United States, outside of the particular circles in which the book circulates, women in that "other" world considered "third world," "developing," non-European/non-US. In other words, the interest stops at the US border, unless it involves immigrant women from over "there." While the project proclaims an interest in empowering "women worldwide" to resist oppression and violence, the phrase means a particular kind of woman, mostly poor women who are living in so-called developing countries, and not women who are living in the privileged "West." The presumption underlying the project and book is that women residing within the US borders do not need empowerment or resources because we/they do not experience oppression and violence, and this presumption, in a sense, is what ultimately enables the nationwide conversation.

Thus, while the enthusiastic *concern* for improving the lives of the "world's women" *feels* genuine, it relies on a narrow and distorted neocolonial lens projected onto the "women worldwide." The popularity of the lens requires keeping the focus on specific groups of women understood as "over there" (meaning women of the global south) with little reflection on our interconnected histories and struggles that would link "here" and "there." The authors offer little critical understanding of the historical, geopolitical, and cultural contexts of the communities referenced, and they seem intent on disconnecting their histories and struggles from those of us in the United States. The stories may *feel* compelling, then, because of the distance created between "us" and "them." The narratives rely on a logic that the roots of the problems are with "them" and have nothing to do with "us." In other words, the authors discourage us from considering how the roots of poverty and violence "over there" are entangled in international and transnational systems of power that shape our interconnected lives. The impulse toward "saving," I would argue, depends on an ignorance of how we ourselves are implicated in the systemic roots of the oppression and violence being addressed, and an ignorance about how these systems are embedded within relationships, institutions, and structures that interconnect our lives. Moreover, I would argue that it is precisely these projects of "saving" that actually strengthen and solidify the very roots of oppression and violence that they are supposedly set up to solve.

In this chapter, I seek to critically engage the stories and logics offered in the book *Half the Sky* in an effort to challenge the imperial lens of so-called benevolence and to offer a perspective on the stories grounded in interconnectedness and accountability. I offer a critical analysis of the us/them logic that frames the project. This is a narrative logic well rehearsed throughout US imperial, white-supremacist, patriarchal, and heteronormative history that has served to produce systemic oppression and violence that it then simultaneously claims to "save" women from. As I critically interrogate the narratives and the subject positions of dominance and subordination that they reproduce in the name of empowerment, I also shift the lens to make more visible the interrelatedness of "us" and "them." I situate the *Half the Sky* project within a neoliberal agenda that obscures the workings of global, white-supremacist, heteronormative capitalism by focusing on the struggles and triumphs of individual women and by locating the roots of the oppression in culture and religion. I make more visible the ways neoliberalism and global capitalism, rather than culture, are integral to poverty, health crises, and violence, rather than a solution to them. Finally, I create some bridges across the shared and interconnected contexts that are lost in the us/them binary of the book, thereby shifting the relational lens between "us" and "them" from one of "saving" to one of accountability.

Storytelling and the Politics of Accountability

Kristof and WuDunn's argument for "turning oppression into opportunity for women worldwide" is developed through their constructed stories of women's struggles and triumphs against incredible odds of poverty and violence in the global south. Each chapter introduces us to individual women that Kristof and WuDunn have met through their work as journalists. The stories they tell read as powerful, compelling, and heart-wrenching—they write them intentionally to pull on the

heartstrings of the US, white, middle- and upper-middle-class readers who are their intended audience. They are written to activate our
pity, our empathy, our outrage, and our dollars, but not necessarily our
accountability and solidarity. The stories ultimately serve their neoliberal and global hegemonic agenda, not the self-/collective determination
of women and their communities in the global south. These stories are
followed by the stories of individual affluent women and men of the
global north who are "helping" women by developing or contributing to
projects on women's empowerment, health, and education. These stories serve as inspiration for readers to join in efforts to save women, to
become problem solvers for "their" problems, as well as to boost their/
our own sense of purpose in life. These are politically constructed stories of brutal poverty and violence from the global south that serve to
reify the affluent heroism of the global north. As Sherene Razack suggests, the stories we tell about people's lives across contexts and power
divides are always embedded in political power relations.[5]

In this chapter, I seek to shift the readers' lens from one oriented
toward "saving" poor women to one that prompts a reflective lens
grounded in accountability. Accountability, Razack writes, is "a process
that begins with a recognition that we are each implicated in systems of
oppression that profoundly structure our understanding of one another.
That is, we come to know and perform ourselves in ways that reproduce
social hierarchies."[6] She argues that we are embedded in hierarchical
arrangements that shape our *understandings*, and that we must be critically reflective of our impulses to *know* those defined as "different" from
us as a way to claim solidarity or alliance. Instead, she suggests that we
shift from a desire to *understand "them"* to a commitment to *understand
our complicity* in the systems of domination that produce the hierarchical differences between us. She writes, "Tracing our complicity in these
systems requires that we shed notions of mastering differences, abandoning the idea that differences are pre-given, knowable and existing in
a social and historical vacuum. Instead, we invest our energies in exploring the histories, social relations, and conditions that structure groups
unequally in relation to one another and *that shape what can be known,
thought, and said."*[7]

Thus the work of accountability is less about acquiring information
about "them" for the purpose of understanding "them," and more about

interrogating what we think we know through turning the lens on our relationship to the systems that are shaping the hierarchical relationship between us. In other words, we might engage in a process of tracing the ways in which we are complicit with, benefit from, and are accountable for the systems that produce the oppression and violence with which we are concerned. This would lend itself to building solidarity along the lines of respect, mutuality, and interconnectedness across our differences, rather than a superiority and righteousness directed toward intervention and "saving."[8] Again, Razack writes, "If we can name the organizing frames, the conceptual formulas, the rhetorical devices that disguise and sustain elites, we can begin to develop responses that bring us closer to social justice."[9] Our work is not just to consider "what we know" but to interrogate "how we know."[10] This requires a methodology that is persistently critical of the "interpretive structures we use to reconstruct events."[11]

With Razack's critical challenges in mind, some of the questions to consider in the reading of *Half the Sky* include the following: Whose stories are being told and from whose perspective? Whom do the stories make into villains or into heroes? Who are the victims, the saviors, and from whose perspective and for whose benefit? Whose power gets reproduced in the stories? What kind of relationships do the stories build within and across power lines? And within the stories, what issues are highlighted, and what issues are not addressed? Whose voices, experiences, and perspectives are missing?

Deconstructing the Us/Them Binary

As I mentioned earlier, *Half the Sky* provides two parallel narratives of "victims" and "saviors." This structure creates an us/them binary of two distinct and separate groups—the helpless victims in the so-called developing world on the one hand and the affluent and benevolent saviors from the United States on the other. While Kristof and WuDunn use the phrase "women worldwide," they are constructing a category of women that they locate in "poor" and "developing" countries. These women are the focus of the first, most dominant narrative—a narrative of brutal oppression, violence, and poverty as well as individual resilience and resistance. These are the women, they argue, who are oppressed primarily by the men (and women) in their local communities and the culture they have created. The individual stories told are of women who have overcome incredible odds and who are working to build a sustainable if meager life for themselves.

The stories Kristof and WuDunn craft from the women they have met are quite familiar to "us" in the "West"—as they are stories of individuals pulling themselves up by their bootstraps. The authors tell stories of individual change and empowerment, rather than of social and political change.[12] The locus of empowerment within the stories told is the individual will and determination of the women themselves, with support from "outsiders" in the form of social entrepreneurs and/or development organizations of the "West."

Because their focus is on individual victimization and individual empowerment, they obscure the structural and geopolitical roots of oppression and the social movements seeking to address them. There are no stories of activist women leaders and participants in community-based, nationalist, feminist, and/or social justice movements. For the most part, they construct a version of women and men of the global south as mostly all the same—the women as victims of cultural male domination, and the men as perpetrators. They bring no attention to the social and political differences within and between communities. For instance, they rarely include the life stories of women with higher social status—by education, class, ethnicity, caste, religion—who also live in these communities or regions. When present, they are distinguished as "supporters" and "helpers" of poor, impoverished women, more connected to the "West," to NGOs, and therefore more like "us," and not presented as women who may share a common history, social context, culture, and/or religion with the women with whom they are working.

As central to the narrative of victimization and powerlessness in the so-called developing world is its parallel—the narrative about "us" (the imagined readers) in the "West" who are assumed to be superior to "them" in poor and developing countries and who are repelled and horrified when learning about "others" and then compelled to action. The "us" is made up of those who, like the authors, are "outsiders," who come from and/or identify with the affluent "West" where "we" who are assumed to embrace and practice gender equality are in the best position to "save the world's women." In this project, this "we" of the "West" have already achieved equality, freedom, wealth, and affluence, except for a few issues that the authors define as minor and trivial.

To a large extent, the authors actually frame women of the global north as no longer in the category of "women" since, according to them, "we" women in the global north are no longer subject to discrimination, mistreatment, and violence. The authors trivialize and minimize any problems related to women's oppression, or any oppression, in the United States, and consistently redirect "us" outside of our own context to one that is seemingly "other" and outside the realm of anything that might happen in this country. As they write, "If you're reading this article, the phrase 'gender discrimination' might conjure thoughts of unequal pay, underfinanced sports teams or unwanted touching from a boss. In the developing world, meanwhile, millions of women and girls are actually enslaved."[13] This trivialization allows privileged, US, white, middle- and upper-middle-class women readers to more firmly and uncritically align ourselves *as individuals* with the white, middle- and upper-class men of the global north into the category of "saviors." By trivializing the few issues they have defined as exemplifying the "West" in one sentence, they erase from the reader's lens the pervasive conditions of poverty, exploitation, and violence in this so-called West. "Our" lives here are contrasted wholesale with those of women in poor countries whose lives they characterize as poverty-stricken and brutally violent because of their backward cultures and/or religions.

At the same time, claiming that the project is about "women worldwide" gives "us" in the United States the right to claim these stories as *our* stories, and to claim a right to interpret, evaluate, and intervene in the name of "helping" and "saving" these *other* women. In other words, making a broad claim of *universal* women's issues creates a space for intervention on behalf of "women worldwide." Sherene Razack again writes about the dangers of such universalizing that operates to sustain rather than challenge the unequal power lines that structure systemic oppression and privilege; she writes, "[R]elying on the notion of an essential woman, the idea that all women share a core of oppression on to which can then be grafted their differences, has enabled a masking of how systems of domination interlock and thus how we, as women, are implicated in one another's lives."[14]

The authors ultimately naturalize the dynamics of hierarchical power within such relationships through their reliance on discourses of culture and religion, rather than lenses that situate the roots of poverty and violence within historical systems of capitalism, colonialism, white supremacy, etc. It is here where the logics of racism and ethnocentrism reveal themselves. As Sherene Razack writes,

> The close connection between assertions of cultural difference and racism has meant that in white societies the smallest reference to cultural differences . . . triggers an instant chain of associations (the veil, female genital mutilation, arranged marriages) that ends with the declared superiority of European culture. . . . Culture clash, where the West has values and modernity and the non-West has culture, consolidates membership in the dominant group.[15]

By constructing women as victims of *other* cultures who need "help," not rights, not self-determination, not revolution, we obscure the power lines created by capitalism, colonialism, imperialism, and militarism that underlie the interconnections between us. Rather than analyzing the geopolitical and structural roots of the problems and tracing the lines that might reveal how we are implicated in the suffering of others and may benefit from its causes, instead we use "their suffering to reconstitute ourselves as white knights and as victims, taking ourselves out of their histories."[16]

The narrative discourse constructs this "we" here and the "they" there with categorically distinct and separate issues, histories, cultures, and contexts. The authors present the lives of women in poor, developing countries as if they were fundamentally different from and disconnected from the lives of women and men in the affluent, developed countries of the "West." There is little to no recognition of how we are interconnected, that the conditions of life "here" are connected to the conditions of life "there," that these connections are forged through the historical and contemporary processes of global capitalism, colonialism, and imperialism.

And when geopolitical, economic, and social interconnections between these contexts of "here" and "there" might be more difficult to hide, Kristof and WuDunn make sure to let the reader know that they are not blaming the "West" for conditions in poor and developing countries. For instance, in the context of sex trafficking and the coercion of poor women, the authors argue that westerners should be involved in an abolitionist movement against sexual slavery not because the "West" is somehow involved, but because it is morally the right thing to do; they assure the readers, "[T]his is not a case where we in the West have a responsibility to lead because we're the source of the problem. Rather, we single out the West because, even though we're peripheral to slavery, our action is necessary to overcome a horrific evil."[17] They are quite quick to claim, without evidence, that "Western men" are not involved in sex trafficking; instead, they claim, "Western men do not play a central role in prostitution in most poor countries. . . . The vast majority are local men. . . . Western men usually go with girls who are more or less voluntary prostitutes, because they want to take the girls back to their hotel rooms, while forced prostitutes are not normally allowed out of the brothels."[18] Of course, this characterization of men of the so-called West is inaccurate, and minimizes the role of western sex tourism as well as the role of the US military in the growth of the sex industry around its military bases, for instance, in the Philippines and in Thailand. Consistently, the potential for any critical reflection about the role of people and/or institutions connected to the United States and to the "West" is evaded and/or minimized.

These lenses of "saving" and "helping" work to solidify "our" sense of superiority and power in relation to "them" and to ward off any sense of our own relationship to or accountability for the issues being addressed. In this *us/them* framework, we are not compelled to understand how "our lives" are intricately related to "their lives" except as outside bystander witnesses to *their* victimization and as potential *saviors* who can help *them* to become *empowered*. This is what Razack describes as the essential colonial encounter—"when powerful narratives turn oppressed peoples into objects, to be held in contempt, or to be saved from their fates by more civilized beings."[19] This is made vividly real, for example, in a video clip that follows actress Eva Mendes as she accompanies Nicholas Kristof to a meeting with young women rape survivors in Sierra Leone. While she admits she has no knowledge or understanding of Sierra Leone, she becomes the lens for the audience's viewing. The audience sees her shock, horror, and sympathy as she visits and engages with women in a rape crisis center in Sierra Leone, a set of emotions that sets her (and the audience) apart from the women—superior, distant, and yet sympathetic (as opposed to empathetic). The project's constructions of "us" are what Razack might refer to as "fantasies of racial superiority" that are reinforced in many "small, quotidian ways."[20] And as she explains, "It is not as monsters that we collude in these brutal acts, but as 'nice' people, living in the nicest place on earth, and as compassionate people traumatized by brutality."[21]

Most significantly, Kristof and WuDunn work hard to tell their readers that "we" (in the "West") have no relationship to, or any responsibility for, the entangled roots of poverty, poor healthcare, lack of access to education, or the development of religious extremism connected with terrorist networks in so-called poor and developing countries. Rather, it is as benevolent, civilized, and privileged "outsiders" that "we" are made to believe that *we* can help to solve *their* problems.

This project of "saving the world's women" (taking from the title of the *New York Times* issue that featured *Half the Sky*) is deeply problematic. It denies women's agency, power, history, knowledge, and perspectives, as well as self-determination, and it implies a relation of superiority and inferiority. As Razack argues, "[T]he paradigm of saving the Other . . . precludes an examination of how we have contributed to their crises and where our responsibility lies. It is a paradigm that allows us to maintain our own sense of superiority. With its emphasis on pity and compassion, saving the Other can be a position that discourages respect and true belief in the personhood of Others."[22] This construct of superiority is what underlies the lens of Kristof and WuDunn, and is key to what needs to be dismantled and undone in forging accountability and solidarity within and across these divides.

Social Entrepreneurship: The Neoliberal Agenda

While Kristof and WuDunn call for a movement to empower women, it is a movement driven by individuals invested in helping the poor and downtrodden, not a collective movement invested in structural change and social justice. Their model is one of social entrepreneurship, rather than social activism, which speaks to the neoliberal ideology that underlies the project. The "helpers"/"saviors" highlighted in the project are affluent women and men from the "West" who get involved in, support, and/or initiate their own efforts that provide support to poor women of the global south to create better lives for themselves and their families. Kristof and WuDunn emphasize how their involvement in "helping" "others" can make a difference in the immediate quality of life for women while also providing personal as well as financial benefits for the "helpers," and ultimately benefits "us" as well. This is the case because the efforts do not challenge the global structures of power that "we" are implicated in and that are often at the roots of the problems they are addressing.

Kristof and WuDunn suggest that young people are orchestrating this "new movement" and are bringing "new approaches to support-ing women in the developing world." Distinct from aid workers, they "create their own context by starting a new organization, company, or movement to address a social problem in a creative way."[23] Kristof and WuDunn also distinguish them from what they call "traditional liberals"—those who are suspicious of capitalism; in fact, many of these social entrepreneurs, they write, "charge for their services and use a busi-ness model to achieve sustainability."[24] What is left out of their narratives is how these projects are situated in and dependent on a transnational network of power lines built by broader forces, institutions, and policies of global capitalism and imperialism. These are the power lines that both produce the endemic issues of poverty, violence, and corruption and then produce a "need" for international development organizations and agendas to intervene. These organizations, then, create opportunities for full staffs of people from the "West" to "help" people cope with the con-sequences of this same global domination and inequity.

Kristof and WuDunn glorify global economic institutions, like the World Bank and the International Monetary Fund, as benevolent care-takers and champions of poor and developing countries and the women and children within them. Their hope is that the *Half the Sky* book and project will galvanize resources for the "women's empowerment" agenda of these international development initiatives that are largely driven by US geopolitical interests in conjunction with the policies and direc-tives of these global economic institutions. They highlight the World Bank's 2001 report, *Engendering Development through Gender Equality in Rights, Resources, and Voice*, which argues that gender equality is the

226 | RESISTING THE "SAVIOR" COMPLEX

solution to world poverty.[25] They applaud the World Bank and corollary development initiatives for creating an intensive focus on the empowerment of women and girls as a key solution to the world's problems—they call it "the girl effect." A release by the NIKE Corporation about a session on "The Girl Effect" at a Global Forum states, "A safe, healthy, educated, economically empowered girl has the power to solve poverty and ignite progress as an economic actor and future mother. With the right opportunities, she alone will unleash the girl effect. She will marry later, have fewer children, and invest nearly all of her income back into her family. Yet today, less than half a cent of every international development dollar is spent on her."[26] Throughout the book and project, Kristof and WuDunn highlight development institutions such as the United Nations Development Programme, UNICEF, and CARE, as well as the NIKE Foundation and the NoVo Foundation, with projects devoted to empowering women and girls and gender equality through a neoliberal agenda that is all about increasing women's ability to access entry into market economies to become "self-sufficient" and "independent" of "their" cultures and within their own contexts.

Again, what remains invisible in the project is the devastation wrought by these same transnational neoliberal institutions and corporations and the global capitalist interests they represent. When Kristof and WuDunn suggest without any evidence, for instance, that families in Mexico are simply *not interested* in sending their children to school, and that outsiders need to *bribe* families to send them to school, they make it seem as if the problem is something inherent to Mexican people and "their" culture. What they fail to mention is that it was the structural adjustment programs of the International Monetary Fund in the 1980s and 1990s that mandated the cutting of social programs, including education. As Winifred Poster and Zakia Salime, in "The Limits of Microcredit: Transnational Feminism and USAID Activities in the United States and Morocco," point out, the IMF's

> programs for allocating loans to poor countries and the attached debt repayment policies have devastated local economies, particularly by requiring governments to devalue their currencies and suspend basic social services like health care and education. Women are hit the hardest by such measures: They face an intensified burden from taking on second

jobs, a reduction in food and clothing as the limited household resources typically go to men, and an increase in violence.[27]

Thus, it is governmental cuts to public education, and the cost of tuition, that make it most difficult for poor families to enroll their children in school. These costs, in fact, are often prohibitive, and so when push comes to shove, if there is a chance at schooling, some choose to send boys rather than girls because of a sexism bolstered by economic constraints within families. In other words, while structures of patriarchy are at work in these decisions, it is the mandated cuts to education by structural adjustment programs that have made access to education a luxury rather than something that is provided to all. And this is across gender lines. Similarly, when Kristof and WuDunn talk about the dire healthcare situation and its impact on women's health, they fail to mention the mandated cutting of public health by the IMF in lieu of these loans, and how this has created less access to healthcare more broadly. These same global institutions are responsible for the privatization of water and energy resources that communities are then unable to access.

In assessing the economic status and treatment of women in the global south, these institutions and policies are as important as, if not more important than, culture or religion. By limiting the lens to one that views women only in relationship to men, they provide the reader with no understanding of the structures that shape the similar as well as different conditions of life of people in the community with attention to class, religion, caste, and other systems of power. Rather than seeing the roots of women's oppression in relation to men through a lens of cultural backwardness, a broader geopolitical lens allows us to see the roots in the transnational and global capitalist systems that are responsible for endemic poverty, interpersonal, state, and militarized violence, and dire health conditions.

Kristof and WuDunn draw our attention to international development organizations whose mission it is to manage the *effects* of poverty, not to transform the social, economic, and political structures that produce poverty and violence. Their goal is to "empower" individual women to participate in free market capitalism to better cope with the conditions produced by global inequities. Development organizations promote involvement in local or transnational economies to provide subsistence living at the local level while creating cheap and accessible products to people, for instance, in the United States, while producing enormous profits for the transnational corporations. And while, on the one hand, the efforts may make a difference in some women's lives—providing necessary subsistence wages—they are structured in such a way as to *not* address the underlying power systems that produce the problems they are addressing. In fact, these efforts are often dependent upon the very systems and institutions that are responsible for the reproduction of the root causes of poverty and oppression. Making women into small business owners, factory workers, and heads of households, not participants and leaders of collective social movements or activists demanding more accountability of the WTO, IMF, or World Bank, these institutions maintain control over the economic growth and development of these countries and provide access to cheap labor, mineral resources, and military bases for the global north while the women themselves remain at or below poverty level.

The call for a "new" movement, then, is not organized toward social-structural change or economic justice, and it is decidedly disconnected from indigenous justice movements and struggles. Readers with little to no knowledge of the histories behind the stories being told would not have any reference points for the women's movements, nationalist movements, labor movements, peasant movements, environmental movements, or social justice movements indigenous to the areas—including within Afghanistan, India, Pakistan, Nigeria, and the Congo. The authors rarely mention the existence of local and/or transnational feminist and social justice movements whose goals are to transform the broader social structures that produce the conditions of people's lives—the interlocking global social, economic, political structures and systems—except to point out their flaws.

As a result, we are meant to understand that the concerns of this "new" movement with regard to sexism and the devaluation and mistreatment of women are in fact "new" to these countries, while they are simultaneously not relevant to the "West." While "feminists" and "women's advocates" show up here and there in the book, they present them as out of touch with the needs and goals of women in "poor" and developing countries. While they pat themselves on the back for supporting "local" leadership, it is a very specific kind of leadership that is made visible—a leadership that does not challenge global networks and institutions of power, but that is solely focused at the individual, local level. The authors consistently downplay the importance of broader social structural change efforts and feminist initiatives that focus on human rights or mass movement building.

Roots of Poverty

Kristof and WuDunn claim that the sexism and misogyny endemic to the cultures of poor and developing countries are *the* root causes of enduring poverty. Correspondingly, they argue that sexism no longer exists in the "West" because of its modernization through capitalism and free market enterprise—which are their solutions to global poverty. Thus, the solution is an influx of global capitalist structures, practices, and values that would specifically support women's individual empowerment, which they define as access to working in whatever market is available.

Kristof and WuDunn argue that empowerment is dependent on women's own individual initiative. They write the stories in ways that have the women disconnecting from and overcoming the cultural barriers imposed by the men and women in their families and communities. According to them, if individual women would just stand up for themselves against poverty and violence and become economically independent, then systemic oppression would go away and global poverty would disappear. In their words,

> One of the reasons that so many women and girls are kidnapped, trafficked, raped, and otherwise abused is that they grin and bear it. Stoic docility—in particular, acceptance of any decree by a man—is drilled into girls in much of the world from the time they are babies, and so they often do as they are instructed, even when the instruction is to smile while being raped twenty times a day. . . . This is not to blame the victims. There are good practical as well as cultural reasons for women to accept abuse rather than fight back and risk being killed. But the reality is that as long as women and girls allow themselves to be prostituted and beaten, the abuse will continue.[28]

To build this argument, they construct stories about individual women who fight back against incredible brutality and work toward economic independence. They argue that with the "help" of international development agencies, these individual women are now better able to support their families and/or to decrease the violence of their husbands. These stories bolster the idea that if individual women work hard and apply themselves, then poverty and violence will be eradicated. Winifred Poster and Zakia Salime call this "a bottom-up approach to development, in which women are responsible for raising their own economic status by means of small amounts of cash."[29]

According to this development approach, individual women can improve the economic conditions of their families if they start up small local businesses within the informal economy through the assistance of microcredit institutions. While it may be true that these economic opportunities might, to some extent, improve individual women's lives, they do not eradicate poverty, nor do they necessarily increase women's economic and political power or their families' within the broader context. Work in the informal economy is mostly "poorly paid, isolating and routine," it is more "insecure," and it often poses "serious risks to women's safety."[30] According to Poster and Salime, contrary to the promises of economic empowerment, "microcredit ultimately traps low-income families in their socioeconomic position rather than enabling mobility."[31] Again, it is instructive to reflect on what is left out of the stories told in *Half the Sky*. For instance, we do not learn about the constraints of these loans—for example, that the interest rates are very high; that some of the risk-sharing arrangements can be very conflictual; and that the conditions of default are quite stifling.[32] They do not help us understand that these opportunities do not eradicate poverty. While some of the women with micro-enterprises have a few more resources to negotiate the conditions of poverty, the basic social conditions of life within their communities remain, and the structural roots of poverty go unaddressed.

Kristof and WuDunn also celebrate women's employment in factories in Southeast Asia; they argue that these factories significantly contribute to poor women's ability to improve the economic conditions of their lives. From their perspective, what is important is that the women are working and contributing to the GNP of their country *and* that we benefit from the mass production of products available to us at much lower costs because of the "cheap labor." They write, "The economic explosion in Asia was, in large part, an outgrowth of the economic empowerment of women. . . . These factories produced the shoes, toys, and shirts that filled America's shopping malls, generating economic growth rates almost unprecedented in the history of the world—and creating the most effective antipoverty program ever recorded."[33] They do not, however, show any evidence that these jobs eliminate poverty—only that they produce a meager living. They minimize the exploitation, harassment, and discrimination that women face within these transnational corporate factories. In fact, to some extent they celebrate the ways in which sexist ideas and discrimination allow for phenomenal profit growth. They quote a manager of a purse factory saying, "'They have smaller fingers, so they're better at stitching. . . . They're obedient and work harder than men. . . . And we can pay them less.'"[34] The authors do not pause for a second at the statement that "they're obedient" and "we can pay them less." They then quickly dismiss the transnational organizing against the exploitation and abuse of workers of these corporations, saying that the mere fact of being able to work for pay is a luxury. For them, the women are lucky to have a job. They write,

> Implicit in what we're saying about China is something that sounds shocking to many Americans: Sweatshops have given women a boost. Americans mostly hear about the inequities of garment factories, and they are real—the forced overtime, the sexual harassment, the dangerous conditions. Yet women and girls still stream to such factories. . . . In most poor countries, women don't have many job options. . . . The factories prefer young women, perhaps because they're more docile and perhaps because their small fingers are more nimble for assembly or sewing. So the rise of manufacturing has generally raised the opportunities and status of women.
>
> The implication is that instead of denouncing sweatshops, we in the West should be encouraging manufacturing in poor countries, particularly in Africa and the Muslim world.[35]

Within this neoliberal paradigm, Kristof and WuDunn rarely address the geopolitical forces that shape the scope of what is possible for women living in northern India, the Congo, or Southeast Asia. Again the authors leave out the broader forces that root these social conditions such as a history of colonialism, a history of imperialist war and invasion. Instead, they portray the problems as rooted in timeless traditional cultures that, for the authors, need to be modernized through the benefits of global capitalism, which is equated with freedom and equality, though it is only a freedom from private and/or cultural confinement and freedom to earn subsistence wages and experience displacement from home communities to be exploited for one's obedience to the demands of transnational corporations.

Roots of Violence

The interpretive lens of Kristof and WuDunn is one that focuses in on an exclusively *gender-divided* world in "developing" and "poor" countries where women are the victims and men are the perpetrators of violence. The authors portray the men from the global south as either inherently brutal and violent, or lazy and irresponsible (both constructions synchronistic with the portrayal of men of color and immigrant men from the global south in the dominant culture of the United States). While they argue that the cultural roots of misogyny are deeply embedded in the men and women living within these particular cultures, they focus on building support, resources, and programming for *women's* empowerment, as opposed to *community* empowerment. In the stories told, the men of the global south are seen mostly as irredeemable, and of course, given this, they are presented as separate and distinct from "western" men. Gender differences between women and men in the global south are presented as predetermined and inevitable, and these differences provide the justification for the focus on supporting and/or rescuing women and girls from their cultures that are dominated by men.

With regard to poverty, for instance, Kristof and WuDunn consistently describe the men of the global south as lazy and selfish. They paint a portrait of adult men drinking away their families' money and resources, and/or frequenting women in prostitution. In one of their most sweeping portraits, they write, "Many African and Indian men now consider beer indispensable and their daughters' education a luxury. The service of a prostitute is deemed essential; a condom is a frill."[36] They conclude, "If poor families spent only as much on educating their children as they do on beer and prostitutes, there would be a breakthrough in the prospects of poor countries."[37]

When not portraying these men as lazy and shiftless, Kristof and WuDunn tell stories about *these* men's propensity for brutal violence against women. Again, they make broad, sweeping statements suggesting that gender-based violence is "ubiquitous in much of the developing world, inflicting far more casualties than any war."[38] The following statements are representative of these overarching racist claims.

> Now it is increasingly common for men in South Asia or Southeast Asia to take sulfuric acid and hurl it in the faces of girls or women who have spurned them.[39]

> In many poor countries, the problem is not so much individual thugs and rapists but an entire culture of sexual predation.[40]

> Ethiopia is "where kidnapping and raping girls is a time-honored tradition."[41]

The authors provide *no evidence* for any of these statements, and yet these claims become the backdrop of the specific stories they tell. Their overarching claims are rooted in a deeply racist, ethnocentric and imperialist culture and context that depends on such ideas for its claims of superiority, of having all the answers, and of justifying any type of intervention when it aligns with its own geopolitical interests. And yet because these ideas are so entrenched, they become "common knowledge" facts, disconnected from geopolitical realities, and are assumed to be representative of entire cultures, regions, and nations.

It can be hard to step outside of the stories in order to critically engage their construction. The stories they construct of rape and violence are compelling and heart-wrenching. The stories are told in ways that elicit both pity and outrage, and their ability to do so is connected to the very particular discourse and logic within which the stories are held, which decontextualize the violence from its social and geopolitical roots.[42] Ethnocentric, racist, and imperialist logics locate the roots of violence, like poverty, in isolated pathological cultures, and obscure historical and contemporary transnational geopolitics. And it is actually the United States' active participation in these geopolitics that generates both their interpretive framework for the violence as well as the gendered oppression and violence that they are simultaneously addressing.

For example, the authors label the Congo as the "world capital of rape"[43] and describe it as a "cauldron of violence and misogyny."[44] No doubt the widespread rape and sexual violence against women in the Congo is horrific, but they explain it as a cultural problem, rather than a social and political problem. They offer imperialist and racist interpretations that invite our pity as "outsiders," with little understanding of how we might be implicated in the problems themselves. They avoid any discussion of the historical and geopolitical context of colonization, imperial interventions, and transnational conflicts for control over the Congo's mineral resources. The result is that they obscure the role of the United States in fueling this endemic violence and the ongoing instability of the country and thus avoid any consideration of US accountability. For example, Kristof and WuDunn do not tell us that our deep dependence on these mineral resources is, in part, what fuels the ongoing conflicts and violence in the region. As Muadi Mukenge with Kady and Stanton, in a Global Fund Report, *Funding a Women's Movement against Sexual Violence in the Democratic Republic of Congo: 2004–2009*, point out, the Congo is home to "80 percent of the world's reserves of coltan—the industrial name for tantalum—and 1/3 percent of its cobalt, the world's largest share."[45] These minerals are integral to the aviation, telecommunications, and defense industries, with the United States as the largest user of cobalt. These mineral resources are at the center of the political and economic conflict in the Congo, not internal ethnic or cultural struggles or misogyny against women, although the struggle over them becomes one where ethnic, gender, class, and religious differences become embedded into the conflicts. In addition, the authors do not address how the United States has been integrally involved in and connected with the Congo's historical development—it is not a separate and distinct country or region from the United States. For example, Kristof and WuDunn do not mention the US-sponsored dictatorship of President Mobutu (1965–1997), an era Mukenge et al. say was "characterized by ruthless repression of political opposition and freedom of expression."[46] Since 1998, with the fall of this dictatorship, "Northeastern Congo . . . has borne the brunt of brutal military campaigns . . . as foreign and local armies vie for control of lucrative mines. The governments of Rwanda and Uganda in particular, with the firm backing of the West, have interfered in Congo's political affairs, committed mass atrocities, and led the plunder of lucrative minerals while serving as a conduit to a plethora of multinationals."[47]

Additionally, as Mukenge points out, the current tactics of sexual violence are not, in fact, *indigenous cultural* practices, but rather they originated with the rule of King Leopold II of Belgium from 1885 to 1908. The colonialists were the ones who introduced sexual violence as a tool of community control; Mukenge et al. write that they used an "unimaginable array of rapes, in front of husbands, forced rapes among family members, sexual torture, the introduction of objects into women's bodies, and kidnappings. . . . The aim of these atrocities is to humiliate everyone involved, assert control, traumatize families and communities, and force the population into obedience."[48]

With a transnational lens on the violence, our understanding of the devastating impact of these militarized conflicts would shift from a focus solely on women to an understanding of women within the context of their communities. Mukenge with Kady and Stanton offer a wider scope of interpretation while continuing to center sexual violence; they write,

> Over the past decade, up to half a million Congolese women and girls have been raped by multiple armies from Congo and neighboring countries, often as part of a strategy to humiliate communities, destroy social structures and norms, and control territory for mining. Weapons that easily make their way across Congo's borders facilitate this terror campaign. The region has seen massive population displacement, disruption of agricultural activities, and acute poverty.[49]

In 2004, the authors report that the systemic rape of women occurred in a context where over three million people had been displaced, unemployment was over 85 percent, 50 percent of children were not in school because of tuition costs, and only 6 percent had access to electricity. Moreover, while sexual violence against women is rampant, so is sexual violence against men and boys. Widening our lens to include the context and the multiple forms of violence mandates further investigation, a more complex interpretive framework, and a different set of responses.

This social, geopolitical, and economic context is essential in any discussion of sexual violence in the region. When we do not understand the political roots and context of the ongoing conflict, and the US relationship to it, we may more readily accept the ethnocentric racism that locates the problem as inherent to Congolese men and Congolese culture. When we do broaden our understanding, we recognize that, in fact, the United States is *not* an innocent and disinterested bystander, and that our "desire" to "help" *them* as if they are the source of the problem must be critically challenged. Instead, we might begin with the recognition of how we contribute to and benefit from the conflict in the Congo, and how US foreign policy has a role in creating and perpetuating it. When we begin from that location of accountability, we are led to different responses.

Organizations and initiatives that seek to cultivate accountability in the United States for our contributions to the war-torn violence in the Congo, including sexual violence and rape, offer alternative responses. They approach solidarity through a lens of respect, mutuality, and reciprocity, rather than through a lens of "saving," which presumes that we are "outsiders," superior, and located completely outside of the context of "their" problems. The Friends of the Congo provide solid critical analysis that situates the roots of violence, including rape and sexual violence, within a broad historical and geopolitical context, rather than within a homogenous, static culture, and their solidarity strategies direct us toward human rights and corporate accountability.[50] Most importantly, they help people in the United States understand our intricate relationship to these issues through our use of cell phones and other technology. In arguing against US militarism as a solution to the brutal violence and massacres in Northeast Congo, they write, "This massacre is directly related to the highly profitable plunder of minerals, such as coltan, tungsten and cobalt, vital to our cell phones and computers."[51] The struggle for control and profit over these minerals that corporations are highly involved in fueling is at the root of this violence, and more militarism or military aid will not contribute to addressing the real needs and hopes of the Congolese people. They urge us to consider our own implication in the violence, and to see ourselves, then, as having a stake in transforming its roots. Another organization, Rights and Accountability in Development (RAID), is also focused on corporate accountability with respect to the human rights responsibilities of companies. RAID "works to hold companies to account for illegal and unethical practices by helping victims to obtain redress, and by campaigning for stronger domestic and international mechanisms of regulation for business."

Roots of Terrorism

Not only do Kristof and WuDunn argue that women's oppression is *the* cause of poverty, but they argue that cultures that oppress women are also ones that breed terrorism and extremism. This links their agenda directly to the US "war on terrorism" and supports US militarism in the service of imperialism. Similar to their analysis of poverty and violence against women, they argue that sexism is a chief cause of terrorism and extremism, as opposed to political, social and/or material causes. This discourse is powerful given that the US media offers little perspective on the root-cause explanations for the terrorist attacks of 9/11. Alsultany, in *Arabs and Muslims in the Media*, argues that the media mostly obscures "the 'why' of the story so that political violence perpetrated by Arabs or Muslims is decontextualized and portrayed as senseless. . . . What commonly stands in for the 'why' is framing Islam as having a propensity for terrorism through a subcoding of race, gender, and sexuality."[52]

Kristof and WuDunn follow this formula as well. They use cultural and religious explanations for terrorism, rather than geopolitical frameworks. There is no reference to the ongoing impacts of colonialism and imperialism, including the role of US foreign policy and global neoliberal capitalism in the conflicts. In *Half the Sky*, the authors single out Islamic cultures and contexts for breeding terrorism, which, they argue, has its roots in the marginalization of women. In their chapter "Is Islam Misogynistic?" their answer is nuanced but decidedly, I would argue that their answer is "yes." Aware that it would be, as they say, "politically incorrect" to say that Islam is inherently misogynistic, the chapter suggests that while Islam may not be misogynistic in the abstract, Muslim cultures have strong tendencies toward misogyny, marginalization, and oppression of women, as well as toward terrorism.[53]

They claim that women's marginalization is more extreme in predominantly Muslim countries, and they suggest that Islamic culture "takes on the testosterone-laden culture of a military camp or a high-school boys' locker room. . . . Indeed, some scholars say they believe the reason Muslim countries have been disproportionately afflicted by terrorism is not Islamic teachings about infidels or violence but rather the low levels of female education and participation in the labor force."[54] One reason they offer for what they call a "boom in Muslim terrorists in recent decades" is what they call a "youth bulge in Islam," which they attribute to "lagging efforts on family planning—and the broader marginalization of women."[55]

These arguments feed into the gendered and orientalist logics deeply entrenched in the "war on terror" orchestrated by the United States since the invasion of Afghanistan in 2001. Within this logic, they uncritically glorify the US military commitment to "saving Afghan women" as evidence of US commitment to gender equity and interest in women's empowerment and in women as a tool in fighting terrorism. They write, "[T]he Joint Chiefs of Staff and international security specialists are puzzling over how to increase girls' education in countries like Afghanistan."[56] This framework provides a very distorted understanding of US foreign policy and the ways it is being implemented in Iraq and Afghanistan, among many other locations. It ignores the extensive US role in the rise of the Taliban and in the political conflict, occupations, and wars of the last forty years, as well as the pervasive sexism, misogyny, and sexual violence in the US military itself, both in terms of sexual harassment and rape of women in the US military as well as sexual harassment and rape of Afghan women. If these geopolitical explanations were drawn upon, it would shift the scrutiny from culture to politics, from an exclusive focus on "them" to an exploration of "our" own involvement, contributions, and accountability for terrorism.[57]

In general, it is unimaginable in the world drawn by Kristof and WuDunn that men in the global south are involved in women's lives in any way but negatively. This too is an extremely narrow lens produced by imperial frameworks. While sexist and patriarchal structures may be operating in communities in the global south, as they are in the so-called West, this does not mean that brutality and violence are the only dynamics that define people's lives in communities. For example, mainstream media in the United States, as in *Half the Sky*, offered a portrayal of a very gender-divided and hostile world for women in Afghanistan under the Taliban. Within the most dominant narrative, it was next to impossible to imagine anything other than brutal and violent Afghan men terrorizing Afghan women. However, this left out the multitudes of Afghan men who never supported the Taliban and who continue to be engaged in resistance to the Taliban's restrictions and brutal treatment of women as well as their brutal treatment of whole communities. And it left out the brutality of US and NATO troops engaged in multiple forms and levels of violence, including sexualized violence against women.

Reading and learning from Afghan women activists who make visible the multiple roots of oppression and violence experienced by women as well as men in Afghanistan, and the multiple trajectories of resistance to it, significantly widen our perspectives.[58] For instance, in Joya's political memoir, *A Woman among Warlords*, she describes the multiple sources of violence against women, fueled by US military occupation, as well as stories of the many men and women in Afghanistan who are involved in daily resistance against oppression and violence brought on by local as well as international forces. Joya makes visible the common struggles Afghan men face along with Afghan women—lack of access to healthcare and education and loss of relatives and friends to the thirty-five-plus years of war, displacement, and sexual abuse, among other traumas.[59] Anne Brodsky, in *With All Our Strength: The Revolutionary Association of the Women of Afghanistan (RAWA)*, offers a detailed analysis of how RAWA works with men as allies and supporters in its struggles against the Taliban as well as against imperial forces, including the United States. She documents stories of men who have resisted the extremist forces and their treatment of women, and who have supported women in their families and communities against the sexism and misogyny of the warlords and militias.[60]

Shared Struggles/Interconnected Contexts

What is most problematic in *Half the Sky* is what is most integral to its popularity and the enthusiastic response it has garnered across the country. And that is the idea that "we" are distinctly and wholly different from and superior to the peoples, cultures, and religions in so-called poor and developing countries. Its resonance for US readers is connected to how deeply embedded these discursive distinctions are to the US image of itself and how this discourse leads to knee-jerk justifications for imperial interventions over "there." These are interventions that are often more about geopolitical interests, but must be couched in an imperial discourse that makes intervention a righteous cause, rather than a brutal takeover to secure control and power over a region. These hegemonic discourses of "us" and "them" serve a number of functions in an unjust and unequal world—they create uncritical justifications for military interventions and occupations, they erase how the United States is implicated in the production of poverty and violence, and they obscure the shared struggles across borders and contexts.

In *Half the Sky*, for instance, the authors describe and decry the brutal violence against poor women in so-called developing countries while presenting the United States as a place of safety, equality, and freedom for women—a postfeminist, postracial, post-inequality environment. The United States is presented as a model of progressive change that they hope to instill over "there." They reference the injustice of slavery, for instance, but as something that is set in the past, with no impact on the present. They ignore, minimize, and deny endemic violence in the United States in order to solidify both US superiority as a model for change and to enlist people from the United States who, because there are no problems "here," have the freedom and opportunity to contribute to the poor and downtrodden over "there."

Their ethnocentric, imperialist logics fall apart when we make visible the endemic violence against women in the United States—in our institutions, including in families, schools, hospitals, prisons, law enforcement, religious institutions (e.g., churches, mosques, synagogues), and in the military. Women of color and immigrants from the global south in the United States experience multilayered surveillance, profiling, abuse, and violence by the police, prison guards, and immigration and homeland security forces.[61] Gender and sexual nonconformity is consistently met with punishment and violence by the police, the schools, and other institutions. Transgendered folks, butch lesbians, effeminate men and boys, in particular people of color, face daily state, street, and institutional violence, as well as higher rates of incarceration—very much connected to gender presentation rooted in histories of colonization and white supremacy.[62] There continue to be pervasive sexual, racial, and homophobic harassment, rape, and violence in schools; child sexual abuse and homophobic violence is pervasive in families; there has been rampant sexual abuse against women and men in the Catholic Church and other religious institutions.[63]

Additionally, the assumption that people in the United States are free to dress, to love, and to engage in sexual activity without negative consequences is untenable. While the US government claims to be "saving" Afghan women from the Taliban for its violence against women who do not wear the *burqa* in public, it is also the case that Muslim women in the United States who wear the *burqa* and other forms of veiling face daily harassment as well as discriminatory treatment in employment, education, and other arenas because of their association with Islam. Gender policing is a significant issue in the United States, albeit it may "look" different. For instance, girls and women in the United States who wear "sexy" clothes are seen as "asking for it" and are blamed for any sexual harassment, rape, and violence that they experience. Queer, gender queer, and trans-identified people who transgress the rigid boundaries of gender in dress are met with hostility and violence as well as being subject to employment and educational discrimination. In the United States, there continues to be an obsessive focus on "virginity" and "chastity" in the form of abstinence-only education, chastity balls, and institutionalized stigma against sexually active girls and women, particularly those involved in the sex trade. That is, there is persistent mistreatment and violence against women categorized as "sluts" and "whores," including transgender women, who then are seen as not rapeable or worth protecting. Poor women in the sex trade are criminalized and incarcerated for their involvement in the sex trade, and this is linked to their vulnerability to sexual violence by law enforcement as well as within prisons.

There is an increased gap between the rich and poor in this country, and like the poor countries referenced in *Half the Sky*, the United States has shifted its approach to social services and education. In the United States, we have seen severe cuts in healthcare, welfare, education, and community mental health projects, and a massive increase in criminalization of poverty, mental illness, and drug addiction, among other social problems. There is a move toward privatization of social services, which means less access to mental health services or support for people experiencing everyday forms of interpersonal physical, sexual, and other forms of violence.

This is not an argument that everything is the same in the United States as it is in the global south; we do not have external military occupation nor an ongoing civil war nor massive displacement. And we must recognize substantial differences; it is not an argument that it is worse or better here or there. As Moraga argues, "There is no hierarchy of oppressions." And yet, a critical consciousness about the endemic inequities and violence "here" shifts our orientation in engaging with those who are struggling and resisting interconnected forces in other parts of the world.

From "Saving" to Accountability

In this chapter, I have sought to offer critical questions regarding the deeply problematic logics of *Half the Sky* and to shift the lens towards a transnational feminism for support and solidarity with women in the global south that is grounded in an ethics and politics of accountability, rather than "saving." As Sherene Razack illuminates, "On the one hand if we understand the realities of groups subordinate to us as different or special, we plunge into hierarchy: we become saviours of less fortunate peoples."[64] A "helping" mentality bolsters the underlying structure of white supremacy. It does not challenge the structure of power as it assumes that the problems reside in the person or group, not in the structures of domination. Razack argues, "Instead of seeking to save women we consider less fortunate than ourselves, we might begin to organize against the racism that structures migration and flight, and that continues to structure the lives of women fleeing to the North."[65]

Such a shift requires us to critically interrogate the interconnectedness of "us" and "them." It requires an analysis that situates our lives, and the social conditions of our lives, as interconnected (not disparate nor isolated) across contexts, as interwoven in the histories of inequality, colonialism, imperialism, and white supremacy that shape the differential relations between and among us. In other words, it requires that we recognize our locations within these systems, and how forging alliances across these divides requires that we relate in ways that do not reproduce these systems based in hierarchy and notions of superiority and inferiority, but rather foster relations of equality, accountability, and reciprocity.

ACKNOWLEDGMENTS

This book reflects the work of many organizers, healers, artists, poets, activists, visionaries, educators, and scholars with whom I have learned, worked, struggled, commiserated, and dreamed. Many of us have experienced harm, and many of us have participated in harm, and many of us are struggling toward individual and collective healing and accountability. It has been in these communities of struggle where I have been able to practice new ways of relating, living, and organizing grounded in collective efforts to build a future with love and justice at its center. The ideas contained within the book have emerged through workshops, conferences, nonferences, teach-ins, community gatherings, circles, classrooms, and more. They also emerge from the collective work of organizations, projects, and initiatives. None of this has been easy because of how deeply entrenched these systems of structural oppression are in our identities, relationships, and communities, and so I have experienced and witnessed such heartbreak, hurt, mistakes, and blunders throughout my time within feminist, queer, antiracist, and anti-imperialist movements. And yet I continue to learn with others, and we continue to practice and build together toward healing, accountability, social change, and transformation.

I cannot begin to thank everyone who has contributed to the ideas, examples, practices, strategies, and more that I explore in the book. I can say without a doubt that these are not *my* ideas, but the ideas that have emerged from the collective work, mostly led by feminists of color and feminists of the global south, as well as queer, trans, and gender-nonconforming feminists, that I have been able to participate in through my reading, organizing, teaching, and activism. This book would not exist without the work and inspiration of Incite! Women of Color Against Violence, Generation Five, Creative Interventions, Critical Resistance, and the Storytelling and Organizing Project, which cultivated a national conversation around community accountability and transformative justice. It would not exist without the knowledge and imagination of the feminists of color, transnational feminists, feminists of the global south, queer and trans feminists, and more who continue to direct us toward feminisms of the future, where no one is left behind, where we can build from our differences, where we can hold the complexities and contradictions of our lives, where we can forge a new way of living with and for one another.

I am more than indebted to the fierce, compassionate, and powerful leadership of Mariame Kaba and Shira Hassan, who have, over the many years I have known them, initiated, led, and developed community accountability and transformative justice spaces and practices in Chicago and beyond. Along with them, I have learned from a wide range of organizers, advocates, scholars, and artists in Chicago, including Kay Ulanday Barrett, Hiranmayi Bhatt, Veronica Bohanon, Mary Scott Boria, Rachel Caidor, Ada Cheng, Mayadet Cruz, Jen Curley, Misty DeBerry, Ana Romero Diaz, Stacy Erenberg, Keisha Farmer-Moore, Iliana Figueroa, Laurie Fuller, Claudia Garcia-Rojas, Cheryl Graves, Sabrina Hampton, Jane Hereth, Tanuja Jagernauth, Alice Kim, Deana Lewis, Erica Meiners, Joey Mogul, Carrie Morris, Pidgeon Pagonis, Manju Rajendran, Barbara Ransby, Sangeetha Ravichandran, Sarah Ji Rhee, Beth Richie, Andrea Ritchie, Lu Rocha, Chez Rumpf, Ora Schub, Erin Tinnon, Michelle VanNatta, Adaku Utah, and Daisy Zamora. And I have grown immensely through my participation in workshops offered in Chicago and beyond by Shakti Butler, Alexis Pauline Gumbs, Rachel Herzing, Isaac Ontiveros, Mimi Kim, and Mia Mingus, among others. I want to thank those whom I interviewed in 2010 and 2011 for being so generous to sit with me and share their stories, struggles, and wisdom around accountability. Unfortunately, the tapes from those interviews were lost in the shuffle of many moves of offices and computers in the last ten years. Still, these conversations continue to shape my ideas and journey. Those interviewed include Lara Brooks, Jen Curley, Shira Hassan, Cyd Jenefsky, Mariame Kaba, Mimi Kim, Brian Ragsdale, Penny Rosenwasser, and Adaku Utah.

I have deep gratitude for the thousands of students in my classes who have taught me how to learn and grow together in community. I want to thank in particular those who have worked with me in the Building Communities, Ending Violence (BCEV) project at DePaul, including

Michele Emery, who cofounded the project with me in 2010, as well as Hannah Arwe, Shana Bahemat, Nihan Can, Satya Chima, N. A. Clark, Asher Diaz, Joy Ellison, Mary Hazboun, Sydney Haliburton, Katie Heinekamp, Jill Kuanfung, Caitlyn Lomonte, Buki Ogundipe, Clare Stuber. BCEV has enjoyed great partnerships with faculty and staff at DePaul, including Misty DeBerry, Stefani Mikos, Michael Riley, and Katy Weseman, among others, as well as from beautiful collaborations with my dear friends and colleagues Misty DeBerry and Laurie Fuller. I have also benefited from a strong community of faculty and staff at DePaul whom I have had the honor of collaborating with on social change and justice projects within and outside of DePaul, including Irene Beck, Enora Brown, Sumi Cho, Valerie Johnson, Amor Kohli, Leo Masalihit, Kalyani Menon, Michele Morano, Christina Rivers, Lourdes Sullivan, and John Zeigler, as well as Katrina Caldwell, Namita Goswami, Harvette Grey, Sandra Jackson, Ted Manley, and Elsa Saeta, who have since left DePaul.

I am also indebted to the many scholars and scholar-activists whose work has been essential in pushing me and stretching me to expand my understanding of the interlocking systems of capitalism, white supremacy, heteronormativity, patriarchy, ableism, and imperialism, among others, as well as the need for developing a praxis of accountability in our feminist work to end violence. There are too many to name here, but you will see their words, insights, and wisdom through the book.

The book represents a collective process and brings together what I have been learning through my work with many community organizations, including at different times the Broadway Youth Center, Community Justice for Youth Institute, Love and Protect, Project Nia, Chicago Freedom School, Just Practice, Survived and Punished, the Women and Girls Collective Action Network and Females United for Action (FUFA), Young Women's Action Team, and the Young Women's Empowerment Project, among many others, as well as the Building Communities, Ending Violence Project and the Difficult Dialogues group connected to the Cultural Center at DePaul in the mid-2000s. I have also deeply benefited from workshops and trainings I have been able to participate in both in and outside of Chicago with Creative Interventions, Communities United Against Violence, Critical Resistance, Generation Five, and the Storytelling and Organizing Project.

I have struggled over many years to write this book, and for some years, was close to giving up. I am deeply appreciative of Ilene Kalish from New York University Press, who provided support, encouragement, and patience as I made my way toward completion of this project. I was very lucky to learn about Kerry Ann Rockquemore's National Center for Faculty Development and Diversity and, in particular, its Faculty Success Program. Thanks to the generous support of Beth Catlett and the Department of Women's and Gender Studies and the former dean of the College of Liberal Arts and Sciences, Chuck Suchar, I was able to obtain the funding to enroll in the Faculty Success Program, where I learned to commit to a daily practice of writing thirty minutes a day. This practice, and the online accountability groups, changed my relationship to writing and to the book. This book would not be where it is today without this program. I am also grateful for the support of the University Research Council for a research leave in 2009–2010, as well as the Summer Research Grant from the College of Liberal Arts and Sciences. These provided me with space and time to work on the project. As I worked to complete the project, I received daily support from students working in the Women's Center, including Victoria Agunod, Olivia LaFlamme, Kiana Lewis, Alexis Redick, Fabiola Rosiles, Sarah Scriven, and Jax Witzig. I also want to thank former student Clare Stuber for her astute editorial guidance and support on the book. And I am appreciative of those at NYU Press, particularly Maryam Arain, Alexia Traganas, and Emily Wright, who guided the book along to publication.

I have deep gratitude for my dear colleagues and friends who nourished me with deep conversations, who pulled me into many projects and initiatives, and who provided me with deep support and care throughout the writing of this book. I want to thank in particular Aimee Carrillo Rowe, Beth Catlett, Amina Chaudhri, Jen Curley, Misty DeBerry, Laila Farah, Laurie Fuller, Cricket Keating, Sheena Malhotra, Erica Meiners, Anne Mitchell, Julie Moody-Freeman, Sanjukta Mukherjee, Penny Rosenwasser, Kathryn Sorrells, Choua Vue, and Daisy Zamora.

I am deeply indebted to my dear friend Lourdes Torres for her ongoing love and support throughout the project. She read many versions of many chapters and provided a great critical eye—often asking deep and hard questions that pushed me to work toward speaking to a wider audience. Through her questions, she made me understand the significant stakes that underlie the book. I have enormous gratitude for my niece Demitria ("Meechie") Pates, who has been a constant source of love and support, and who reminds me daily of the importance of showing up and being there for one another. I would also like to thank the members of my beloved family, Laura Castaneda, Philip and Phyliss Royster, Rebecca Royster, Nicholas Russo, and Mark and Becky Russo, and Cheryl L. West as well as Michele and John Carruthers, Tara Hamilton, Alexandra Pates, Rusel-Busisiwe Quaery, Rose and Steve Rosdahl, Barry Shuchter and Shirin Lee, and John and Susan Russo, who have provided beautiful support and encouragement over these many years.

This book would simply not have been possible without the deep love and daily support of my partner in life, Francesca ("Frannie") Royster. She inspires me daily with her never-ending and unconditional love, her everyday brilliance, her generous and vibrant spirit, and the eternal sunshine she brings to whatever is before us. She read chapters, pulled me out of the many self-doubt-generated doldrums I experienced over these years, brought incredible joy and fun into our lives, and inspired me with her own dedication to the work of writing! Finally, I have such gratitude for my dear daughter, Cece, who brings continuous joy, love, and laughter into our lives, and whose future is very much at the heart of this book's communal and transformative project and vision.

NOTES

INTRODUCTION

1 I use the term "we" and "us" in the book to indicate my own participation in these movements and thus to implicate myself in the dynamics of which I am talking rather than presuming that I am outside of the critical analyses as well as practices that I am proposing.

2 Aimee Carrillo Rowe, *Power Lines: On the Subject of Feminist Alliances* (Durham, NC: Duke University Press, 2008), 3.

3 Morgan Bassichis, "Reclaiming Queer and Trans Safety," in *The Revolution Starts at Home: Confronting Intimate Violence within Activist Communities*, edited by Ching-In Chen, Jai Dulani, Leah Lakshmi Piepzna-Samarasinha (Oakland, CA: AK Press, 2016), 3–24.

4 E.g., M. Jacqui Alexander, *Pedagogies of Crossing* (Durham, NC: Duke University Press, 2006), Patricia Hill Collins, *Black Feminist Thought* (New York: Routledge, 1990); Kimberlé Crenshaw, "Mapping the Margins: Intersectionality, Identity Politics, and Violence against Women," *Stanford Law Review* 43, no. 6 (1991): 1244–91; Audre Lorde, *Sister Outsider* (Toronto, Canada: Crossing Press, 1994 [2007]), Cherríe Moraga and Gloria Anzaldúa, eds., *This Bridge Called My Back: Writings by Radical Women of Color* (Albany, NY: Kitchen Table: Women of Color Press, 1981), Chandra Talpade Mohanty, Ann Russo, Lourdes Torres, eds., *Third World Women and the Politics of Feminism* (Bloomington: Indiana University Press, 1991); Chandra Talpade Mohanty, *Feminism without Borders* (Durham, NC: Duke University Press, 2003), Sherene Razack, *Looking White People in the Eye: Gender, Race, and Culture in Classrooms and Courtrooms* (Toronto: University of Toronto Press, 1998), among many others.

5 Mary Louise Fellows and Sherene Razack, "Race to Innocence: Confronting Hierarchical Relations among Women," *Journal of Gender, Race & Justice* 1 (1997): 335.

6 Carrillo Rowe, *Power Lines*.

7 Mary Elizabeth Hobgood, *Dismantling Privilege: An Ethics of Accountability* (Cleveland, OH: Pilgrim Paperback, 2000), 16.

8 Beth Richie, *Arrested Justice: Black Women, Violence, and the Prison Nation* (New York: NYU Press, 2012); Ann Russo, *Taking Back Our Lives* (New York: Routledge, 2001).

9 Razack, *Looking White People*, 10.

10 Ibid., 159.

11 Simona Sharoni, *Gender and the Israeli-Palestinian Conflict: The Politics of Women's Resistance* (Syracuse, NY: Syracuse University Press, 1995).

12 Ibid., 141.

13 Ibid., 145.

14 Razack, *Looking White People.*

CHAPTER 1. BUILDING COMMUNITIES

1 Connie Burk, "Think. Re-Think: Accountable Communities," in *The Revolution Starts at Home: Confronting Intimate Violence within Activist Communities* (Oakland, CA: AK Press, 2016), 267.

2 Carolyn Boyes-Watson, *Peacemaking Circles and Urban Youth* (St. Paul, MN: Living Justice Press, 2013), 110–11.

3 Ibid., 112.

4 bell hooks, *Teaching Community* (New York: Routledge, 2003), 36.

5 Chris Crass, *Towards Collective Liberation: Anti-Racist Organizing, Feminist Praxis, and Movement Building Strategy* (Oakland, CA: PM Press, 2013).

6 Sharon Welch, *Sweet Dreams in America: Making Ethics and Spirituality Work* (New York: Routledge, 1999), 26.

7 Ellen Kaye Scott, "From Race Cognizance to Racism Cognizance," in *Feminism and Antiracism: International Struggles for Justice*, edited by Kathleen Blee and Frances Winddance Twine (New York: NYU Press, 2001), 126.

8 Tema Okun, *The Emperor Has No Clothes: Teaching about Race and Racism to People Who Don't Want to Know* (Charlotte, NC: Information Age Publishing, 2010), 58.

9 Fellows and Razack, "Race to Innocence."

10 Scott, "From Race Cognizance," 125.

11 Fellows and Razack, "Race to Innocence," 338.

12 Aurora Levins Morales, *Medicine Stories* (Boston: South End Press, 1998), 76.

13 Ibid.

14 Ibid.

15 This group no longer exists; it was a group of white queer activists in Chicago in the late 1990s and early 2000s, who collaborated with a queer people of color group—the Color Triangle, which was connected to Horizons, an LGBT service and activist organization in Chicago.

16 Derrick Bell, *Faces at the Bottom of the Well* (New York: Basic Books, 1993); Reginald Hudlin and Warrington Hudlin, directors, *Space Traders* (HBO, 1994).

17 Ibid.

18 Leslie Roman, "White Is a Color! White Defensiveness, Postmodernism, and Anti-racist Pedagogy," in *Race, Identity, and Representation in Education*, 2nd ed., edited by Cameron McCarthy and Warren Crichlow (New York: Routledge, 2005), 84.

19 Shakti Butler's talk given at DePaul University during a premier showing of her film, *Cracking the Codes: The System of Racial Inequity* (World Trust, 2012), https://crackingthecodes.org.

20 Peggy McIntosh, "White Privilege: Unpacking the Invisible Knapsack," *Peace and Freedom* (July–August 1989): 10–12; Michael Kimmel and Abby Ferber, eds., *Privilege: A Reader* (Boulder, CO: Westview, 2003).

21 Mia McKenzie, *Black Girl Dangerous* (Oakland, CA: BGD Press, 2014), 140.

22 Mab Segrest, *Born to Belonging: Writings on Spirit and Justice* (New Brunswick, NJ: Rutgers University Press, 2002), 158.

23 Mariame Kaba, Panel on "Making Connections and Building Alliances," DePaul University, 11 February 2015.

24 hooks, *Teaching Community*, 61.

25 Twelfth annual White Privilege conference, "This Land Is Whose Land? Defining Citizenship, Understanding Access, Taking Action," in Minneapolis, Minnesota. www.whiteprivilegeconference.com.

26 Welch, *Sweet Dreams*, 33.

27 White Privilege Conference Caucuses, explained on White Privilege Conference website, www.whiteprivilegeconference.com.

28 Welch, *Sweet Dreams*, 44.

29 Ngoc Loan Trân, "Calling IN: A Less Disposable Way of Holding Each Other Accountable," *Black Girl Dangerous*, 18 December 2013, http://www.blackgirldangerous.org.

30 Ibid.

31 Ibid.

32 Okun, *The Emperor Has No Clothes*, 93.

33 Ibid., 97.

34 Sangtin Writers and Richa Nagar, *Playing with Fire* (Minneapolis: University of Minnesota Press, 2006).

35 Ibid.

36 Carillo Rowe, *Power Lines*, 10–11.

37 Dorothy Allison, *Skin: Essays on Sex, Class, and Literature* (Whittier, NC: Firebrand Press, 1994).

38 Welch, *Sweet Dreams*, 26.

CHAPTER 2. NAVIGATING SPEECH AND SILENCE

1 Carrillo Rowe, *Power Lines*.

2 Maria Lugones and Elizabeth Spelman, "Have We Got a Theory for You! Feminist Theory, Cultural Imperialism, and the Demand for 'The Woman's Voice,'" *Women's Studies International Forum* 6, no. 6 (1983): 580.

3 Lynet Uttal, "Nods That Silence," in *Making Face/Making Soul: Haciendo Caras*, edited by Gloria Anzaldúa (San Francisco: Aunt Lute Books), 319.

4 Megan Boler, *Feeling Power: Emotions and Education* (New York: Routledge, 1999), 164.

5 Ibid., 166.

6 Audrey Thompson, "Listening and Its Asymmetries," *Curriculum Inquiry* 33, no. 1 (2003): 86.

7 Ibid.
8 Ibid., 86–87.
9 Ibid., 86.
10 Cynthia Enloe, *The Curious Feminist: Searching for Women in a New Age of Empire* (Berkeley: University of California Press, 2004), 2.
11 M. Jacqui Alexander, *Pedagogies of Crossing: Meditations on Feminism, Sexual Politics, Memory, and the Sacred* (Durham, NC: Duke University Press, 2005), 109–10.
12 Ibid., 109.
13 See Lisa A. Mazzei, "Silence Speaks: Whiteness Revealed in the Absence of Voice," *Teaching and Teacher Education* 24 (2008): 1125–36.
14 See Cricket Keating, "Building Coalitional Consciousness," *NWSA Journal* 17, no. 2 (2005): 86–103.
15 See Aimee Carrillo Rowe's book, *Power Lines*, for an incisive analysis of how whiteness and heterosociality inform the alliances of a significant number of the white academic feminists she interviewed. In part she found that white feminists tended to have a different approach to alliances from feminist academics of color. For many of the white feminists, though not all, they approached alliances as a method of advancing their own careers, including within women's studies, whereas alliances, for the feminists of color, were more about creating support as well as solidarity for change.
16 Scott, "From Race Cognizance," 134.
17 Ibid., 125–49.
18 hooks, *Teaching Community*, 63.
19 Ibid., 61.
20 Cathy Cohen, "Punks, Bulldaggers, and Welfare Queens: The Radical Potential of Queer Politics," *GLQ: A Journal of Lesbian and Gay Studies* 3, no. 4 (1997): 437–65.
21 Peggy McIntosh, "White Privilege and Male Privilege," in *Privilege*, edited by Michael S. Kimmel and Abbey L. Ferber (Boulder, CO: Westview, 2003), 147–60.
22 Mazzei, "Silence Speaks," 1132; also drawing on Elizabeth Ellsworth, "Double Binds of Whiteness," in *Off White: Readings on Race, Power, and Society*, edited by Michelle Fine, Lois Weis, Linda C. Powell, and L. Mun Wong (New York: Routledge, 1997), 259–69.
23 Ibid., 1134–35.
24 Thandeka, *Learning to Be White* (New York: Continuum, 2005).
25 Ibid., 3.
26 Ibid., 4.
27 Sarita Srivastava, "Tears, Fears, and Careers: Anti-racism and Emotion in Social Movement Organizations," *Canadian Journal of Sociology/Cahiers Canadiens de Sociologie* 31, no. 1 (2006): 55–90.
28 Ibid., 83.
29 Gail Griffin, "Speaking of Whiteness: Disrupting White Innocence," *Journal of the Midwest Modern Language Association* 31, no. 3 (1998): 12.

30 Srivastava, *Tears, Fears*, 83.

31 Ibid., 85.

32 Ann Russo and Melissa Spatz, "Stop the False Race-Gender Divide," in *Who Should Be the First? Feminists Speak Out on the 2008 Presidential Campaign*, edited by Beverly Guy-Sheftall and Johnetta Cole (Albany: SUNY Press, 2010), 17–20.

33 Jennifer L. Eichstedt, "White Identities and the Search for Racial Justice," *Sociological Forum* 16, no. 3 (September 2001): 445–70.

34 Ibid., 466–67.

35 bell hooks, "beloved community," in *Killing Rage, Ending Racism* (New York: Holt, 1996), 262–73.

CHAPTER 3. DISRUPTING WHITENESS

1 Carrillo Rowe, *Power Lines*.

2 Segrest, *Born to Belonging*, 162.

3 Ibid.

4 Mary Hobgood, *Dismantling Privilege*, 37, quoting Maria Lugones, "*Hablando cara a cara*/Speaking Face to Face: An Exploration of Ethnocentric Racism," in *Making Face, Making Soul: Creative and Critical Perspectives by Feminists of Color*, edited by Gloria Anzaldua (San Francisco: Aunt Lute Books, 1990), 48–49.

5 Ibid., 36.

6 Lorde, *Sister Outsider*, 39.

7 Thandeka, *Learning to Be White*.

8 "Bleeding Heart" in *The Free Dictionary*, www.thefreedictionary.com.

9 I heard this idea of the "gravitational pull of white supremacy" from Chris Crass in his keynote address, "Collective Liberation," to the sixteenth annual White Privilege Conference, "Resistance, Action, Courage, and Equity," on 13 March 2015, in Louisville, Kentucky.

10 Morales, *Medicine Stories*, 13.

11 For instance, it was quite revealing to me that when Milo Yiannopoulis visited DePaul University on 24 May 2016, his speech, "feminism is cancer," was a put-down of women's and gender studies classes that have students sit in circles, share stories, feelings, and analyses of systems of oppression, and offer art as a form of expression.

12 Chris Crass, "For White Activists Devastated and Feeling Defeated by Racist Violence," *Good Men Project*, 31 July 2015, goodmenproject.com.

13 Cherrié Moraga, "La Guerra," in *This Bridge Called My Back* (Albany, NY: Kitchen Table: Women of Color Press, 1981), 26.

14 Autumn Brown and Maryse Mitchell-Brody with contributions from Adaku Utah, Leah Lakshmi Piepzna-Samarasinha, Susan Raffo, and Triana Kazaleh Sirdenis, and drawing on the work of many organizers for healing justice. "Healing Justice Practice Spaces: A How-To Guide," available online at https://justhealing.files.wordpress.com.

15 Morales, *Medicine Stories*, 20.

16 Ibid., 19.

17 Sharon H. Chang, "Trump Supporter Milo Yiannopoulis Furthers Racial Hatred at DePaul," *ThinkProgress*, 7 June 2016, https://thinkprogress.org.

18 Mariame Kaba, J. Cyriac Mathew, and Nathan Haines, eds., *Something Is Wrong: Exploring the Roots of Youth Violence*, 2010, project-nia.org, accessed 13 December 2017.

CHAPTER 4. SHIFTING PARADIGMS TO END VIOLENCE

1 CARA (Communities Against Rape and Abuse), "Taking Risks: Implementing Grassroots Community Accountability Strategies," in *Color of Violence*, edited by Incite! Women of Color Against Violence (Boston: South End Press, 2006), 250.

2 Beth Richie, *Arrested Justice*; K. Bumiller, *In an Abusive State: How Neoliberalism Appropriated the Feminist Movement against Sexual Violence* (Durham, NC: Duke University Press, 2008).

3 Nancy Matthews, *Confronting Rape: The Feminist Anti-Rape Movement and the State* (New York: Routledge, 1994); Paul Kivel, "Social Service or Social Change?" in *The Revolution Will Not Be Funded: Beyond the Non-profit Industrial Complex*, edited by Incite! Women of Color Against Violence (Cambridge, MA: South End Press, 2007), 129–50.

4 Richie, *Arrested Justice*.

5 Anannya Bhattacharjee, *Whose Safety? Women of Color and the Violence of Law Enforcement*, American Friends Service Committee, 2001, www.afsc.org.

6 Incite! Women of Color Against Violence, *Color of Violence: The Incite! Anthology* (Cambridge, MA: South End Press, 2006); Incite!, *The Revolution*.

7 Richie, *Arrested Justice*.

8 Andrea J. Ritchie, *Invisible No More: Police Violence against Black Women and Women of Color* (Boston: Beacon, 2017).

9 Generation Five, "Toward Transformative Justice: A Liberatory Approach to Child Sexual Abuse and Other Forms of Intimate and Community Violence; A Call to Action for the Left and the Sexual and Domestic Violence Sectors," Executive Summary, 2007, 11, www.generationfive.org.

10 Incite! *Color of Violence*.

11 Generation Five, "Toward Transformative Justice," 11.

12 Paul Kivel, "Social Service or Social Change?"; Ann Russo, *Taking Back Our Lives*.

13 Generation Five, "Toward Transformative Justice," 21.

14 Incite! *Color of Violence*.

15 Young Women's Empowerment Project (YWEP), *Girls Do What They Have to Do to Survive: Illuminating Methods Used by Girls in the Sex Trade and Street Economy to Fight Back and Heal*. Report of YWEP (Chicago: YWEP, Fall 2009), 6.

16 YWEP and FUFA are no longer active as organizations, though their work lives on in Chicago and broader communities.

17 YWEP, *Girls Do What They Have to Do to Survive*, 5.

18 Ibid., 8.

19 Ibid., 9.

20 Ibid., 7.

21 Ibid.

22 LaToya Peterson, "The Not Rape Epidemic," in *Yes Means Yes! Visions of Female Sexual Power and a World without Rape*, edited by Jaclyn Friedman and Jessica Valenti (Lebanon, IN: Seal Press, 2008), 209.

23 Ibid., 212.

24 Lynn Phillips, *Flirting with Danger* (New York: NYU Press, 2000).

25 Lori Girshick, *Woman to Woman Sexual Violence: Does She Call It Rape?* (Boston: Northeastern University Press, 2002).

26 Emi Koyama, "Disloyal to Feminism: Abuse of Survivors within the Domestic Violence Shelter System," in *Incite! Color of Violence*, 217.

27 Ann Russo, *Taking Back Our Lives*.

28 Generation Five, "Toward Transformative Justice," 35.

29 Ubuntu, "Documents: About Ubuntu," *make/shift: feminisms in motion* 2 (Fall/Winter 2007–2008): 12–13.

30 Ibid., 12.

31 hooks, *Teaching Community*, 75.

32 Jen Curley, member of FIRE, quoted in Ann Russo and Melissa Spatz, *Communities Engaged in Resisting Violence*, Report of the Women and Girls Collective Action Network, 2007, https://www.transformativejustice.eu.

33 Young Women's Empowerment Project, *Girls Do What They Have to Do to Survive*, 12.

34 Incite! *The Revolution Will Not Be Funded*; Frances Winddance Twine and Kathleen Blee, eds., *Feminism and Antiracism: International Struggles for Justice* (New York: NYU Press, 2009).

35 Lara Brooks, quoted in Russo and Spatz, *Communities Engaged in Resisting Violence*.

36 Broadway Youth Center, "Responding to Violence: Community Healing, Accountability, Capacity, and Transformation in the BYC's Drop in Program" (Chicago: Broadway Youth Center, 2010).

37 Carolyn Boyes-Watson, *Peacemaking Circles and Urban Youth: Bringing Justice Home* (St. Paul, MN: Living Justice Press, 2008).

38 Beth Richie, Natalie J. Sokoloff, and C. Pratt, eds., *Domestic Violence at the Margins: Readings on Race, Class, Gender, and Culture* (New Brunswick, NJ: Rutgers University Press, 2005); Russo, *Taking Back Our Lives*.

39 Janice Ristock, *No More Secrets: Violence in Lesbian Relationships* (New York: Routledge, 2002).

40 Ibid.; Russo, *Taking Back Our Lives*; Richie, *Arrested Justice*.

41 Young Women's Empowerment Project, *Girls Do What They Have to Do to Survive*, 16.

42 Illinois Safe Schools Alliance, "IL Teachers and Social Workers Still Unprepared to Address LGBTQ Issues," *Visibility Matters*, 2 March 2012, www.ilsafeschools.org.

43 Critical Resistance and Incite! "Gender Violence and the Prison-Industrial Complex," in Incite! *Color of Violence*, 224.
44 Young Women's Empowerment Project, *Girls Do*, 5–6.
45 Ibid., 6.
46 Ibid., 7.
47 Young Women's Empowerment Project, *Bad Encounters* (Chicago: YWEP, 2012).
48 Morgan Bassichis, "Reclaiming Queer and Trans Safety," in *Revolution Starts at Home*, edited by Ching-In Chen, Jai Dulani, and Leah Lakshmi Piepzna-Samarasinha (Boston: South End Press, 2011), 14.
49 GABRIELA Chicago is no longer active, but its work and all those involved continue in other forms.
50 Generation Five, "Toward Transformative Justice," 2.
51 Chen et al., *Revolution*.
52 Burk, "Think. Re-Think," 273.
53 Ibid., 267.
54 Ibid., 267.

CHAPTER 5. COLLECTIVE AND COMMUNAL SUPPORT

1 Richie, *Arrested Justice*; Young Women's Empowerment Project, *Girls Do* and *Bad Encounters*.
2 Jake Fawcett, *Up to Us: Lessons Learned and Goals for Change after Thirteen Years of the Washington State Domestic Violence Fatality Review* (Seattle: Washington State Coalition Against Domestic Violence, 2010), 20–32.
3 Timothy Colman, "Violence among Us: Facing Sexual Assault in Our Communities and Movements," *make/shift: feminisms in motion* 5 (Spring/Summer 2009):16.
4 "Why FAR Out?" farout.org, accessed 21 July 2012.
5 Alexis Pauline Gumbs, "Interview with Leah Piepzna-Samarasinha," in *The Revolution Starts at Home: Partner Abuse in Activist Communities* (2009), 80; in the original zine available at www.incite-national.org.
6 Colman, "Violence among Us," 16.
7 Gumbs, "Interview," 80.
8 Gumbs, "Interview," 81.
9 Chen et al., *Revolution*, 14.
10 Gumbs, "Interview," 81.
11 Farr, *The Revolution Starts at Home*, xxxix.
12 "A Few Words about F.A.R. Out," *Friends Help Friends Survive* (blog), farout.org, accessed 21 July 2012.
13 Burk, "Think. Re-Think," 277; also, "A Few Words about F.A.R. Out," 2. Questions posed: "How does support happen within your group? How has domestic violence impacted relationships with my friends? How can we hold ourselves, and each other, accountable in our relationships? What would it take to build friendships that are more resilient than and outlast abusive relationships?"

14 Burk, "Think. Re-Think," 277.

15 Nathaniel Shara, "Mapping Our (Collective) Wellness," *Friends Help Friends Survive* (blog), farout.org, accessed 2 February 2015.

16 Jen Curley, from Russo and Spatz, *Communities Engaged.*

17 Shannon Perez Darby, "'We're Going to the Jersey Shore!': To Connect with Friends and Family," *Friends Help Friends Survive* (blog), farout.org, accessed 2 February 2015.

18 See Kay Pranis, Mark Wedge, and Barry Stuart, *Peacemaking Circles: From Crime to Community* (Minneapolis, MN: Living Justice Press, 2003); Kay Pranis, *The Little Book of Circle Processes* (Brattleboro, VT: Good Books, 2005).

19 The circular process is guided by a talking piece that travels clockwise around the group and provides a space for each person to speak, without interruption, to an issue or question.

20 The Building Communities, Ending Violence Project was cofounded and developed with Michelle Emery, who was a graduate student at DePaul in women's and gender studies (WGS). She helped me build the project for the first year, and then many graduate assistants worked with me thereafter, including Hannah Arwe, Shana Bahemat, Nihan Can, N. A. Clark, Asher Diaz, Joy Ellison, Sydney Haliburton, Mary Hazboun, Katie Heinekamp, Jill Kuanfung, Buki Ogundipe, and Clare Stuber, among many other graduate and undergraduate students in WGS who have helped me to build the project since.

21 Gumbs, "Interview," 81.

22 Generation Five, "Toward Transformative Justice," 23.

23 Ibid.

24 Tala Khanmalek, "'Revolution Capable of Healing Our Wounds': An Interview with Aurora Levins Morales," *nineteen sixty nine: an ethnic studies journal* 2, no. 1 (2013): 4, escholarship.org.

25 Generation Five, "Toward Transformative Justice," 25.

26 Ibid., 23.

27 Tanuja Jagernauth, quoted by Mariame Kaba, in "The Toll It Takes: Activism and the Need for Healing Justice," *Prison Culture* (blog), 15 December 2010, www.usprisonculture.com, accessed 3 February 2015.

CHAPTER 6. EVERYDAY RESPONSES TO EVERYDAY VIOLENCE

1 Generation Five, "Toward Transformative Justice," 12.

2 Kaethe Weingarten, *Common Shock* (New York: NAL Trade, 2004), 161.

3 Weingarten, *Common Shock*, 20–21.

4 Stop It Now! *Let's Talk: Speaking Up to Prevent Child Sexual Abuse*, 2006, www.stopitnow.org, accessed 26 November 2013.

5 Stop It Now, press release, 10 October 2012, www.stopitnow.org.

6 Generation Five, "Toward Transformative Justice," 29.

7 Grace Poore, "Every Breath You Take," SHaKTI Productions, theshaktiproductions.net, accessed 15 October 2009.

8 Weingarten, *Common Shock*, 161.

9 Poore, "Every Breath," 2.

10 Weingarten, *Common Shock*, 37.

11 Shakti Butler, *Cracking the Codes*.

12 Joy DeGruy, *Post Traumatic Slave Syndrome* (N.p.: Joy DeGruy Publications, 2005).

13 Weingarten, *Common Shock*, 36.

14 Creative Interventions, http://www.stopviolenceeveryday.org, accessed 7 May 2018.

15 Story Telling and Organizing Project, "Telling Our Stories: Storytelling as Community Organizing," www.stopviolenceeveryday.org, accessed 4 April 2018.

16 Mimi Kim, "Moving beyond Critique: Creative Interventions and Reconstructions of Communities," *Social Justice* 37, no. 4 (2011/2012): 18. Accessed 7 January 2014.

17 Phoebe, "A Community Response to Racist Violence," Story Telling and Organizing Project, www.stopviolenceeveryday.org, accessed 7 May 2018.

18 Di Grennell, "He Korero Iti: A Small Story," www.stopviolenceeveryday.org.

19 Storytelling and Organizing Project, "Telling Our Stories," www.stopviolenceeveryday.org.

20 DiGrennell, "He Korero Iti".

21 Storytelling and Organizing Project, 4.

22 Ibid.

23 Morgan Bassichis, "Reclaiming Queer," 18.

24 Ibid.

25 Inspiration for these strategy sessions comes from the work of Creative Interventions and its Storytelling and Organizing Project (STOP) and that of Communities United Against Violence (CUAV), both in the Bay Area. As Bassichis describes in "Reclaiming Queer and Trans Safety," CUAV organizes "Safety Labs" that create space where "people come together to imagine and practice grounded community responses to violence that do not rely on the prison industrial complex (PIC) or its tactics of shame, punishment, and isolation" (Bassichis, "Reclaiming Queer," 6).

26 See Laura Van Dernoot Lipsky, *Trauma Stewardship* (Oakland, CA: Berrett-Koehler Publishers, 2009).

27 Breakthrough "Ring the Bell" Campaign, us.breakthrough.tv.

28 Mallika Dutt, "Admirable: Successful 'Ring the Bell Campaign Goes Global,'" us.breakthrough.tv, accessed 8 November 2013.

29 Dutt, "Violence against Women: We're Asking Men the Wrong Question," 26 June 2013, us.breakthrough.tv.

30 Patricia Williams, *Seeing a Colorblind Future* (New York: Farrar, Straus, and Giroux, 1998), 32.

31 Mari Matsuda, *Where Is Your Body?* (Boston: Beacon, 1997).

32 Stop It Now! *Let's Talk*, 2.

33 Ibid., 6–7.

34 Ibid., 15.

35 Stop It Now! *Don't Wait*, www.stopitnow.org.

36 Peter Pollard, "Marketing Sexual Abuse Prevention," *Behavioral Health* 26, no. 5 (2006): 8–9.

37 Ibid.

38 Ibid.

39 Stop It Now! *Let's Talk*, 2.

CHAPTER 7. FROM PUNISHMENT TO ACCOUNTABILITY

1 They also say that "[w]hile we support survivors in seeking assistance and legal remedy through the court system if they desire to do so, our work will not wait on or be silenced by legal processes." Ubuntu, "Documents: About Ubuntu," *make/ shift: feminisms in motion* 2 (Fall/Winter 2007–2008): 13.

2 Bhattacharjee, *Whose Safety?*; Richie, *Arrested Justice*; Incite! *Color of Violence.*

3 Lee Madigan, *The Second Rape: Society's Continued Betrayal of the Victim* (New York: Macmillan, 1991); Rebecca Campbell and Sheela Raja, "Secondary Victimization of Rape Victims: Insights from Mental Health Professionals Who Treat Survivors of Violence," in *Violence and Victims* 14, no. 3 (1999): 261–75.

4 Also see James Ptacek, *Battered Women in the Courtroom: The Power of Judicial Responses* (Boston: Northeastern University Press, 1999).

5 Andrea Ritchie, *Invisible No More! Police Violence against Black Women and Women of Color* (Boston: Beacon, 2017).

6 Mariame Kaba, *No Selves to Defend*, June 2014, https://noselves2defend.wordpress.com; Ritchie, *Invisible No More.*

7 Boyes-Watson, *Peacemaking Circles*, 110–11.

8 Adrienne Maree Brown, "What Is/Isn't Transformative Justice?" 9 July 2015, adriennemareebrown.net.

9 Ibid., 114.

10 Morales, *Medicine Stories*, 112.

11 Ibid., 114.

12 Thich Nhat Hanh, *Being Peace*, 2nd ed. (Berkeley, CA: Parallax Press, 2005).

13 Hanh, *Being Peace*, 61–62.

14 Ana Clarissa Rojas Durazo, "In Our Hands: Community Accountability as Pedagogical Strategy," *Social Justice* 37, no. 4 (2010–2011): 78.

15 Ibid., 50.

16 Ibid., 79–80.

17 Creative Interventions, "Tools," www.creative-interventions.org.

18 Esteban Lance Kelly, "Philly Stands Up: Inside the Politics and Poetics of Transformative Justice and Community Accountability in Sexual Assault Situations," *Social Justice* 37, no. 4 (2010–2011): 53.

19 Incite! *Color of Violence*, 84.

20 CARA (Communities Against Rape and Abuse), "Taking Risks: Implementing Grassroots Community Accountability Strategies," in Incite! *Color of Violence*, 251–55.

21 Ibid., 250.

22 Terrence Crowley, "The Lie of Entitlement," in *Transforming a Rape Culture*, 2nd ed., edited by Emilie Buchwald, Pamela R. Fletcher, and Martha Roth (Minneapolis, MN: Milkweed Editions, 2005), 301–9.

23 Ibid., 303

24 Ibid., 303–4.

25 Ibid.

26 Robin DiAngelo, *What Does It Mean to Be White? Developing White Racial Literacy* (New York: Peter Lang, 2012).

27 Morales, *Medicine Stories*, 76.

28 Philly Stands Up, "What to Do When . . . ," www.phillystandsup.com.

29 Ibid.

30 Generation Five, "Toward Transformative Justice," 35.

31 Kelly, "Philly Stands Up," 48–49.

32 Durazo, "In Our Hands," 85.

33 Ibid.

34 Ibid., 86.

35 Ibid.

36 Restorative justice has expanded in the broader culture to the point where even some judicial courts and schools are now implementing restorative justice processes into their systems as a way to divert young people from incarceration and as a way to prevent future violence. Within these institutional arenas, many times the practices are coopted, diluted, and then mainstreamed into a system that continues to be punitive.

37 Pranis, Stuart, and Wedge, *Peacemaking Circles*, 10.

38 Ibid., 11.

39 Ibid.

40 Ibid., 12.

41 Ibid.

42 Roca, Inc., "Our Story," Rocainc.org, accessed 13 December 2013.

43 Boyes-Watson, *Peacemaking Circles*, 19.

44 Ibid., 20.

45 Ibid., 136.

46 Ibid.

47 Ibid., 206.

48 Ibid., 207.

49 Kim, "Moving beyond Critique," 21–22.

50 Ibid., 29.

51 Ibid.

52 Bench Ansfield and Jenna Peters-Golden, "How We Learned *Not* to Succeed in Transformative Justice," *Make/Shift* 12 (2012): 31.

53 Summary Statement Re Community Accountability, *Transforming Harm*, 17 March 2017, http://transformharm.tumblr.com.

54 Ibid.

55 See Russo and Spatz, *Communities Engaged.*

56 Bench Ansfield and Timothy Colman, "Confronting Sexual Assault: Transformative Justice on the Ground in Philadelphia," *Tikkun* 27, no. 1 (Winter 2012): 41–44.

57 Alexis Pauline Gumbs, "Freedom Seeds: Growing Abolition in Durham," in *Abolition Now! 10 Years of Strategy and Struggle against the Prison Industrial Complex*
(Oakland, CA: AK Press, 2008), 145–56.

CHAPTER 8. DISENTANGLING US FEMINISM FROM US IMPERIALISM

1 Miriam Arghandiwal, "Afghan Group Accuses Police of Significant Violence
against Women," Reuters, 10 June 2013, www.reuters.com.

2 "Afghan Women Rally against Domestic Violence," *USA Today*, 13 February 2014,
www.usatoday.com.

3 Feminist Majority Foundation, "Stop Gender Apartheid in Afghanistan," www.
feminist.com.

4 Sherene Razack, *Looking White People*, 10.

5 Mohanty, *Feminism without Borders*, 242.

6 M. Jacqui Alexander and Chandra Talpade Mohanty, "Introduction," in *Feminist
Genealogies, Colonial Legacies, Democratic Futures* (New York: Routledge, 1997):
xv–xlii.

7 Mohanty, *Feminism without Borders*, 242.

8 Ibid.

9 Nupur Chaudhuri and Margaret Strobel, *Western Women and Imperialism:
Complicity and Resistance* (Bloomington: Indiana University Press, 1992); Leila
Ahmed, *Gender and Islam: Historical Roots of a Modern Debate* (New Haven, CT:
Yale University Press, 1993); Louise Michele Newman, *White Women's Rights: The
Racial Origins of Feminism in the United States* (New York: Oxford University
Press, 1999).

10 Corinne Mason, "Global Violence against Women as a National Security 'Emer-
gency,'" *Feminist Formations* 25, no. 2 (Summer 2013): 56.

11 Ibid.

12 Ibid., 57.

13 Cyra Akila Choudhury, "Empowerment or Estrangement? Liberal Feminism's Visions of the 'Progress' of Muslim Women," *University of Baltimore Law Forum* 39,
no. 2 (2009): 168.

14 Evelyn Alsultany, *Arabs and Muslims in the Media.*

15 Ibid., 73.

16 Razack, *Looking White People*, 132.

17 Lila Abu Lughod, "Do Muslim Women Need Saving?" *American Anthropologist*
104, no. 3 (2002): 783–90; Zillah Eisenstein, *Against Empire* (New York: Palgrave
Press, 2004); Sherene Razack, *Casting Out: The Eviction of Muslims from Western
Law and Politics* (Toronto: University of Toronto Press, 2008); Evelyn Alsultany,
Arabs and Muslims in the Media: Race and Representation after 9/11 (New York:

NYU Press, 2012); Sonali Kolhatkar and James Ingalls, *Bleeding Afghanistan: Washington, Warlords, and the Propaganda of Silence* (New York: Seven Stories Press, 2006).

18 Alsultany, *Arabs and Muslims.*

19 Kolhatkar and Ingalls, *Bleeding Afghanistan,* 12.

20 Ibid., 13.

21 Ibid.

22 Malalai Joya, *A Woman among Warlords* (New York: Simon and Schuster, 2009).

23 Jasmin Zine, "Between Orientalism and Fundamentalism: The Politics of Muslim Women's Feminist Engagement," *Muslim World Journal of Human Rights* 3, no. 1 (2006): 11.

24 See Nancy Gallagher, "The International Campaign against Gender Apartheid in Afghanistan," *UCLA Journal of International Law & Foreign Affairs* 5 (2000–2001): 369–70.

25 See J. Fluri, "Sexual Misconduct and International Aid Workers: An Afghanistan Case Study," *Wagadu: A Journal of Transnational Women's and Gender Studies* 10 (2012): 72–101.

26 Sima Wali, Elizabeth Gould, and Paul Fitzgerald, "The Impact of Political Conflict on Women: The Case of Afghanistan," *American Journal of Public Health* 89, no. 10 (1999): 1474–76.

27 The Landmine Monitor Report, "Afghanistan: Casualties and Victim Assistance," 18 October 2014, www.the-monitor.org.

28 Kolhatkar and Ingalls, *Bleeding Afghanistan,* 53.

29 Ibid.

30 Ibid., 55.

31 UNHCR (United Nations High Commissioner on Refugees), "Afghanistan 2012," www.unhcr.org.

32 "Afghanistan the Worst Place to Be a Woman, Finds Survey by TrustLaw Woman," 15 June 2011, www.news.com.au.

33 Lyric Thompson, "The World's Worst Places to Be a Woman," *Amnesty International* blog, 17 June 2011, www.blog.amnestyusa.org.

34 Mina Habib, "Violence against Women 'More Extreme,'" *Institute for War and Peace Reporting,* 29 November 2012, www.iwpr.net.

35 Lisa Anderson, "Afghanistan Most Dangerous Country for Women," *Globe and Mail,* 15 June 2011, www.theglobeandmail.com.

36 Fariba Nawa, "Stop Knee-Jerk Blaming of Afghan Men and Culture," *Women's E-news,* 4 June 2013, womensenews.org.

37 Human Rights Watch, "Just Don't Call It Militia," 12 September 2011, www.hrw.org.

38 Ibid.

39 Ibid.

40 Jawad Sukhanyar and Alissa J. Rubin, "4 Members of Afghan Police Found Guilty of Rape," *New York Times,* November 7, 2012, www.nytimes.com; and Alissa J. Ru-

bin, "Rape Case, in Public, Cites Abuse by Armed Groups in Afghanistan," *New York Times*, 1 June 2012, www.nytimes.com.

41 "US Force Rape Women in Northern Afghanistan: Locals," *Press TV*, 4 December 2012, www.presstv.ir.

42 Gordon Duff, "US Forces Rape Women in Northern Afghanistan: Locals," *Veterans Today*, 4 December 2012, www.veteranstoday.com.

43 Stephen Lendman, "Rape and Murder in Afghanistan," 19 March 2012, www.stephenlendman.org.

44 Women's Bureau, US Department of Labor, *Trauma-Informed Care for Women Veterans Experiencing Homelessness: A Guide for Service Providers*, www.dol.gov, accessed 27 October 2012; Molly O'Toole, "Military Sexual Assault Epidemic Continues to Claim Victims as Defense Department Fails Females," *Huffington Post*, 6 October 2012, www.huffingtonpost.com.

45 Naomi Wolf, "A Culture of Coverup: Rape in the Ranks of the US Military," *Guardian*, 14 June 2012, www.theguardian.com.

46 Derek J. Burks, "Lesbian, Gay, and Bisexual Victimization in the Military: The Unintended Consequence of 'Don't Ask, Don't Tell,'" *American Psychologist* 66, no. 7 (2011): 604–13; Matthew Kerrigan, "Transgender Discrimination in the Military: The New Don't Ask, Don't Tell," *Psychology, Public Policy, and Law* 18, no. 3 (2012): 500–518.

47 K. J. Ayotte and M. Hussain. "Securing Afghan Women: Neocolonialism, Epistemic Violence, and the Rhetoric of the Veil," *NWSA Journal* 17, no. 3 (2005): 112–33.

48 Razack, *Looking White People*, 7.

49 Alsultany, *Arabs and Muslims*, 80.

50 Loretta Kensinger, "Plugged in Praxis: Critical Reflections on U.S. Feminism, Internet Activism, and Solidarity with Women in Afghanistan," *Journal of International Women's Studies* 5, no. 1 (2003): 8.

51 Abu Lughod, "Do Muslim," 787–88.

52 Alsultany, *Arabs and Muslims*, 84.

53 Shahnaz Khan, "Between Here and There: Feminist Solidarity and Afghan Women," *Genders* 33 (2001), www.genders.org; S. Banks, "Donning Scarves in Solidarity," *Los Angeles Times*, 25 September 2002, www.articles.latimes.com; S. Benet, "Muslim, Asian Women Target of Insults," *Women's E-News*, 21 September 2001, www.womensenews.com; S. Shah, "Veiled Solidarity," *Progressive*, January 2002, 28–30.

54 "CAIR Report Shows 2017 on Track to Becoming One of Worst Years Ever for Anti-Muslim Hate Crimes," Council on American-Islamic Relations, https://www.cair.com.

55 Benet, "Muslim, Asian Women."

56 ACLU, "Discrimination against Muslim Women—Fact Sheet," 29 May 2008, http://www.aclu.org.

57 Christina Cauterucci, "String of New York Attacks Show the Tie between Islamophobia and Misogyny," *Slate*, 13 September 2016, www.slate.com.

58 Dermana Seta, *The Forgotten Women: The Impact of Islamophobia on Muslim Women* (Brussels: European Network Against Racism, May 2016), http://enar-eu.org.
59 European Network Against Racism in Europe, "Women Are the First to Pay the Price of Islamophobia in Europe," Press Release, 26 May 2016, http://enar-eu.org.
60 Seta, *Forgotten Women.*
61 Zine, "Between Orientalism," 10.
62 Mona Eltahawy, "Muslim Women, Caught between Islamophobes and 'Our Men,'" *New York Times* Op-Ed, 19 November 2017, www.nytimes.com.
63 Ibid.
64 Chandra Talpade Mohanty, "Under Western Eyes," in *Third World Women and the Politics of Feminism* (Bloomington: Indiana University Press, 1991), 56.
65 M. A. Franks, "Obscene Undersides: Women and Evil between the Taliban and the United States," *Hypatia* 18, no. 1 (2003): 136.
66 Ibid., 150.
67 Joey Mogul, Andrea Ritchie, and Kay Whitlock, *Queer (In)Justice: The Criminalization of LGBT People in the U.S.* (Boston: Beacon, 2012).
68 Ibid.
69 J. Fluri, "Sexual Misconduct and International Aid Workers: An Afghanistan Case Study," *Wagadu: A Journal of Transnational Women's and Gender Studies* 10 (2012): 72–101.
70 Cyra Akila Choudhury, "Empowerment or Estrangement?"
71 *View from a Grain of Sand*, written and directed by Meena Nanji (Ecesis Production, 2008), http://viewgrainofsand.com.
72 Niloufar Pourzand, "Afghan Refugee Women's Organizations in Pakistan (1980–2001): Struggles in Adversity," *Resources for Feminist Research* 30, no. 3 (2003): 65–81.
73 Ibid.
74 Ibid.
75 Ibid.
76 "Working in Partnership with Afghan Women," *Herizons* 18, no. 4 (Spring 2005), http://www.herizons.ca.
77 Pourzand, "Afghan Refugee."
78 Zine, "Between Orientalism," 1.
79 Zine, "Between Orientalism," 14; referencing Miriam Cooke, *Women Claim Islam* (New York: Routledge, 2001).
80 Choudhury, "Empowerment or Estrangement?" 162.
81 Choudhury, "Empowerment or Estrangement?" 170.
82 M. Nayak, "Orientalism and 'Saving' US State Identity after 9/11," *International Feminist Journal of Politics* 8, no. 1 (March 2006): 48.

CHAPTER 9. RESISTING THE "SAVIOR" COMPLEX

1 Nicholas D. Kristof and Sheryl WuDunn, *Half the Sky: Turning Oppression into Opportunity for Women Worldwide* (New York: Knopf, 2009), xxii.

2 Marcia G. Yerman, "*Half the Sky* Live Event Brings Awareness to Women's Issues," *Huffington Post*, 26 April 2010, www.huffingtonpost.com.
3 Half the Sky Movement, www.halftheskymovement.org.
4 Ibid.
5 Razack, *Looking White People*.
6 Ibid., 10.
7 Ibid., 10.
8 Razack, *Looking White People*; Mohanty, *Feminism without Borders*.
9 Razack, *Looking White People*, 16.
10 Ibid., 54–55.
11 Kimberlé Crenshaw, quoted by Razack, *Looking White People*, 55.
12 Kristof and WuDunn, *Half the Sky*, xxii.
13 Nicholas Kristof and Sheryl WuDunn, "Saving the World's Women: The Women's Crusade," *New York Times Magazine*, 17 August 2009, http://www.nytimes.com.
14 Razack, *Looking White People*, 21.
15 Razack, *Casting Out*, 88.
16 Razack, *Looking White People*, 166.
17 Kristof and WuDunn, *Half the Sky*, 25.
18 Ibid., 24.
19 Razack, *Looking White People*, 3.
20 Razack, *Casting Out*, 156.
21 Ibid., 156.
22 Ibid., 155.
23 Kristof and WuDunn, *Half the Sky*, 54.
24 Ibid.
25 World Bank, "Engendering Development through Gender Equality, Resources, and Voice" (World Bank and Oxford University Press, 2001), http://www-wds.worldbank.org.
26 NIKE, "World Economic Forum Gives Adolescent Girls a Voice Globally," 30 January 2009, http://news.nike.com.
27 Winifred Poster and Zakia Salime, "The Limits of Microcredit: Transnational Feminism and USAID Activities in the United States and Morocco," in *Women's Activism and Globalization: Linking Local Struggles and Transnational Politics*, edited by Nancy A. Naples and Manisha Desai (New York: Routledge, 2002), 190.
28 Kristof and WuDunn, *Half the Sky*, 47.
29 Poster and Salime, "The Limits of Microcredit," 194.
30 Ibid., 196.
31 Ibid., 197.
32 See Mary E. Hawkesworth, *Globalization and Feminist Activism* (New York: Rowman and Littlefield, 2006).
33 Kristof and WuDunn, *Half the Sky*, xix.
34 Ibid., xix.
35 Ibid., 210.

36 Ibid., 193.

37 Ibid.

38 Ibid., 61.

39 Ibid., 62.

40 Ibid.

41 Ibid.

42 Alsultany, *Arabs and Muslims*.

43 Kristof and WuDunn, *Half the Sky*, 84.

44 Ibid., 88.

45 Muadi Mukenge with Aimee Mwade Kady and Caitlin Stanton, *Funding a Women's Movement against Sexual Violence in the Democratic Republic of Congo: 2004–2009* (Global Fund for Women, February 2010), 9, http://www.globalfundforwomen.org.

46 Ibid., 9.

47 Ibid., 10.

48 Ibid., 11.

49 Ibid., 10.

50 Friends of the Congo, "Coltan," http://www.friendsofthecongo.org, accessed 12 August 2014.

51 Noelle Barber, "Increased Military Presence and Aid Alone Will Not Prevent Another Makombo Massacre," *Friends of the Congo* blog, 9 April 2010, http://congofriends.blogspot.com.

52 Evelyn Alsultany, *Arabs and Muslims*, 103.

53 Kristof and WuDunn, *Half the Sky*, 149.

54 Kristof and WuDunn, "Saving the World's Women."

55 Kristof and WuDunn, *Half the Sky*, 157–58.

56 Kristof and WuDunn, "Saving the World's Women."

57 Alsultany, *Arabs and Muslims*, 104–9.

58 Joya, *A Woman among Warlords*.

59 Ibid.

60 Anne E. Brodsky, *With All Our Strength: The Revolutionary Association of the Women of Afghanistan* (London: Psychology Press, 2003).

61 See Bhattacharjee, *Whose Safety?*; Beth Richie, *Arrested Justice*.

62 Mogul, Ritchie, and Whitlock, *Queer (In)Justice*; Ritchie, *Invisible No More*; Gail Mason, *The Spectacle of Violence: Homophobia, Gender, and Knowledge* (New York: Routledge, 2001); Eric A. Stanley and Nat Smith, eds., *Captive Genders: Trans Embodiment and the Prison Industrial Complex* (Oakland, CA: AK Press, 2015).

63 L. Ben-Moshe, C. Chapman, and A. Carey, *Disability Incarcerated: Imprisonment and Disability in the U.S. and Canada* (New York: Palgrave, 2014); Therese Quinn and Erica Meiners, *Flaunt It! Queers Organizing for Public Education and Justice* (New York: Peter Lang, 2009); Regina Rahimi and Delores Liston, *Pervasive Vulnerabilities: Sexual Harassment in Schools* (New York: Peter Lang, 2011); Mica Pol-

lack, *Everyday Racism: Getting Real about Race in Schools* (New York: New Press, 2008); Noemi Pareda, Georgina Gilara, Maria Forns, and Juana Gomez-Benito, "The Prevalence of Child Sexual Abuse in Community and Student Samples," *Clinical Psychology Review* 24, no. 4 (2009): 328–38; Marije Stoltenborgh, Marinus H. van IJzendoorn, Eveline M. Euser, and Marian J. Bakermans-Kranenburg, "A Global Perspective on Child Sexual Abuse: Meta-Analysis of Prevalence around the World," *Child Maltreatment* 16, no. 2 (2011): 79–101; *Child Sexual Abuse and the Catholic Church: Gender, Power, and Organizational Culture* (London: Oxford University Press, 2011).

64 Razack, *Looking White People*, 20.

65 Ibid., 159–60.

INDEX

Abu-Lughod, Lila, 191, 201
Accountable communities, 21, 107, 119
ACLU, American Civil Liberties Union, 201, 202
Afghan Independent Human Rights Commission, 196
Afghan Women's Media Center, 210
Afghan Women's Network, 210
Alexander, M. Jacqui, 46
Ally, 26, 27
Alsultany, Evelyn, 190, 200, 201, 237
Amnesty International, 196
Anaesthetic aesthetic, 59
Ansfield, Bench, 176
Antiviolence movement, 6, 85–87, 101, 119, 157
Assata's Daughters, 4
Audre Lorde Project, 89
Ayotte, Kevin, 191

Bassichis, Morgan, 2, 104, 142, 143, 206
Bay Area Transformative Justice Collective, 166
Bell, Derrick, 23
Bhattacharjee, Annanya, 87, 103, 159
Blame: default response, 32, 108, 129, 170; individualized, 33, 35; self-blame, 80, 95; victim-blaming, 97, 108, 159, 178, 241
Boler, Megan, 44
Boussiani, Cherif, 198
Boyes-Watson, Carolyn, 19, 100, 162, 174, 175
Breakthrough, 147

Broadway Youth Center, 90, 254
Brodsky, Anne, 197, 239
Brooks, Lara, 99
Brown, Adrienne Maree, 163
Brown, Autumn, 69
Building Communities, Ending Violence (BCEV), 12, 125, 144, 244, 245
Burk, Connie, 19, 107, 118
Butler, Shakti, 25, 139
BYP 100 (Black Youth Project), 176, 177, 180, 184
Bystanders, 133, 136, 147, 223, 236

Calling in, 33
Calling out, 10, 32
Callous disregard, 14, 27, 61
Cantoni, Clementina, 196
Carceral feminism, 3, 4, 10, 161
Carceral logic, 19, 21, 22, 29, 31, 33
CARE, 6, 214, 226
Carillo Rowe, Aimee, 2, 38
Cauterucci, Christina, 202
Chen, Ching-In, 117, 166
Chicago Freedom School, 78
Choudhury, Cyra Akila, 189, 191, 212
Coalitional consciousness, 50, 149
Cohen, Cathy, 50
Collusion, 132
Colman, Timothy, 111, 181
Colonization, 187, 190, 234, 240
Communities Against Rape and Abuse (CARA), 86, 167
Communities United Against Violence (CUAV), 2, 13, 89, 104, 142

Jagernauth, Tanuja, 12, 130
Joya, Malalai, 192, 197, 208, 209, 239
Just Practice, 34, 89, 109, 166, 167, 245

Kaba, Mariame, 27, 34, 71, 78, 156, 167, 176, 177, 206
Kady, Aimee Mwade, 234, 235
Keating, Cricket, 50,
Kelly, Esteban Lance, 167, 172
Kim, Mimi, 140, 167, 176
Kolhaktar, Sonali, 191, 192
Koyama, Emi, 96

Law enforcement, 86, 161,177; violence, 61, 87, 156, 202, 204, 241
Legal advocacy, 3, 85, 88, 89, 157
Liberal feminism, 9, 39, 186, 189, 211
Listening, 42–47, 56, 71, 79–80, 129; as support, 113, 117, 121
Lorde, Audre, 61
Lugones, Maria, 43, 61

Mango Tribe, 180
Mason, Corinne, 189
Matsuda, Mari, 149
Mazzei, Lisa, 50
McKenzie, Mia, 26
Microcredit, 226, 230
Militarism, 7, 190, 194–99, 236, 237; feminism and, 3, 186, 213
Minimization, 111, 134, 143, 150, 176
Mistakes: and accountability, 49, 108, 163, learning from, 19, 20, 28–31, 109, 167; and systemic oppression, 21, 33; and zero tolerance 19, 32
Mitchell-Brody, Maryse, 69
Mogul, Joey, 205, 206
Mohanty, Chandra Talpade, 187, 188, 204
Morales, Aurora Levins, 23, 57, 63, 70, 110, 129, 163, 164, 170
Movement building, 128
Mukenge, Muade, 234, 235
Muslim feminisms, 211

Muslim women, 200, 203, constructed as "other," 199, 200, feminism and accountability, 211, 212, 241, and "liberating," 190, 193, 199; violence in US, 199, 200, 201–203, 206, 241

Nagar, Richa, 36
Nanji, Meena, 209
Nawa, Fariba, 196, 197
Nayak, M., 213
Neoliberalism, 3, 6, 86, 91, 217–218, 224–229, 231
NGOs, 37, 220
NIKE, 226
Normative logics, 21, 32, 63, 205; of imperialism, 186, 191, 194, 212, 222, 233, 240; of retributive justice, 170
Northwest Network, 19, 92, 107, 112, 118

Okun, Tema, 22, 35
Organization for Promoting Afghan Women's Capabilities, 208
Orientalism, 190, 194, 205, 211, 213
Outsiders, 27, 47–50, 187, 191, 213, 220, 234

Page, Cara, 130
Peace circles, 70–76, 100, 120–128, 173–75, 179
Perez-Darby, Shannon, 120
Peters-Golden, Jenna, 176
Perpetrators, 70, 97–100, 147, 164, 196, 220
Peterson, Latoya, 94
Phillips, Lynn, 95
Philly Stands Up, 105, 166, 167, 171, 172
Pity, 15, 190, 218, 224, 233, 234,
Police brutality and violence, 3, 87, 88, 100, 104, 160, 197, 205; reliance on, 72, 86, 134, 140, 146, 158, 189; surveillance, 64, 101; untrustworthy, 101, 103, 134, 158–59, 177, 181
Policing, 4, 86, 88, 204–206, 241
Poore, Grace, 135
Poster, Winifred, 226, 230,

Stop It Now!, 13, 134, 152, 153, 154

Storytelling, 36–38, 77, 140; and accountability, 217–19; circles, 70–76, 123, 126,
175

Storytelling and Organizing Project
(STOP), 140, 142, 243

Stuart, Barry, 173, 174

Support, 67, 72, 77, 80, 104, 146, 152,
159; communal, 88, 137, 142, 145, 154,
178; individualized, 86, 102; of those
harmed and those who did the harm,
98, 100, 105; of those impacted by
violence, 110–31; toward accountability,
31–32, 36, 108, 166–175

Take Back the Night (TBTN), 124, 125,

Teachers for Social Justice, 78

Thandeka, 51, 54, 61

Thompson, Audrey, 44

Tran, Ngoc Loan, 32,

Transnational accountability, 190, 212

Transnational feminism

Trauma, 3, 57, 59, 111, 163, 173; and collective struggle, 130, 131; cumulative and
collective impact, 129, 157; and healing,
69, 70, 110, 126; and isolation, 114, 128;
systemic, 60

Trivialization, 221

Ubuntu, 13, 89, 98, 116, 117, 119, 156, 158

UNICEF, 226

Us/them binary: and imperialism, 188,
190, 200, 206, 216; relationship to
accountability, 217, 218, 219–224, 238,

240; and victim/perpetrator binary,
99, 107

Uttal, Lynet, 43

Values: and accountability, 36, 168, 174;
shared, 32–35, 71, 92, 100, 108, 118–119,
143, 186

Veil and veiling, 186, 187, 199–207; 241

Victim/perpetrator binary, 76. *See also*
Perpetrators

Violence Against Women Act (VAWA),
86; International VAWA, 189

Wedge, Mark, 173–174

Weingarten, Kaethe, 133, 135, 136, 140

Welch, Sharon, 21, 30, 31, 40

Whiteness, 31, 47–49, 57–81

White privilege, 1, 27, 43, 50, 150; and accountability, 31, 139

White Privilege Conference, 29–31, 36

Whitlock, Kay, 205,

Williams, Patricia, 149

Women and Girls Collective Action Network (WGCAN), 89

Women's human rights, 185, 188, 198, 214,
216

Young Women's Action Team (YWAT),
13, 89

Young Women's Empowerment Project,
13, 89, 92, 99, 101, 104

Zero tolerance, 19, 34, 150, 163

Zine, Jasmin, 191, 193, 203, 211

ABOUT THE AUTHOR

Ann Russo is Associate Professor in the Department of Women's and Gender Studies and the Director of the Women's Center at DePaul University. She focuses on queer, antiracist, and feminist movement building to end violence and to build socially just and caring communities. Her scholarly and activist work engages transformative justice theories and practices that cultivate communal healing, intervention, accountability, and transformation in response to systemic interpersonal, community, and state violence. She is the author of *Taking Back Our Lives: A Call to Action in the Feminist Movement* (2001) and co-editor of *Talking Back, Acting Out: Women Negotiating the Media across Cultures*, with Sandra Jackson (2002), and *Third World Women and the Politics of Feminism*, with Chandra Talpade Mohanty and Lourdes Torres (1991).

Lightning Source UK Ltd.
Milton Keynes UK
UKHW010425300820
368968UK00015B/419